The ℱ

CM0825189

FAMINE IN COUNTY DOWN.

TO THE EDITOR OF THE VINDICATOR,

DEAR SIR,—I have not troubled you for a length of
time with anything relative to the state of the
poor in and about the Seven Towns; indeed,
it appeared almost an act of supererogation to
talk of their condition at all, seeing that it could
not be worse than that of their fellow-suffer-
ers in other parts of the county; nor would I refer
to it now but that there seems to be a total disregard, or, to say the least of it, apathy, on the part of
the wealthy of the district in question. We had a
relief meeting in Castlewellan, to be sure, but, literally speaking, nothing was done. The landlords
were, as they ever have been, absent when either honour or duty calls; let it not be disguised, there is
no real sympathy among them for the starving people. Mr. Moore tested them to the core, and showed
that what I have stated is a simple fact. The able-
bodied men are going about idle; every day adds to
their misery. Their wives and children are becoming feeble and weak, through sheer hunger. Owing
to the extraordinary wetness of the season, turf
cannot be procured—coals are out of the question,
and the poor have thus the double pressure of hunger
and cold to bear up against; while the rich wrap
themselves up in their own importance, and shun their
dependants as a plague. The continual cry among the
small farmers is, " What in the world are we to do!"
The rent is being called for, in some instances, with
merciless perseverance. Add the prospect of being
turned out of their holdings, to that of depriving
themselves of the means of sustenance, and you will
be able to form an opinion of the feelings of the poor
farmers in this district. The bodings of the cottiers
and day labourers are melancholy in the extreme;
their accustomed food is gone, and no substitute
forthcoming. Their usual wages would require to be
trebled to be of any sufficient service whatever; it
is provokingly barbarous to offer them 8d or 10d per
day, and yet none of the farmer class is able to pay
more. My own impression is, that a regular list of
all the landlords of the locality should be made out,
and each of them called on to attend another meeting,
to be convened in the same place, as soon as possible,
so as to see their tenants in person, and hear what
is the real state of the question. It will not pass to
" shab" away to England, with their people's money in
their pockets, and leave them to the tender mercies
of heartless, ignorant bog-bailiffs, and screwing
agents, whose pay depends on the amount wrung
from the unfortunate class committed to their charge.

A COUNTY DOWN MAN.

Castlewellan, October 22, 1846.

The
Famine
in ULSTER
the regional impact

Edited by
**CHRISTINE KINEALY
& TREVOR PARKHILL**

**ULSTER
HISTORICAL FOUNDATION**

First Published 1997
by the Ulster Historical Foundation
12 College Square East, Belfast, BT1 6DD

All rights reserved. No part of this publication may be produced, stored in a
retrieval system or transmitted in any form or by any means, mechanical or
otherwise without permission of the publisher.

©1997 Ulster Historical Foundation
ISBN 0-901905-68-2 (paperback)
ISBN 0-901905-81-X (hardback)

Typeset by the Ulster Historical Foundation
Printed by ColourBooks Ltd, Dublin
Cover and Design by Dunbar Design

This book has received support from the Cultural Traditions Programme of
the Community Relations Council, which aims to encourage acceptance and
understanding of cultural diversity

Front cover illustration: background scene, Slemish Mountain, Co Antrim

CONTENTS

ACKNOWLEDGEMENTS   vi

CONTRIBUTORS   vii

INTRODUCTION   1
CHRISTINE KINEALY

THE FAMINE IN COUNTY ANTRIM   15
CAHAL DALLAT

THE FAMINE IN COUNTY ARMAGH   35
GERARD McATASNEY

THE FAMINE IN COUNTY CAVAN   59
FR DAN GALLOGLY

THE FAMINE IN COUNTY DONEGAL   77
ANTHONY BEGLEY AND SOINBHE LALLY

THE FAMINE IN COUNTY DOWN   99
TREVOR McCAVERY

THE FAMINE IN COUNTY FERMANAGH   129
JOHN CUNNINGHAM

THE FAMINE IN COUNTY LONDONDERRY   147
TREVOR PARKHILL

THE FAMINE IN COUNTY MONAGHAN   169
PATRICK DUFFY

THE FAMINE IN COUNTY TYRONE   197
JIM GRANT

SOURCES AND BIBLIOGRAPHY   223

INDEX   238

vi

ACKNOWLEDGEMENTS

The idea for this volume of essays on the Famine in Ulster was initiated by Gerard MacAtasney and the editors, on behalf of the Ulster Historical Foundation, are glad of this opportunity to acknowledge his role.

The editors wish, on their own behalf and of behalf of their fellow contributors, to acknowledge the valued help of a number of people for advice on sources and information based on their research: Dr Bill Crawford, Federation for Ulster Local Studies; Mrs Brenda Collins, Irish Linen Centre, Lisburn Museum; Dr Margaret Crawford, Department of Economic and Social History, QUB; Mr John Dooher, Strabane Historical Society; Mr Seamus Hasson, Benbradagh Historical Society (Dungiven); Mr Roddy Hegarty, Familia: Ulster Heritage Centre; Mr Robert Heslip, Ulster Museum; Mr John Killen, Linen Hall Library; Miss Catherine Loney, Banbridge Academy; Mr Neil MacAtamney, Clogher Historical Society; Mr Robert McClure, Belfast; Mr Malachy McRoe, Tempo Historical Society; Mr Osborne Morton, Ulster Museum; the staff of the National Archives, Dublin, in particular Miss Catriona Crowe and Mr Donal Moore; Dr Roger Strong, Mrs Heather Stanley and Mr Philip Smith and staff of the Public Search Room, Public Record Office of Northern Ireland; Dr Peter Solar, Brussels; Dr Brian Trainor, Chairman, Irish Manuscripts Commission.

The editors would also take this opportunity to thank the following for their permission to include quotations from records in their care: Major J.H. Shirley; the Director, National Archives, Dublin; the Deputy Keeper of the Records, Public Record Office of Northern Ireland and the Acting Director, Ulster Museum.

This publication has been assisted by grants from the Cultural Traditions Group of the Community Relations Council and the Elizabeth Ellison Trust.

Christine Kinealy
Trevor Parkhill

CONTRIBUTORS

ANTHONY BEGLEY

Is a Trustee of County Donegal Historical Society and a member of the editorial board of *The Donegal Annual* to which he is a regular contributor.

JOHN CUNNINGHAM

Is a retired Belleek school principal who has written extensively on local history in Co. Fermanagh.

DR CAHAL DALLAT

Is a retired Ballycastle, Co. Antrim, school principal and a prominent member of the Glens of Antrim Historical Society.

DR PATRICK DUFFY

Lectures in the Department of Geography, St. Patrick's College, Maynooth and has published widely on his native Co. Monaghan and on aspects of Irish historical geography.

FATHER DAN GALLOGLY

Is editor of *Breifne*, Journal of Breifne Historical Society, Cavan and is writing a history of the Diocese of Kilmore.

DR JIM GRANT

Is a retired Senior Lecturer, St Mary's College, Belfast, whose doctoral thesis (QUB 1986) was on the mechanisms of Famine relief.

DR CHRISTINE KINEALY

Is a fellow of the University of Liverpool. She is author of *This Great Calamity: The Irish Famine 1845-52*, (1994) and *A Death-Dealing Famine: The Great Hunger in Ireland*.

SIONBHE LALLY

Is a member of Ballyshannon Workhouse Research Group and is the author of two children's novels and several radio plays.

GERARD MacATASNEY

Is researching a doctoral thesis on the Famine in Co. Armagh and is the author of *This Dreadful Visitation: The Famine in Lurgan and Portadown*.

DR TREVOR McCAVERY

Is Head of History at Regent House School, Newtownards and the author of *Newtown: history of Newtownards*.

TREVOR PARKHILL

Is Keeper of History, Ulster Museum, and editor of *Familia: Ulster Genealogcal Review*.

INTRODUCTION

CHRISTINE KINEALY

The Irish Famine of 1845-52 is central to an understanding of the development of modern Ireland. In affecting the whole of Ireland, the crisis displayed significant regional variations. The local dimensions of the tragedy have only recently begun to be examined in greater depth and a more textured view of the Famine is now beginning to emerge.[1] Whilst there is no doubt that the consequences of the Famine were most severe in the west and south, other parts of the country also suffered greatly. Even Belfast, the flagship of Ireland's industrial and commercial progress, was affected.

The one-hundred-and-fiftieth anniversary of the Famine has resulted in a renewed popular and academic interest in the event. New publications have emerged at an unprecedented rate. Nonetheless, the range of documentary evidence that has survived from the Famine period has been little researched until recently; in particular, the impact of the potato blight in Ulster has been largely ignored.[2] This has contributed to a widespread belief that there was no famine in Ulster, a belief that has its roots in the event itself. This volume of essays, which is based on new evidence, fresh perspectives, and an informed local knowledge of the nine counties of Ulster by each author, is a valuable addition to this body of research. Each essay clearly demonstrates that there was famine in Ulster, although its impact varied from county to county and even, within a county, from district to district.

A number of themes recur in these accounts of the Ulster experience of the Famine. The first is that famine and food shortages had been experienced by the people of Ulster even before the crisis of the late 1840s. Secondly, the economy of the whole of Ireland was undergoing a period of readjustment. In parts of rural Ulster this had resulted in a process of 'de-industrialisation' as industry became more concentrated in a number of key towns, most notably Belfast. Thirdly, poverty in Ulster mirrored poverty in the south and west of the country. Fourthly, although various relief mechanisms were put in place by the government, local circumstances gave a distinct character to the provision of relief. In spite of many examples of individual generosity, much of this relief was inadequate. Fifthly, the consequences of the Famine – distress, disease, emigration, evictions and excess mortality – were evident throughout Ulster. Whilst mortality rates were highest in the provinces of Connaught and Munster, Ulster was also affected severely. Finally, the folk memory of the Famine has remained strong and enduring in Ulster (if sometimes unreliable).

Before the Famine, the Irish economy had gone through a series of readjustments which were to the disadvantage of small tenants and cottiers. In many parts of Ireland, but notably in Ulster, there was a decline in the domestic spinning industry, due largely to the development of new technology. As a consequence, the textile industry, especially linen, was becoming more concentrated in Belfast and other towns in Ulster. In general, incomes fell and small-holders were denied access to alternative sources of revenue. In Co. Londonderry, Trevor Parkhill notes that the decline of the domestic linen industry had contributed to an increase in migration and emigration from the county in the pre-Famine decades, a characteristic that was evident in other counties, particularly Armagh, Cavan, Derry and Monaghan.

In Co. Armagh, Gerard MacAtasney observes that the impact of technological changes was to increase the economic vulnerability of weavers whilst increasing their dependence on potatoes. At the same time, he notes, there was a large number of people who did not even have access to this form of supplementary income and eked out an existence on the 'margin' of economic survival. The transformation in linen production coincided with attempts by a number of landlords and their agents to modernise their estates. A pre-condition of this transformation was that the sub-division of farms should be ended and reversed. The process of consolidation of holdings was evident in many parts of Ulster even before the potato blight but it was accelerated during the Famine years, facilitated by deaths, emigration, evictions and the voluntary surrender of land.

Paddy Duffy's study of Co. Monaghan focuses on changes in the rural landscape and society. On the eve of the Famine, there was considerable rural overcrowding within the county as land had become fragmented and farms sub-divided. The sub-division of land had been facilitated by the expansion of the linen industry in the eighteenth century, the possession of a loom making small-holdings of land economically more viable. By 1841, the decline of the domestic linen industry left a large number of people without the safety net of a supplementary income. As a consequence, in the years before the Famine many of the poor existed on the verge of destitution. They periodically had to seek assistance, usually in the form of rent rebates, blankets or food. The role of large estates, such as the Shirley estate in Co. Monaghan, in providing this form of intermittent welfare was significant. However, the introduction of the Poor Law in 1838 contributed to a decline in private charity.

In contrast to the process of de-industrialisation evident in many parts of the countryside, on the eve of the Famine the town of Belfast had become the centre of Ireland's industrial development. The Act of Union of 1800 had resulted in the gradual erosion of trade barriers between Britain and Ireland. This had disadvantaged a number of Irish industries which were unable to compete with the industrial might of Britain, although Belfast clearly benefited from links with the wider British and colonial markets. Even in Belfast, however, there were districts such as Smithfield which remained vulnerable; vagrants were so commonplace that people were employed to keep them off the streets.

There were many parallels between pre-Famine rural poverty in the west and in the north of the country, especially in areas where the population was dense. At the beginning of the nineteenth century, Co. Armagh was the most densely populated county in the country and the competition for land resulted in a growth of sectarian conflict.[3] Rural overcrowding also existed in other parts of Ulster. For example, Paddy Duffy demonstrates that on the eve of the Famine there were 400 people per square mile in parts of Co. Monaghan, a population density similar to the west of the country. Moreover, as is evident in many of these chapters, the life of the poor of Ulster mirrored that of the poor in the west of Ireland. There was a high dependence on the potato amongst the rural poor of Ulster; not the 'lumper' variety which was consumed throughout the rest of the country, but 'cups', 'doe blacks', 'red downs' or 'black seedlings'. In Co. Cavan, Father Gallogly describes the poverty of a large portion of the rural population, which manifested itself in poor housing, ragged and inadequate clothing, and increasing dependence on potatoes. Gerard MacAtasney quotes the observation of the Rev. Ives of Tartaraghan near Lurgan that the poor in the district frequently ate potatoes for breakfast, dinner and supper. Thus, in the midst of industrial prosperity, economic vulnerability and extreme destitution were apparent.

Even before the Great Famine, subsistence crises and famines had occurred intermittently in Ireland. In the years between 1800 and 1850, it has been estimated that there were eight subsistence crises and three famines within the country.[4] These food shortages could be viewed as an early-warning signal of the vulnerability of the Irish economy. Cahal Dallat believes that the administrative and fund-raising experiences which the local gentry gained on earlier relief committees, especially in 1817 and 1831, proved invaluable during the Great Famine. This experience was evident, for example, in the private soup kitchens set up in Co. Antrim in 1847. James Grant agrees that this experience of previous food shortages was useful because it meant that 'the mechanism of government-supported local effort was well established and had already been activated in 1845'. Trevor Parkhill's study of Co. Londonderry describes how, following the first appearance of blight in the county, the traditional providers of relief – clergy, landlords, large farmers – initiated steps to provide assistance to the destitute.

A feature which made the Famine of the 1840s distinct from earlier and subsequent famines was the longevity of the potato disease. Reports of the mysterious potato blight first appeared in Irish newspapers on 6 September 1845. The same blight had already appeared in parts of Belgium,

France, Germany, England and the Netherlands during the summer of 1845, and in America in the previous year. Ireland was unique, however, for its high level of dependence of the population on potatoes, which were the staple food of an estimated two fifths of the population. The concurrent food shortages in Europe after 1845 provided a ready market for Irish grain products throughout the Famine years.

One of the earliest confirmed sightings of the blight in Ireland was in Florence Court in Co. Fermanagh, where the local constabulary reported that a whole field had been destroyed.[5] However, as Trevor Parkhill points out, there were sightings of the disease in Co. Londonderry even earlier. In 1845, the damage caused by the potato blight was uneven throughout the Ulster countryside. This is evident in Co. Antrim where blight destroyed the potato crops in the Antrim, Ballycastle, Ballymoney and Lisburn Unions. In the nearby Larne Union, much of the crop was sound. In Co. Down, the turnip crop also was ruined by the same 'rot' that had destroyed the potatoes. By October 1845, many Ulster Boards of Guardians – the local relief officials – concerned about the blight, began to consider alternative types of food for the inmates of the workhouses. Rice, oats, bread or soup began to replace the traditional potato diet. In general, the first year of potato blight was managed by the local relief mechanisms established throughout Ulster and there was little need to ask for government assistance. However, as is clear from Father Gallogly's account of the Famine in Co. Cavan, in the spring of 1846 there existed many instances of extreme privation and suffering, and a portion of the local population were close to starvation.

In 1846, the blight returned to Ireland and was far more widespread than in the previous year. There were recorded sightings as early as July. A journalist from a Dublin newspaper travelling through Ulster in September 1846 reported that the disease had already destroyed the crop in counties Down, Antrim, Derry, Tyrone, Armagh and Monaghan. There were only two exceptions, the Cave Hill in Belfast and the neighbourhood of Glenarm. He also reported that the local hotels were no longer able to serve potatoes and rice was given in their place.[6]

The second and more extensive appearance of the potato blight in 1846 marks the real onset of the Famine in Ireland. In June 1846, Peel's Tory government had fallen from power. The new Whig administration, led by Lord John Russell, modified the relief policies of the previous year and decided to make public works the main mechanism for providing relief.[7]

This policy was not only costly but was ineffective in providing immediate relief. James Grant demonstrates that even in Co. Tyrone, one of the counties least affected by the Famine, the public works administration was unable to deal with the demands being placed on it. A meeting calling for public works to be introduced into the area was held in East Omagh on 13 October 1846. It took a further two months before the necessary bureaucratic procedures had been completed and an initial grant of money could be provided. Another month passed before the whole money was made available. As James Grant points out, the process of establishing drainage works for the same purpose was even slower. By the time the relief works were operational, many of the people already were suffering from fever, dysentery and diarrhoea. Furthermore, the wages paid on the works were too low to support a family so that more pressure was thrown back onto the local relief committees. For example, the Clogher relief committee gave supplementary relief to those working on the public works by giving them cut-price grain.

The role of the local relief committees in providing food to the destitute was important. The insistence by the government that food could not be sold below the local market price was generally disliked and was ignored by a number of committees. Within Co. Tyrone, this policy was most vigorously opposed by the Moy and Dunnamanagh committees. Initially, the relief administrators in Dublin responded by refusing to make a grant allocation to committees who did not obey this ruling. But, James Grant notes, as the situation deteriorated at the end of 1846, a more flexible approach became apparent.

In the wake of the second failure of the potato crop, the horrors of famine were not confined to the west of the country. Trevor McCavery shows that, by the beginning of 1847, suffering and starvation in parts of Co. Down were being likened to the situation in the Skibbereen in Co. Cork. This comparison was disliked by a number of local landlords and gentry who prided themselves on residing in the most economically successful part of the country. However, McCavery's detailed study of the Newtownards Union, which was praised by the government for its financial independence, clearly demonstrates the pervasiveness of the crisis. The failure of the potato crop in 1846 coincided with a slump in the linen industry which drastically reduced the incomes of many handloom weavers. In the Newtownards Union the destitution manifested itself through the setting up of public works, the establishment of relief committees, increased pressure for admittance to the local workhouse and the opening of privately-funded soup kitchens. These actions paralleled what was taking place in many other parts of the country. In Newtownards and some of its neighbouring unions, these relief measures were mostly provided without the financial assistance of government, thus avoiding costly repayments at a later date. But the poverty of the local people was redolent of the scenes of destitution elsewhere. Trevor McCavery provides a contemporary description of people queuing at a soup kitchen in Newtownards as 'emaciated and half-famished souls' many of whom were without sufficient clothes to cover them.

These scenes of suffering were repeated in other parts of Ulster. The Lurgan Union, which was at the centre of one of the most industrially advanced parts of the country, also contained pockets of extreme destitution. Gerard MacAtasney identifies a case of death from starvation as early as January 1847. In the first week of February, mortality in the Lurgan workhouse was the highest in Ulster. In the same week, the workhouse was closed to further admissions. A member of the Society of Friends who visited the union in April 1847 described what he saw as approaching the distressing situation in Co. Cork.

A major part of famine relief was provided through the local workhouses. The Poor Law system, which had operated in England since the sixteenth century, had been introduced to Ireland in 1838. As a consequence of the Act, the country was divided into 130 unions (collections of townlands) and each union had its own workhouse and elected Boards of Guardians. The 1838 Poor Law ignored county boundaries and some unions had portions in two, three, or occasionally four, counties. The workhouses varied greatly in size, ranging from the Cavan workhouse (which could accommodate 1,200 paupers) to the Armagh, Belfast and Downpatrick workhouses (each built to accommodate 1,000 paupers) to the Castlederg and Gortin workhouses (both built to accommodate 200 inmates).

Initially, the workhouses were to play a secondary role in the provision of famine relief. However, following the second failure of the potato crop in 1846, pressure increased on local workhouses throughout the country, including Ulster. By the end of the year, 21 of the 43 workhouses in the province were full to capacity and they had to be extended, or additional buildings rented, so that they could cope with the extra pressure for relief.

The demand for workhouse relief varied from union to union. In the Magherafelt Union in Co. Londonderry, Trevor Parkhill estimates that there was a 413 per cent increase in the number of workhouse inmates in 1847 compared with the previous year. Inevitably, poor rates – the taxes paid for the upkeep of the local workhouses – increased dramatically.

Overcrowding within the workhouses resulted in a sharp increase in sickness, especially dysentery and fever, and a corresponding increase in mortality. During Christmas week 1846, for example, 23 inmates of the Omagh workhouse, including 16 children, died. By February 1847, the situation had deteriorated further and the central Board of Commissioners ordered that the workhouse should take no new admissions. This workhouse remained closed until July 1847. The preponderance of children aged under 15 in the workhouses was a feature common to the whole country but, as Trevor Parkhill points out, the proportion was especially high in Ulster and by 1848 children accounted for over half of the total workhouse population.

In some cases, the pressure of providing extra relief brought the Guardians into conflict with the central Board of Commissioners. The Cookstown Guardians asked if they could give food to destitute people for whom they were unable to provide workhouse relief. Their request was refused. One of the most notorious examples of conflict was with the Lowtherstown Board of Guardians in Co. Fermanagh who were eventually dismissed and replaced by paid officials. This union was described as the worst administered in Ireland. The Armagh Union, in contrast, was regarded by the Poor Law Commissioners as the best administered in the country. The neighbouring Lurgan Union, on the other hand, was beset by inefficient and incompetent management. In his account of the union, Gerard MacAtasney points out that in two years from May 1845 to May 1847 the workhouse had seven different masters. During the same period, many of the guardians showed little interest in the workhouse, the medical officer was incompetent, the workhouse was insanitary and disease-ridden and the diet was deemed to be inadequate.

Life for workhouse officers, and all relief workers, could be hazardous. In the Cavan workhouse, two successive matrons died of fever. Furthermore, as Father Gallogly observes, fever was no respecter of social status and in the town of Cavan it killed more rich than poor people. The fear of catching this disease occasionally led to acts of inhumanity. For example, the temporary fever hospital in Belturbet, Co. Cavan, was burnt down deliberately in April 1847.

In their chapter on the Famine in Co. Donegal, Anthony Begley and Soinbhe Lally consider in detail the Ballyshannon Poor Law Union. As early as November 1846, the workhouse stopped admitting paupers. A member of the Society of Friends who visited the workhouse in the winter of 1846 described it as being 'in about as bad a condition as any we have seen'. Inefficient administration and lack of finances had a detrimental effect on the guardians' ability to provide relief. This was manifested in the high mortality rates in the workhouse which the guardians attributed to poor diet and lack of clothes. The winter of 1846-47 was particularly cold, with snow falling in Donegal as late as April 1847. The master of the workhouse reported that during this freezing weather, paupers were working outdoors without shoes and stockings. The authors also analyse the religious denomination of the paupers. They conclude that the increased influx of Protestants into the workhouse could be gauged by the purchase of additional Protestant prayer books and Bibles throughout 1847. It is ironic that these items were purchased at a time when inmates who died in the workhouse were being buried coffin-less and in mass graves due to lack of funds.

The problems in the administration of the workhouses made the Poor Law less able to cope with the calamity that confronted them after 1846. Even unions previously praised for their good management could fall foul of the central Commissioners. For example, the Ballycastle Guardians in Co. Antrim responded to their workhouse becoming full by opening up soup kitchens in the locality. The Coleraine Guardians also considered adopting this emergency form of relief. The provision of outdoor relief had been strictly forbidden by the 1838 Poor Law Act and the Commissioners threatened to take legal action against the guardians. Nonetheless, at the beginning of 1847, the government announced that they were replacing the failed public works system with soup kitchens.

The Temporary Relief Act of February 1847, which provided for the establishment of government soup kitchens throughout the country, was probably one of the most successful of all of the relief policies introduced by the British government during the Famine. By July 1847, over three million people were receiving free daily rations of food. Nonetheless, the regional variations were marked. In parts of the west of the country, such as Gort, Swinford and Westport, over 80 per cent of the local population depended on this form of relief in the summer of 1847. In contrast, in the unions of Antrim, Belfast and Newtownards, no government soup kitchens were opened (although privately-funded ones continued to operate).[8] Indeed, the town of Belfast – which was engaged in raising subscriptions for other, poorer parts of the country – prided itself on not having recourse to financial assistance from the government.

The need for additional workhouse accommodation became even more critical after the autumn of 1847 when the Poor Law was made responsible for both 'ordinary' and famine relief. In recognition of the fact that a number of unions would still require financial assistance from the government, 22 unions were declared to be officially 'distressed'. The majority of these unions were situated in the south and west of the country. The Glenties Union in Co. Donegal was also placed in this category. Although there had been little potato blight in 1847, only a small crop had been sown. Moreover, a slump in the British economy in 1846-47 had repercussions in Belfast and its industrial hinterland, especially for the linen industry. In Co. Armagh, Gerard MacAtasney observes that the general industrial recession combined with a poor flax and oats harvest left the local weavers (many of whom were already impoverished) without any resources. In Belfast too, many workers became temporarily unemployed or were placed on lower wages. All of this served to put pressure on the local workhouses and, in 1848, over one million people throughout the country were in receipt of Poor Law relief.

In some instances, the boardrooms within the workhouses became the venues for ideological battles regarding the nature of destitution and how it should be treated. In the Newtownards Union, for example, Trevor McCavery discovered that the majority of Guardians voted not to give outdoor relief following the passage of the Poor Law Amendment Act in 1847 which made it legal for the first time. This decision led to the resignation of the chairman, William Sharman Crawford, who described the ruling as 'unjust, uncharitable and unchristian'. McCavery identifies the poor as the real victims of these decisions which meant that they could not receive relief until they were already weakened in health and almost at starvation point.

The increase in Poor Law taxation during the Famine contributed to the indebtedness of a number of Ulster unions. John Cunningham, who examines the impact of the blight in Co. Fermanagh, observes that by May

1847 the Enniskillen Union was £5,000 in debt. A few months later, the Enniskillen Guardians were dismissed. Their successors – paid officials appointed by the central Commissioners – found the financial difficulties of the union no less intractable. Within Ulster, four boards of guardians were disbanded (Cavan, Cootehill, Enniskillen and Lowtherstown) two of which were in Co. Fermanagh. The dismissal of the Lowtherstown Union was locally resisted and resulted in a parliamentary enquiry into the case.[9]

In 1848 a Commission was set up to recommend the creation of new workhouses. Thirty-three new unions were formed making a total of 163. Most of the new unions were in the south and west of the country, where blight had been as extensive in 1848 as it had been in 1846. Only three were proposed in Ulster. They were Bawnboy Union (which was created from parts of the Enniskillen and Cavan Unions), Killybegs Union (mostly situated in the Glenties Union) and Kilrea (created from Ballymoney, Coleraine, and Magherafelt Unions).[10]

The continuation of distress in parts of Ireland after 1848 resulted in a further change of policy by the government. In May 1849 a new tax, known as the Rate-in-Aid, was imposed on Irish Poor Law unions for the purpose of the more prosperous unions in the east of the country subsidising relief expenditure in the financially insolvent unions in the west. Whilst some areas in Ulster were beginning to emerge from the worst effects of the Famine, a number of unions were still suffering extreme privation, caused by a combination of hunger, homelessness, disease and exhaustion. Father Gallogly's study of Cavan town, for example, demonstrates that deaths from fever were higher in 1849 than they had been in 1847, and that workhouse mortality was higher in 1849 than at any point during the Famine. The situation in the town alarmed the Bishop of Kilmore who called for relief committees to be re-established in the area.

The Rate-in-Aid tax was unpopular with boards of guardians in Ulster who felt that they were being financially penalised for the poverty and bad management of the western unions.[11] The Ulster guardians mounted a vigorous campaign in which they opposed the new policy. Some of the debate was expressed in divisive terms, a distinction being drawn between the impact of the potato blight in the south and west compared with the north of the country. John Cunningham notes that the Lisnaskea Board of Guardians in Co. Fermanagh objected to the Rate-in-Aid tax being imposed on 'the peaceable and industrious inhabitants of the north of Ireland for

the support of the lazy, vicious and indolent population of the south and
west'. Gerard MacAtasney records the outcome of a meeting held in Lurgan
in May 1849 which attributed the suffering of the people in the west and
south of the country to 'laziness and idleness', in contrast to the
'industriousness' of the people of the north. Yet, as his research indicates,
only two years earlier the suffering of the poor in parts of Co. Armagh had
equalled the worst scenes in the west of the country.

The role of the landlords during the Famine has traditionally been
criticised although recent research has revealed that it was, in fact, diverse.
Elsewhere, Jim Donnnelly has suggested that the response of landlords,
especially in relation to evictions, was motivated by a desire to reform and
modernise their estates. After 1847 there was an added financial incentive
to evict impoverished small-holders as tax burdens on landlords increased
considerably. The clearance of the land was viewed as a necessary pre-
condition for improved estate management. The social dislocation and
upheaval of the Famine, provided an opportunity for evictions, removals
and land consolidation to take place.[12] In Co. Londonderry, there appears
to have been fewer evictions than in other parts of the country but there
was widespread evidence of landlords assisting their tenants to emigrate
and thus clearing their properties. Trevor Parkhill cites the agent of the
London Companies (landowners in the county) who advised that, 'there
never was in the memory of man so good an opportunity of improving the
estates in this country as at present'. This sentiment was echoed by Lord
Londonderry's agent in Co. Down who stated, 'My plan and object is to
press those who are destitute of means to sell and emigrate'.

The response of even neighbouring landlords could vary greatly. Within
Co. Down, for example, Trevor McCavery identifies the different reactions
of two landlords, William Sharman Crawford and Lord Londonderry. The
former responded to the news of the potato blight by reducing his rents and
promising further assistance to his tenants. In contrast, Lord Londonderry
resisted this action on the grounds that a rent reduction would result in
'personal inconvenience ... and the inconvenience of others'. Shortly
afterwards, Lord Londonderry found himself at the centre of a public
controversy when a local newspaper criticised him and his wife for
contributing only £30 to famine relief. The newspaper quipped that his
Lordship's pockets had been locked with 'one of Chubb's double bolters'.
Both Lord Londonderry and his agent vigorously defended his donations –

though they did increase in response to this negative publicity. McCavery also notes that, in 1848, Lord Londonderry made extensive and expensive alterations to his mansion at Mount Stewart and also to Holdernesse House, his London home, while Cahal Dallat describes Lady Londonderry's building of Garron Tower in Co. Antrim.

There is a general consensus that, where the landlords resided on their estates or took an active interest in its affairs, the local population seemed to fare less badly. The involvement of local landlords on the relief committees appears to have been largely beneficial. The clergyman at Ballinderry Glebe in Co. Londonderry complained that a consequence of absenteeism was that the local relief committee was without funds and the local poor at a disadvantage. The indifference of absentee landlords was noted by the Society of Friends who visited Ireland in the winter of 1846-47.[13] Gerard MacAtasney quotes the Rev. Clements of Co. Armagh as attributing the poverty evident in Tartaraghan to 'the evil effects of absenteeism'. James Grant, however, points out that most resident landlords were concerned only with their own estates and they had little interest in what occurred beyond that. This was partly due to financial reasons as most of the burden for financing the relief schemes fell on the local landlords. The most vulnerable areas appeared to be those where there were many different landlords, the land was highly sub-divided (and therefore liable to a higher level of taxation) or the landlords were absentee and neither they nor their agents were involved in relief provision.

The role of merchants and professionals during the Famine has been little researched. These groups were often active on the local relief committees and as guardians of the local workhouses. Their behaviour, however, was not always altruistic. Father Gallogly describes how the food shortages during the Famine were used by some merchants and businessmen in Cavan as an opportunity for profiteering. He records instances of retailers deliberately holding back supplies of corn in order to create a scarcity, or charging exorbitant prices for foodstuffs.

The role of clergymen of all denominations during the Famine was generally exemplary. This was the case both in Ulster and in the country as a whole. Within Ulster, Anglican, Catholic and Presbyterian ministers worked together on relief committees to lessen the impact of what was frequently viewed as 'God's visitation'. Their role was important in raising funds, distributing them (either in money or kind), and pricking the conscience of the local gentry. They were also an important intermediary between the local providers of relief and officials in Dublin and London.

It is impossible to pinpoint when the Famine ended in Ulster. After 1848, the blight had started to disappear from most parts of Ireland although there were still local instances, mainly in the south-west of the country. In Ulster, the return of good harvests coincided with the ending of the trade depression. But blight had not totally disappeared from Ulster and, as Cahal Dallat points out, it reappeared in Co. Antrim as late as 1852. Moreover, the social indicators of the Famine – emigration, evictions, disease and mortality – were all higher than their pre-Famine levels.

The population losses which resulted from the Famine are one of the clearest indicators of the distress and suffering of the Irish people during those years. Between 1845 and 1851 at least one million people died from starvation or famine-related diseases and a further one million people emigrated. Again, there was considerable regional variation. In Kilrush in Co. Clare, for example, population losses were estimated to be over 50 per cent of the population. Throughout the province of Ulster, the average population losses were 17 per cent, although in counties Cavan, Fermanagh and Monaghan they ranged between 25 and 30 per cent. In a number of localities, such as the Inniskeen and Killsherdony townlands in Co. Cavan, the population fell by 36 per cent. In addition to high rates of mortality, the Famine resulted in a widespread social collapse of small farmers, many of whom emigrated. The Famine also expedited the decline of the domestic linen industry and, by 1851, this sector had disappeared from many parts of the countryside.

Trevor McCavery identifies in the relatively prosperous Newtownards Union the impact of the Famine on the social and cultural life of the people. Whilst this dimension is hard to quantify, a local recollection provides an insight into post-Famine Ireland, 'the weavers after the famine were not the same men as they were before it ... many of them felt that they had something else to live for than to eat, drink and be merry'. The Famine did not end when good harvests returned to Ireland and its impact on the people, their culture, the economy and the landscape is still felt today.

THE FAMINE
IN
COUNTY ANTRIM

CAHAL DALLAT

John Lanktree, the Marchioness of Londonderry's agent of her Carnlough and Garron Tower estates in Co. Antrim from 1832 to 1850, first mentioned the potato blight in his annual report to Lady Frances Anne in late 1845. Like most of his contemporaries, he was baffled by what some referred to as this 'cholera of the potatoes', and it is from his pen that we get a first-hand attempt to describe and explain the potato disease which was to have such cataclysmic consequences. 'The year 1845 has been unusually rainy and has proved ungenial to the potato crop – which being a native of the sunny regions of South America and requiring warm weather for ripening, has contracted a strange disease hitherto unknown to agriculturists, which I am sorry to report has been very prevalent throughout the whole estate.'[1] (Curiously, there is a folklore account which runs directly counter to this. Rathlin man, Frank Craig's father, had a contrary explanation: 'My father talked of what he had heard too. It was only in wet ground, strange to say, that any potatoes were got at all; if the ground was in anyway dry they all rotted away'.[2]) Lanktree's report continued:

To the poor tenantry on the mountain farms it has been a source of great
alarm and anxiety and may I fear be subjected to great privations in
consequence of it, but Divine Providence whose care extends even to the
humblest of his children will bring good out of this calamity by awakening
them to necessity of making greater efforts for obtaining a more generous
diet in future years.[3]

By the late summer of 1845, the first traces of potato blight were
beginning to show in several regions of Ireland. Boards of Guardians became
immediately concerned with the implications this news would have for the
feeding of the workhouse population, the workhouses' diet being largely
dependent on the potato. Nowhere was this issue addressed earlier than in
Ballycastle. At a meeting of the Board of Guardians of the Ballycastle
Union held in the courthouse on 3 August 1845:

> It was unanimously resolved: that the Board of Guardians form themselves
> into a Committee for the purpose of purchasing food for the poor, on the
> cheapest terms. It was further resolved that the money should be obtained
> by private subscriptions, and that Mr McElheran's services etc. be retained
> for that purpose and the spare rooms in the Workhouse and machinery be
> so appropriated; the Guardians being of the opinion that much good may
> be done by instructing farmers and the poor in the mode of preparing potato
> starch and mixing it with oatmeal or flour and making it into bread.[4]

Elsewhere in Co. Antrim, the patchiness of the spread of blight is
apparent. Although the master of Antrim workhouse reported in July 1845
that, in consequence of the inferior quality of the potatoes supplied, he had
found it necessary to serve oatmeal for dinner on Tuesday and Wednesday,
the full seriousness of the potato disease took longer to surface.[5] Antrim
Board of Guardians accepted Mr Millar's tender for supplying the
workhouse with potatoes from 1 November 1844 to 31 December 1845 –
'Cups' for the months of June and July, 'Red Downs' for August and 'Black
Seedlings' for the remainder of the contract at 1s 10d per hundredweight.[6]
There was no mention in this list of a breed of potatoes known as 'Doe
Backs' or 'Doe Blacks' which were believed to be immune from the blight.
(This belief is frequently quoted as one of the reasons why the Famine was
not as severe in Antrim as in other places).

In the meantime the Ballymoney Board of Guardians were becoming
more aware of the stress being caused by the failure of the potato crop. At
a meeting on 17 August 1845 a letter was received from George Macartney
of Lisanoure Castle suggesting that they try the preparation of Indian corn-

meal as food for the poor. After some discussion it was agreed that the master should purchase two hundredweight of Indian corn-meal to see if it could be cooked into proper food for the paupers.[7] At a subsequent meeting the master reported that he had tried Indian corn-meal mixed in equal parts with oatmeal and in general the inmates were well pleased with it. It was then agreed that one hundredweight of Indian corn-meal be purchased for the next week's consumption at 12s 6d per bag.[8]

At the same meeting, in early 7 September 1845, the master at Ballymoney was concerned that:

> the potatoes at the Workhouse field were entirely unfit for eating and that none of them had been used for the past five or six days. It had been necessary to substitute whatever Board of Guardians considered best in their place. He had tried both yellow and white Indian meal in equal quantites with oatmeal in stirabout. The latter was preferred. There was request from the Officers of the Workhouse asking what they would be allowed in place of potatoes for dinner. It was resolved that they should get one shilling's worth of bread in lieu of potatoes.[9]

In October 1845, the master of Ballymoney workhouse advised the Board of Guardians that 'it would be a saving to the Union to purchase potatoes at one shilling a bushel and not to use those growing in the workhouse grounds when they can be purchased at the above price. It was resolved that the master purchase potatoes at a price not higher than one shilling per bushel until further notice'.[10]

At the following meeting held on 8 October 1845 Robert Bogle, the master, 'reported that on the previous Saturday there was one third of the potatoes which could not be used because of the rot which was prevalent and he asked if he was to allow any additional quantity if the potatoes continue to be bad'. It was resolved that the master should allow the additional quantity if he considered it necessary. At the same meeting, ominously, a tender was received from James Cameron for seven coffins at 5s 0d and for 'dead dresses' [shrouds?] £1.10s.4d.[11]

By October 1845, it was evident that the failure of the potato crop could no longer be ignored. It was resolved that a full meeting of the Ballymoney Board of Guardians be summoned for Thursday 12 October to take into consideration the objectionable description of potatoes now being supplied by the contractor and the best means to be adopted under these cases.[12] It would almost seem as if the Ballymoney Guardians were unaware of the scarcity of good potatoes and all the blame was being laid at the door of the supplier who was probably doing his utmost to fulfil the conditions of his contract in almost impossible circumstances.

On 7 October the Poor Law Commissioners authorised all unions in Ireland, in consequence of the prevailing epidemic in the potato crop, to depart from the established dietaries by substituting the use of oatmeal, rice, bread or other food in lieu of potatoes, whenever the guardians deemed it advisable to do so. A letter from the Poor Law Commissioners in Dublin was accompanied by an order allowing changes in the 'dietary' of the workhouses when the potatoes were too bad to be used and instead try soup made of vegetables, oatmeal, rice or pudding made of any grain. By early December the master, Robert Bogle, reported that he had tried a starch made from potatoes in place of meal; that he had given 10 lbs of starch in lieu of 14 lbs of oatmeal and that the stirabout was equally good: that he had given onions four days in the week and deducted a small quantity of milk in place of them. It was resolved that the master's conduct in trying the experience with the starch in place of meal and onions be approved and when the potatoes were bad that he follow the same course.[13] Clearly Bogle was delighted to have the approval of the Ballymoney Guardians and a letter written by him appeared subsequently in the *Coleraine Chronicle*, giving details of his method of making starch flour.[14]

The same sense of desperation was, however, visibly missing in the town of Antrim. At their meeting of 6 November, the Antrim Board of Guardians resolved 'that, as the potatoes now being supplied by the contractor appear to be generally of a sound description, the use of same for dinner be resumed for the current month, adult paupers being allowed 4lbs and children 2lbs, with soup as at present viz. 3 days in the week.' The proposal to allocate 4lbs of potatoes for an able-bodied man at dinner was a marked increase on the standard diet.[15]

The Guardians were a little premature in deciding that potatoes were very much improved for, at the meeting of the following week:

> the Master having reported that in consequence of the unsound quality of the potatoes being supplied during the week he had been obliged to supply bread in lieu thereof for the first three days. It was ordered that as the Guardians are of the opinion that proper exertion is not evidenced on the part of the contractor to procure good potatoes, the additional expense incurred as above be charged to his account.[16]

At the same meeting a circular letter was received from the Poor Law

Commissioners recommending employment of certain classes of inmates in the workhouse in the manufacture of potato flour or of starch and pulp from diseased potatoes, that the same could be done very much along the lines as had been adopted already by the Ballymoney Guardians.

> It was ordered that the Poor Law Commissioners be informed in reference to the above that a public meeting had been arranged for that very day to take into consideration the propriety of establishing by subscription a starch manufactory on an extensive scale... The Guardians hope that such arrangement will be made thereat as it will obviate the necessity of the existing regulations being interfered with at present for such a purpose.[17]

In the master's requirements for the week beginning 20 November 1845 there was a considerable increase in the quantity of potatoes (6,000 lbs), suggesting that there was optimism about the improving quality of the crop still to be delivered. However, at the meeting of the Board of Guardians in the following week it was reported that the contractor had been supplying potatoes which were well below standard. It was decided to take legal action and that the relevant bond should be given into the hands of the Board's solicitor with instructions to write to the contractor and his sureties accordingly. In the meantime, the master was authorised 'to purchase the necessary supply until further orders'. In such cases the suppliers could well have bankrupted themselves in an endeavour to fulfil their contracts.[18]

The onset of the blight in Lisburn had a slightly bizarre twist. In October the local landlord, the Marquess of Hertford, '...visited the house and was much pleased with the order and regularity of it, stating in the visitors' book that it was not excelled by any similar institution in England'. He then 'ordered a comfortable dinner to be provided for the paupers at his expense, consisting of beef, carrots and soup and afterwards tea and currant buns'.[19] Although potatoes were not on the menu, they clearly were not at that time a problem, as the minute of the first meeting in November of the Guardians showed: it reported the receipt of 'a letter on the subject of the disease in the potato crop' accompanied by a further letter with an 'order permitting a change of dietary in consequence of the potato disease'. However, the Guardians took the view that 'as the contractor to this Union continues to supply good potatoes to the house...the Board did not think it necessary to make any change as yet'.[20] By January things had changed somewhat and Mr Clark, the contractor for the potatoes, wrote to the Board 'stating that he had now delivered all the potatoes he had at his disposal as the disease had destroyed a large quantity.'[20] He asked to be relieved from his contract which was to expire on 8 March. The Board, 'taking into consideration also the unprecedented disease', duly resolved to release Mr Clark from his contract for potatoes. By late February the shortage was sufficient for the Guardians to direct the master 'to give soup and bread for dinner 4 days in each week and stirabout for 3 days each week till potatoes can be procured...'.[22]

This was evidently the beginning of difficult times for Boards of Guardians in the county as they searched for a suitable substitute for potatoes. Antrim Board had ordered 'bread composed of one half Indian meal and one half of flour but it was found to be unfit for use and the contractor stated that he was unable to furnish an article so composed, which he could recommend. It was resolved that the supply of such bread be discontinued and that common brown bread be substituted in its place.'[23] Only the Larne Guardians appear to have been spared the anxieties of a full-scale shortage of potatoes. Indeed, the Visiting Committee found, in April 1846, 'potatoes and milk of the best quantity'. The committee also heard great complaints against the Indian meal from paupers' and recommended that it be used 'sparingly'.[24]

In spite of the inconsistency in the manifestation of the blight in the north and south of the county, as evidenced in the Ballymoney, Ballycastle, Antrim and Lisburn workhouse experiences, there was an overall consistency in the readiness of guardians to respond to the threat of famine, whenever it came. The experiences of local communities in Co. Antrim in responding to occasional food shortages in the generation before the Famine may contribute to an explanation of this. The 30 years prior to 1845, as had been the case throughout Ulster, had been characterised by hard economic times, beginning with the post-Napoleonic war agricultural depression. The near-famine which had taken root in Co. Antrim and elsewhere had been accompanied by severe fever. By 1823 a number of the gentry of Ballycastle had come together for the purpose of setting up a dispensary which was funded by the members' subscriptions. The first year's subscriptions amounted to £23 4s 9d, with subsequent years being on a similar scale.[25] By 1831 an act of parliament empowered the Grand Jury to match pound for pound any such amount raised by voluntary subscription. Encouraged by this increase in funding the Ballycastle Dispensary Committee set up a temporary fever hospital at Bathlodge on the Shore

Road. The building used had been a salt store, part of the salt industry which had existed in the previous century. Seemingly there was a belief that the residue of salt in the store would act as a cure for the fever. The first year's report mentions that 'there are twelve patients; of these two have been dismissed cured, the remainder may be pronounced convalescent. By the timely removal of the first persons attacked from the town of Ballycastle, the proper disinfection of the house in which they were resident, the spread of the disease has been arrested.' The argument this statement affords for having a proper place for the reception of the first cases of an infectious disease is so strong as to require no comment. In 1839 there were 720 home visits. The number of fever cases was 101. The Ballycastle workhouse opened on 18 March 1843 but the Dispensary Committee continued with its work. In the report for the year ending 1 June 1845 the number of patients attending was given as 714, of whom 10 had died.[26]

A fund for the relief of the poor had been established in Glenarm in 1817 during the severe shortages experienced that year and the gentry subscribed generously to it. As had been the case in Ballycastle, it continued to operate and, by 1841, the situation had changed and it was decided that it would be more beneficial to spend the money received for the purchase of food in bulk. This was the beginning of the Glenarm Soup Kitchen. Jimmy Irvine has described the establishment and operation of this attempt to cope with localised pre-Famine poverty:

> Money immediately subscribed by the Countess of Antrim (£25), Mr Hector McGimney (£10) and Mr Francis Turnly (£20) enabled the Committee to buy stores and equipment. Early bills included oatmeal £1.12s.0d; the boiler 6s.0d plus 10d carriages; nails and cord for hanging scales 4d; a shovel 1s.3d; one quire of paper and quills 11d; three tin spoons 1s.3d and one tin measure 11d. The cook, Jane Hamill, was paid 5s.10d a week or 10d daily for a seven day week, to which was added later the cinders belonging to the Soup House.[27]

Initially the management of the soup kitchen had lain in the hands of the Court of Vestry but in the course of time the committee was extended to include the Presbyterian minister, Rev. Alexander Montgomery and the parish priest, Rev. Michael O'Hagan.[28] As a result, by the time the 1847 Famine struck, all four churches in Glenarm village were able to work together in the face of the common threat. So successful was the scheme that the Glenarm soup kitchen was able to continue without having to seek grant aid from the government under the terms of the Relief Act. There

were, in fact, a number of soup-kitchens established in Ballintoy,
Ballyvennaght, Dunourgan near Cushendun and at the top of Coole Brae
in a building which later became a school; and each of these was generally
referred to as 'the Hungry House'. In the Ballymena area there were kitchens
in Dundermot, Ahoghill, Clough, Broughshane, Kells in Tamneybrake and
Toome in Grange. Cooking days were to be three in each week and on one
day raw meal was to be given.[28] The usefulness of soup kitchens as a practical
means of providing local support for those affected by dearth was, by the
time the potato blight began to threaten seriously tenants in North Antrim,
already widely recognised.

The Brochan House at Moyarget, near Ballycastle.
Brochan was the Gaelic name for porridge or stirabout.

In December 1846 Mr Moore, a member of the Ballycastle Board of
Guardians, attended the meeting of the Coleraine Board of Guardians 'to
explain that great advantage had been derived in the Ballycastle Union
from having ovens erected in the Workhouse and the soup shops throughout
the Union in connection with the workhouse'.[29] The Coleraine Guardians

had spent a considerable amount of time debating the wisdom of providing ovens and soup kitchens. At the next meeting it was reported that a:

> letter was received from the Poor Law Commissioners with reference to the minutes of the previous meeting with respect to the resolution to consider the propriety of establishing soup kitchens throughout the Union in connection with the Workhouse, the Commissioners pointing out that such a thing would be illegal. As a result the Board of Guardians resolved that no soup kitchens in connection with the workhouse be established throughout the Union and that the propriety of erecting ovens in the workhouse for baking bread for the inmates be considered previous to the expiration of the present contract for bread.

In spite of the suggested illegality, Ballycastle Guardians had gone ahead and erected several soup kitchens and an article in the *Coleraine Chronicle* early in 1847 described the Ballycastle workhouse as 'ranking amongst the best managed in Ireland because Guardians had set a noble example to other Unions in this country by passing resolutions in the month of November last, directing soup kitchens to be immediately established in different parts of the Union where the poor could be relieved.'[31] The Poor Law Commissioners, alarmed at the boldness of the step, sent their inspector, Mr Edward Senior, to remonstrate on the consequences; the Guardians remained were firm and did not give way until they found that the Commissioners were likely to institute a suit in Chancery against them. But within a month the situation had become so serious that the government was obliged to change its policy and the Poor Law Commissioners rushed through special legislation towards the end of January 1847. This was the Temporary Relief of Destitute Persons (Ireland) Act (known as the Soup Kitchen Act) for the setting up of relief committees under the auspices of a new relief commission throughout the country to provide food for those unable to gain admission to the workhouse. The relief was to be confined to those attending in person (excepting only sick children) and there was to be no preference.

After the failure of the potato crop for the second time in 1846 a great flood of people, starving and emaciated, crowded into the dreaded workhouses, preferring to accept the miserable conditions on offer (including loss of property, break-up of family and segregation of couples) rather than starve to death in their cottages. In December 1846 the Home Secretary was informed that 56 of the 130 workhouses in the country were already filled with far more paupers than they had been built to accommodate.

This alarmed the government and they had to devise some means of controlling this new situation. The Ballymoney Board of Guardians at their meeting on 21 December 1846 held a lengthy discussion respecting the establishment of soup kitchens. It was proposed that the expenses be defrayed out of the rates. It was considered that the gentlemen in the areas where these kitchens were to be established should cess themselves a rate of 3d in the pound on the Poor Law valuation for the purpose of defraying the expenses of the said soup kitchens in place of making an illegal charge on the rates.[32]

A notice in the *Coleraine Chronicle* in early June 1847 stated that the Board of Guardians in Ballycastle had been obliged to close the doors of the workhouse against the entry of any more paupers. 'There are presently 520 inmates in a building which was erected to accommodate 300'.[33] Those who had earlier complained about the under-utilisation of the workhouses had had their answer. The following week the Board of Guardians found it necessary to hold a public meeting in Ballycastle courthouse for the purpose of raising money for Outdoor Relief. After considerable discussion it was proposed and agreed that tenants should subscribe sixpence in the pound and landlords one shilling in the pound based on the Poor Law valuation of their property.

In point of fact, the statistical evidence, extracted from the reports and returns of the Poor Law Commissioners, shows that of the seven workhouses which served Co. Antrim – Antrim, Ballycastle, Ballymena, Ballymoney, Belfast, Larne, Lisburn – only Ballycastle exceeded its limit (300) when the impact of the Famine was at its worst in 1847 and 1848. At Larne, Ballymena, Antrim and Ballymoney, however, the numbers were so close to the official limit that the pressure was clearly evident as the table of numbers in the county's workhouses in December 1846, 1847 and 1848 shows.[34]

WORKHOUSE	ACCOMMODATION	30 DEC 1846	30 DEC. 1847	30 DEC. 1848
Antrim	700 (+350)	569	813	705
Ballycastle	300 (+40)	362	416	396
Ballymena	900 (+130)	921	993	760
Ballymoney	700 (+50)	562	706	670
Belfast	1000 (+2370)	1334	2355	2867
Larne	400 (+380)	513	627	564
Lisburn	800 (+410)	720	774	664

Much of the pressure on workhouses had, until 1847-8, been seasonal, with the winter months attracting most. The pressure, however, continued into the spring and early summer of 1848 when the presence of fever added to the numbers seeking continued shelter in the workhouses.[35]

WORKHOUSE	ACCOMMODATION	APRIL '48	MAY '48	JUNE '48
Antrim	1050	833	793	757
Ballycastle	340	429	433	429
Ballymena	1150	931	899	876
Ballymoney	750	731	696	704
Belfast	2922	2850	2668	2607
Larne	780	559	553	544
Lisburn	1450	822	729	685

Evidence for the continuation of Co. Antrim workhouses remaining under pressure the following year, 1849, is apparent in the testimony of Edward Senior, Poor Law Commissioner with responsibility for some 17 unions in the northern district, to the Select Committee on Poor Laws (Ireland) in March of that year. He used the example of Antrim workhouses to demonstrate his worry that, increasingly, the workhouse population was dominated by women, young people and males incapable of supporting themselves, thus making it impossible to expect the workhouse population to support itself by labouring:

Of 1,000 inmates in a workhouse, you will not find 10 able-bodied males; the greater part will consist of very old and of very young people. On 15th of February [1849] Antrim workhouse contained 780 inmates, of which there were male adults 125 and of female adults 205, or a total of 330 adults; the boys were 231, the girls 204, the infants 25, total 450. There were at that time about 20 able-bodied men...[36]

In tandem with the workhouses, the other principal means of providing relief centred on the role of the landlords of the county. As well as their additional contributions, based on the valuation of their property, the biggest landlords in Co. Antrim – the Marchioness of Londonderry, Lord Antrim and Lord Hertford – all responded variously to meeting the needs of their tenants' distress. John Lanktree kept the Londonderrys informed, though they were absent from their Co. Antrim estate for a large part of the year. Having drawn their attention to the early appearance of the blight in 1845, his report to Lady Frances Anne the following year lamented that the previous year's meagre crop of potatoes had been exhausted as early as March 1846: 'The Potato Plague is beginning to be acutely felt here. In the Drumcrow district of this Estate the greater number of tenants have not had a potato to eat for some weeks...' .[37] Later in the year he wrote to the Marchioness referring to Sir Robert Peel's decision to import £100,000 worth of Indian meal from America and stated: 'I had your Ladyship's approbation to purchase a few tons of oatmeal to lend among them, but did not lay out any money yet in the hope that in a few weeks Sir Robert Peel's measure might enable this to be done on easier terms'.[38]

It is evident that Lanktree had some difficulty in compiling the annual report for 1847 when he wrote:

> The Report of the management of the Antrim Estate for the year 1847 is unfortunately barren of any detail of improvement. During this year it has pleased Divine Providence to visit our unhappy country with a famine unparalled in the annals of human suffering... To those who lived among them, the daily observation of their actual state was very painful. Pallor and anxiety appeared on every face, and hunger knowing no law forced many an individual of previous good character into crime. No class felt the loss of the potato crop more keenly than the small farmers such as the bulk of the tenants on this Estate, who cultivating small patches on the mountain-side depended wholly upon it for their living.[39]

The Marquess and Marchioness of Londonderry had estates throughout Ulster, in Down, Donegal and Londonderry as well as Antrim, and lived for most of the year at either of their houses, Wynyard Park in Co. Durham or Holdernesse House in London. They paid their first visit to their Glens of Antrim estate in December 1846 and, according to Lanktree, 'The respectful deputations from the several districts vying with each other in the loyalty of their addresses – the amateur band of the Estate, the triumphal arches, the discharge of muskets, the blazing bonfires – all evidenced the delight of the warm-hearted people'.[40] During their tour the Londonderrys visited their tenants in the townland of Ballymacaldrick in Dunloy. The tenants must have been aware of their intending visit and welcomed them with a specially prepared address which was particularly obsequious lest it would offend visitors. Much of the address lauded the kindness of the landlords in deigning to visit the area and criticised former landlords who little dreamed of so cherishing their lowly tenants. In the penultimate paragraph they addressed a harsher reality:

> We will not cloud the joyful occasion of this visit by any enumeration of

our present wants and of the great distress with which it has pleased Almighty God to visit us at this time for our sins. Our potato crop, which was the staff of life – the sole sustenance of ourselves, our wives and children – has been totally blighted by an unseen but merciful hand and how we shall pass through the coming season or make up our rents is only known to God – but we know that we are cared for him by Him and by you both – and we commit ourselves to your benevolent consideration.[41]

Their landlord's response was:

Lady Londonderry and I take the liveliest interest in your welfare and participate sincerely in the distress caused by the failure of the potato crop. We must all bow to the will of God.... . Lady Londonderry rejoices that the clothing, blankets, and other arrangements for your comfort, cleanliness, and convenience, have been acceptable. Circumstances over which we have had no control have prevented hitherto our visting our tenantry in this district, but in a time of trouble, in an inclement season, we have personally come amongst you to ascertain your distress and condition... We have ordered that the rents be remitted from the lands lately under the potato crop, which have wholly failed, and the agent will see that employment and encouragement is given to all those who require it, and are really unable to support their families and themselves.

In addition to the remission of rents, seed corn was distributed in the Spring to the poor tenants who had consumed all their grain. Turnip, carrot, and parsnip seeds were allowed to all and a large supply of guano was provided to force the cultivation of green crops, in which it succeeded beyond my expectation.[42]

Following this an estate relief committee was established in the Glencloy district. Lady Frances Anne also organised a number of charitable functions in England for the relief of the Irish. She and her husband hosted a 'Grand Military Bazaar at the Regent's park Barracks for the Distressed Irish' which raised £300 for the relief of distress in Ireland.

John Lanktree's report for 1848 reflected the continuing problems which the successive potato crop failures had brought:

In my last report I had the painful task of recording a period of great trial and difficulty to your tenantry here. To many small farmers it was so ruinous that they abandoned their lands and emigrated to America in the spring of 1848. It is very sad to write that it was the smallest number of those who so went away that succeeded. Some from Ballymacaldrick were in the unfortunate ship, *Exmouth* which, driven by a storm on the rocky coast of one of the Scottish Isles, went to the bottom within grasp of land and left not one passenger of hundreds to tell the tale; others, chiefly from Drumcrow, after landing safely in America were seized with fever which.raged there in an unprecedented manner and [they] perished ere they found a home.[43]

In the same year Hugh Gullian of Ballymacaldrick died of starvation. Another victim was a woman from Ballymacaldrick and when a post mortem was performed there was not one item of food in her stomach. Charles Kelly of Ballyvaddy, near Carnlough, the father of a large family who owned four cows, two horses and a flock of sheep. Rather than part with any of these he went through the country begging for himself, leaving his family to fend for themselves. Unfortunately he got little support or sympathy and died on the road.[44]

Lanktree, as did most agents who were interested in the more efficient management of their estates, saw the benefits which might arise from the Famine when he wrote about small farms being vacated:

> Generally speaking these thinnings were for the good. They enlarged some farms in the hands of better labourers than the emigrants had been; and if many more should go away of which there is a prospect, it will be all the better for the Estate, for without the potato crop it is quite impossible for small farmers to live and pay rent especially on poor soil.[45]

In spite of the Marchioness of Londonderry's apparent concern for her tenants she pushed ahead with her cherished project, the erection of the mansion of Garron Tower in 1848, a year in which she and Lord Londonderry also extensively and lavishly refurbished Holdernesse House, their London home.[46] As if to commemorate her own bounty to her tenants during the Famine, she caused to be smoothed and inscribed the huge block of limestone which is now known as the Famine Stone. It stands along the side of the Antrim Coast Road, just below Garron Tower. It was her intention that the stone should be 'an imperishable memorial of Ireland's affliction and England's generosity in the year 1846/47', a year she described as 'unparalleled in the annals of human suffering'.[47]

A less considerate side of her personality was exposed a year or two later, however. While John Lanktree had been acting as agent for her he had acquired the tenancy of land in the townland of Stoney Hill. Unfortunately, like many other tenants, he found himself in arrears of rent. As agent he had clearly tried to serve the interests of his landlord but, as a tenant, he was inclined to support the cause of his fellow tenants and found himself requesting a reduction in rent in the estate. Lady Londonderry's scathing reply, like all those who saw the Famine as an excuse for whining, was: 'Lanktree's principle seems to be that tenants should have the land as a free gift and pay no rent as we have not received 6d.' Lanktree in his reply on 2 July 1850 pointed out that:

> The advice that I have given would be supported by everyone who knows the actual state of the country and by anyone who wished Lord and Lady Londonderry well. It could not be opposed by any, except by a person ignorant of the country, or having personal object in giving contrary advice; or above all, by an enemy, who would like to see the tenants alienated from an allegiance which they have been fond to maintain. No one ever risked more in giving honest advice on this painful subject.[48]

Unfortunately, Lanktree was to find he had indeed risked everything. The Marchioness acted immediately to have him evicted and sought immediate payment of his debts. On 1 February 1851 he was forced to sell off his property and became a bankrupt. He subsequently emigrated with his family to Australia.[49]

Other landlords, nevertheless, did show compassion to their tenants by abating rents during the worst years of the Famine of land under the potato. One of these was Lord O'Neill of Randalstown, who also was generous in making grants to local voluntary societies. A newspaper report describes how Lord Massereene of Antrim 'sold some potatoes, in the ground, at the high price of £36 per acre. They looked very well; but so extensive has been the ravages of the rot, that the purchasers are greatly disappointed, and would gladly withdraw their agreement.'[50] A subsequent report in the *Belfast Protestant Journal* pointed out that as soon as his lordship was made aware of the fact that the field was tainted by the prevalent disease, he gave orders to his steward to release all parties, who wished it, from the engagements they had entered into for payments. Lord Massereene was congratulated for his well-timed liberality and humane consideration.[51]

It might be expected that Rathlin Island, which is separated from the mainland by a seven-mile stretch of water, could have escaped the ravages of the potato blight but that was not the case. In 1851, Mrs Catherine Gage, wife of Rev. Robert Gage, Church of Ireland rector and landlord of Rathlin, wrote a history of the island. Writing in the final years of the Famine she had this to say:

> A few went [to America] every year from that time until 1846 when the potato failure set in, and the number of emigrants in the following spring amounted to 107, leaving the population of the island considerably diminished; smaller than there is any record of its ever having been in

modern times. In the beginning of 1847 the distress of the people was very great; their entire crop of potatoes rotted in the ground and they had no visible means of support, but an overwhelming providence raised up a few friends in their hour of need.[52]

Obviously the Gages were well connected and their appeals for relief had met with a generous response. A letter was received from a firm of underwriters in Glasgow apologising that they could only assist people who had been shipwrecked; nevertheless, they enclosed a donation of £10 in recognition of the islanders' honesty in dealing with shipwrecks.

In April 1847, J. and J. Cooke, merchants and shipowners, wrote from Derry to Rev. Robert Gage of Rathlin, pointing out that the number of people whom Gage was proposing to send to America was too great for one ship.[53] The letter refers to Mrs Gage's correspondence in which she 'states that there will be eighty persons or thereabouts emigrating...in your list there is above 100. If we could take them all in our ship we would do so with pleasure; but the number going and anxious to get away this spring is so great...we could not take all yours'.[54] Mrs Gage's subsequent reference to 107 people emigrating in the spring of 1847 would appear to confirm that J. and J. Cooke was in fact able to accommodate all the Rathlin Islanders fleeing the Famine after the dark winter of 1846-7.[55] There is a stone at the upper end of the island known as the *Cloch na Scriobach* which means the 'writing stone' and this contained the names of a large group of people who emigrated from the island at this time. The passenger lists of J. and J. Cooke show that eight people sailed on the *Sir Charles Napier* for St John's, Newfoundland on 23 April 1847, and five members of the family of Andy Black sailed on the *John Clarke* for St John's on 18 May 1847.[56]

The population of the island, interestingly, had begun to decline even before the onset of famine: it dropped from 1,100 in 1831 to 1,010 by 1841 and to 753 in 1851. By 1861, its pre-Famine population had been more than halved, at 453, a percentage well in excess of that in the rest of Ireland.[57] On Rathlin Island Frank Craig's father remembered:

> ...the *Erin's Hope*, a ship from America, coming in to the island. The Irish had sent the ship from America with yellow meal on board. Gage got that. Now, listen to this! Gage was the landlord; the Irish in America paid for that yellow meal, but Gage made the people pay for it; that's true for I heard it told here. My father's father, my grandfather, was a blacksmith, so he went for his share of the meal off Gage. So what did Gage do? Says he: 'You're well fit to pay for it, you have money; get the money and you'll

get your share of the meal'. My grandfather had a forge in Fallyack. And there were other friends (relatives) above where Sandy Maguire lives now. They went for their share of the meal and age says 'Yous have money. Pay for your share'. They told him that they had no money. 'Well yous have friends that have money. Get it off your friends and pay for it.' He had money out of that and it given free.[58]

This description of the landlord of Rathlin does not tally with that given by Rev. H. I. Law, who wrote: 'The Rev. Robert Gage proved himself conscientious and faithful in the performance of his duties, both to his tenants and parishioners... During the potato Famine of 1848-47 he was tireless in his efforts to relieve distress among his tenants'.[59] Gage's own account is very matter-of-fact:

Sloop *Annie* arrived here yesterday when the Master handed me your favour of the 20th with cheque for £50 and agreeably to your request I have purchased 32 barrels of Indian corn meal, American ground, at 31s per barrel. I have also purchased the rice, viz., 3 tons Caroline at £28 10s per ton, and 2 tons broken Patna at £25 per ton both excellent quality. They will commence loading this afternoon or to-morrow morning and when all are shipped I shall get Bills of Lading and forward you them with account of Rice and Meal...[60]

A letter of Rev. J .H. Todd, from London, to Gage in 1848 gives some idea of some people's reaction to the Famine in Ireland: 'I have been over here for the last week on business, the nature of which you may guess from the enclosed; but I find it very hard to get money for any Irish object – people are thoroughly disgusted with Ireland – and if the potatoes should again fail this year, I do think that English sympathy will be found to have entirely dried up.'[61]

An intriguing consideration is the extent to which memories and recollections of the Famine on Rathlin have survived. They are, in themselves, a unique source of information. Frank Craig recalled:

I mind (remember) old people here who remembered the Famine...I heard them tell that here some of the people when they saw the blight on top of the stalks, the tops, they started too pull them off to keep the blight from going down. But they'd been better, they said, to let them stay on (remain), and not touch them. The ones they did that with went quicker than ever. Some people here plucked whole fields like that and lost the whole lot; they went far worse.[62]

Frank Craig explained how they managed for food:

They pulled sloak [an edible seaweed] along the shore and they boiled that
with whatever potatoes they had. My father told me that no one had whole
potatoes; they cut the bad part off and used the rest. Yes, they cut the bad
part off and boiled them with the Sloak and ate it. I mind my father telling
how that brought out a rash on people, probably the cholera.[63]

People living in the coastal areas spent a lot of time gathering any sea-
food which would supplement their diet. A range of items not normally
eaten were pressed into service. Limpets were prised off the rocks and used
in the making of limpet soup; sloak was boiled and eaten along with
dumplings made out of oatmeal; whelks were boiled but being small it
took a lot of them to make a meal; dulse, which was purple in colour when
harvested and turned green when it was boiled, made a lovely meal with
potatoes but in the absence of potatoes it can have been a poor substitute.
Carrigeen moss, another type of seaweed, was generally used as a medicine
but in the Famine years it was used as a food. Those who could fish could
get lythe, glashan, codling, mackerel and crabs but with so many searching
for the same items the catches must have been small. Maggie McKinley,
Craigmacagan, Rathlin Island, recollected:

My grandmother minded (remembered) the Famine. She said there was a
boat come into the bay here that took away over a hundred people,whole
families. She had five or six sisters and two brothers and they went away.
A wild lot died on the boat going over. From here they went to East Port,
Maine, and a lot went to Boston.[64]

Folklore memories of the Famine on the mainland part of Co. Antrim
are equally interesting. Joe McConaghy of Mullarts, Ballycastle, born in
1892, had heard his mother talking of the Famine period:

She [mother] talked of people being in a coma. They would be waking
them [holding a wake] and they wouldn't be dead at all. She talked of
some man from Carry that was burying his wife that time and the man
noticed some movement in the coffin; and took the lid off and his wife was
there wondering where she was. She said he had nothing but his overcoat
to put round her and take her home and she lived for a long time after that.
It was true enough that, and there were others like it.[65]

The Donegans of Ballintoy, Co. Antrim, remembered the soup kitchens:

There was a soup-kitchen run by people named McKinnan in the townland
of Cloughcorr. They called them the 'Brochan-men'. It was porridge they
would give you if you would change your religion. At the time there were
a lot of youngsters and these big people, the gentry, would take them to some

RANDALSTOWN SOUP KITCHEN.

At a MEETING of the Inhabitants of RANDALS-TOWN, and vicinity, held on Saturday, 23rd January instant, to take into consideration the state of the suffering Poor, **John B. Hartwell, Esq. in the Chair,**

It was unanimously Resolved that a *Soup Kitchen* be immediately established, for the purpose of relieving their present urgent distress, and that the following Gentlemen be appointed a Committee to carry the objects of the meeting into effect.

Hon. George Hancock,	Dr. Neeson,	Dr. O'Neill,
John B. Hartwell, Esq.	Mr. Alexander Crawford,	Mr. B. Macauley,
Alexander Markham, Esq.	Adam Dickey, Esq.	Mr. John Martin.
Sampson Courtney Esq.	Lieut. Col. Kennedy,	
Dr. Laughlin,	P. Macauley Esq.	

RESOLVED. That the Distribution of the Soup shall be by TICKETS, to be had of the Secretary; and that each person subscribing *One Pound*, shall be entitled to 12 Tickets per week; and so on in proportion, for the First Eight Weeks; after that period the Tickets to be sold to them, the same as to non-subscribers, at 2s. per sheet of 24 Tickets.

RESOLVED. That TUESDAYS, THURSDAYS, and SATURDAYS, be the days for distributing the Soup, and that one, at least, of the Committee attend on each of those days, to see it distributed.

RESOLVED. That a SUBSCRIPTION LIST be now opened; and that Mr. COURTNEY be requested to act as *Treasurer and Secretary.*

RESOLVED. That the following Gentlemen be requested to solicit Subscriptions in Randalstown and its immediate vicinity, viz:—Mr. CRAWFORD, Dr. LAUGHLIN, Dr. NEESON, Mr. COURTNEY; and that a further MEETING be held in the *Court-House,* on MONDAY the 1st FEBRUARY, for the purpose of receiving Subscriptions; and the several Landholders, Farmers, and others, are earnestly entreated to attend, and contribute liberally; otherwise it will be impossible to continue the establishment; the consequence of which will be a vast increase to the Poor Rates.

RESOLVED. That the Secretary forward copies of these resolutions to the Clergymen of all religious denominations in the parish; soliciting their co-operation in carrying out the objects of the Meeting.

RESOLVED. That a GENERAL MEETING be held on the first day of each Month, to audit accounts and that no alteration be made in these resolutions, except at such Meeting.

☞ Subscriptions will be received by the Secretary or any member of the Committee.

J. B. HARTWELL, Chairman.

Dated 23rd January, 1847.

Subscriptions Received at the Meeting.

Lord O'Neill,	£50	Rev. S. S. Heatly,	£5	Mr. Crawford,	£3	Dr. O'Neill,	£1
Hon. G. Handcock,	20	Dr. Neeson,	4	Alex. Markham, Esq.,	2	Mr. John Scott,	1
J. B. Hartwell, Esq.,	5	Sampson Courtney, Esq.	4	Mr. B. M'Auley,	1		
P. M'Auley, Esq.,	10	Dr. Laughlin,	3	Mr. Spiers,	1		

White, Printer, Ballymena

(PRONI T.2890/38/1)

place and give them food. The children would bless themselves before they would eat; and these ones would have their hands tied behind their backs so's they couldn't bless themselves. This happened round here as far as I heard.[66]

The Famine has been customarily referred to as having taken place in 1845 to 1847. However, there is evidence to suggest that signs of the potato blight lingered in Co. Antrim until the early 1850s. On 21 December 1850 'it was resolved by the Lisburn Board of Guardians that stirabout should be subsituted for dinner instead of potatoes on Tuesdays.[67] Greater apprehension was observed in Antrim Union in September 1851 when it recorded: 'From the reports of the Relieving Officers it appeared that the potato crop throughout the Union had suffered to a large extent from disease, especially during the last fortnight but that in general the grain crops of all descriptions looked well and were ripening...'.[68] Exactly one year later, in September 1852, 'The relieving officers reported that so far as they have been able to ascertain the potato blight appears to be more extensive and severe throughout the Union at present than in any year since 1846'.[69]

There is detectable in these comments something of the continuing dread of Famine that would last for generations.

THE FAMINE
IN
COUNTY ARMAGH

GERARD MacATASNEY

It is true that the potato has failed in Connacht and Munster; but it has
failed just as much in Ulster; therefore, if the failure of the potato has
produced all the distress, in the South and West, why has it not caused the
same misery here? It is because we are a painstaking, industrious, laborious
people, who desire to work and to pay our just debts, and the blessing of
the Almighty is upon our labour. If the people of the South had been equally
industrious with those of the North, they would not have so much misery
among them.[1]

Robert Dolling's observation, at a meeting in Lurgan in 1849, implied
that those suffering the ravages of famine had brought it upon themselves
through laziness and indolence. Inherent in his comments was the claim
that the Famine did not affect the 'industrious' people of the north due to
their ability to sustain themselves in such situations. It is all the more
ironic then, to discover that two years previously the population of north

Armagh was suffering as severely as their counterparts in the south and west, with little assistance forthcoming from gentlemen such as Mr Dolling. Indeed, by the 1840s, Co. Armagh was the most densely-populated county in Ireland. It had also experienced the mounting problems which faced rural communities following the Napoleonic wars. In the years prior to the Famine, technical innovations severely undermined the economic well-being of weavers and their families. Moreover, the years 1846-8 witnessed a slump in trade, especially in the demand for linen and cotton. The Belfast papers reported the abandonment of mill-construction in the city; while those partially built were left unfinished. So serious was the situation that, in May 1847, the *Northern Whig* proclaimed 'productive industry is paralysed and the working population are thrown out of employment and left dependent on charity.'[2]

In March, the same paper reported how the new flax crop had proved to be much smaller than usual with the result that 'Flax is so dear and scarce that it cannot be had, even if the spinners could afford to pay the very highest prices.'[3] Allied to such occurrences was the fact that the oat crop, used by weaving families as an alternative to potatoes, proved to be 'much more deficient than was at first calculated upon'. In fact, by March 1847 prices of oats had more than doubled to 20s 6d per hundredweight.[4] Hence, an unlikely combination of a slump in demand together with poor flax and oat harvests served only to accentuate the problems already being experienced by weaving communities.

The Lurgan Poor Law Union was constituted under the Irish Poor Law Act of 1838. Covering much of north Armagh together with parts of counties Antrim and Down, it contained in 1841 a population of 71,128 living in an area of 79,201 acres. The area was characterised by a multiplicity of weavers' cottages attached to small plots of land. Landholdings of one acre or less accounted for over one third of the total number of landowners in the union. This fact was, in the opinion of many, directly related to the dominance of the linen industry in the locality. John Hancock, agent to Charles Brownlow, the local landlord, offered the following explanation to the Devon Commission in 1844: 'Linen manufacture offers the strongest inducement to subdivision, because a small portion of ground, in addition to looms, will support a family'.[5]

Alongside the weavers, however, there lived a substantial number of people who lived on the margins. Indeed, over one third of the population just managed to eke out an existence as basic as anywhere else in the country.

For this class employment was only to be had in the harvest months from March to June and August to November. Their wages averaged about one shilling per day and when unemployed they either relied on the charity of others or resorted to begging, with one observer remarking: 'In such cases mendicancy is not infrequently the habitual trade of the children and sometimes of the wife too'.[6] They lived in one-roomed mud cabins with little furniture, whilst their clothing was described as ranging from 'tolerantly good' to 'wretched beyond description'.[7] Crucially though, the diet of this class consisted almost exclusively of potatoes, meal and milk, with occasional additions of salted herrings, oatbread and stirabout. The inclusion of meal was virtually unheard of and it would appear that the Rev. Ivers of Tartaraghan was stating the rule rather than the exception when he commented: 'Sometimes their breakfast, dinner and supper consist of potatoes'.[8] Thus, although the Lurgan area had a reputation as a thriving linen district, it contained a substantial proportion of people who were existing at the lowest level.

The Lurgan workhouse, with a capacity for 800 paupers, was opened on 22 February 1841. However, from then until 1845 the institution was less than one quarter filled. A husband and wife fulfilled the roles of master and matron and a sound administrative structure was maintained in these years. In May 1845, however, the husband and wife were dismissed for alleged 'levity of conduct'.[9] This event proved to be highly significant as the following year saw the appointment of three different masters, doing little to ensure a smooth-running administration. Ironically, in the midst of such constant change the workhouse received its first test with the outbreak of fever in June 1846. For the first time the house was substantially filled with almost 500 paupers, many of them in the fever hospital. The situation warranted a visit from Dr Stevens of the Fever Commissioners in Dublin. In his report Stevens gave details of how the medical officer, Dr Bell, had been allowing healthy children to enter the hospital with their sick parents, thus exacerbating an already deteriorating situation.

The Commissioners wrote to the Lurgan Board of Guardians to demand the resignation of Bell. The Guardians were incensed by what they believed to be interference in their internal affairs and presented a vigorous defence of their officer – so vigorous in fact that the Commissioners, although not exonerating Bell, left the final decision to the guardians themselves. They responded by increasing his salary by £20 *per annum*.[10] However, unbeknown to the Guardians, the negligence of their medical officer in this episode was to have far-reaching consequences in the months ahead, when many more people were to resort to the workhouse for relief.

LURGAN POOR LAW UNION 1847

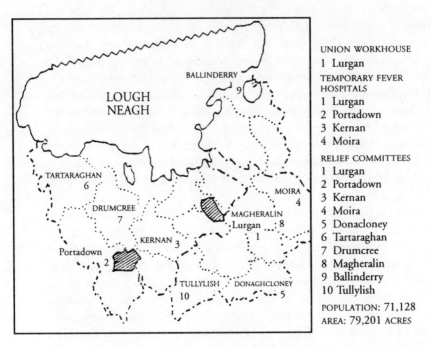

UNION WORKHOUSE
1 Lurgan
TEMPORARY FEVER HOSPITALS
1 Lurgan
2 Portadown
3 Kernan
4 Moira
RELIEF COMMITTEES
1 Lurgan
2 Portadown
3 Kernan
4 Moira
5 Donacloney
6 Tartaraghan
7 Drumcree
8 Magheralin
9 Ballinderry
10 Tullylish
POPULATION: 71,128
AREA: 79,201 ACRES

III

The first failure of the potato crop in 1845, although not as serious as in other areas, did have an impact in Lurgan Union. James Woodhouse, a local businessman, reported a loss of between one quarter and one third of the crop in the Portadown area.[11] At the same time, a supply of potatoes to the Lurgan workhouse from Joseph Berry of Moira was found to be 'very insufficient, there being a great number of rotten and of very small size.'[12] One of the major consequences of the blight was an increase in the price of potatoes per hundredweight – from 1s 11d in April 1845 to 2s 3d in March 1846. This was reflected in a gradual reduction of potatoes in the workhouse diet, being replaced at first by bread and then by meal. Thus, in April 1846, dinner consisted of a few ounces of meal made into stirabout.[13] More significantly, though, the partial failure of 1845 resulted in a shortfall of some ten per cent in the supply of seed potatoes for the following year.[14]

Nevertheless, in early 1846, the new crop appeared to be blight-free and a local constabulary report revealed that 'many persons had decided on not planting potatoes to the same extent; but they have changed their minds, finding those planted to appear healthy and vigorous in their growth.'[15] In April, the Grand Jurors of the county reported 'favourably' on the state of the crop.[16]

Any such optimism about the new season proved to be ill-founded, however, as in July and August the blight struck again – this time with widespread and devastating effect. The *Northern Whig*, quoting from the Armagh agricultural report for August, gave the following account of the destruction:

> Mostly every potato field the eye could light on had the appearance of having been blighted by frost, and in most instances, the petals of the blossoms of the late planted potatoes were observed to wither and shed, in the course of a few hours at times, by day and by night.[17]

This report was corroborated by a Mr Brown from Donacloney who informed the Lurgan Union Farming Society that, on travelling from Warrenpoint to Lurgan, he could 'scarcely believe the smell along the road arising from the decomposition of the potatoes.'[18] Proof that the Lurgan Union did not escape the blight was given in reply to a circular sent by the Commissioners. George Greer, on behalf of the Guardians, remarked that the blight had reappeared in every electoral division of the union and had affected the entire crop.[19]

The most noticeable manifestation of the failure was the increase in the number of people entering the workhouse. At the end of September 1846 the number was 313; by October this reached 432; by November 598 and by the end of December the workhouse was full to capacity with 805 inmates.[20] This increase in admission rates was accompanied by a corresponding rise in the number of deaths.[21] Throughout the year the average number of deaths per month was about 14 but, in November 1846, 31 paupers died and, in December, 58 deaths occurred.[22]

It may be argued that the Poor Law was overwhelmed by the huge numbers applying for relief. Doubtless, workhouses were not built to cater for a calamity on the scale of that of the Famine. Nevertheless, there seemed to be an inability to comprehend the disaster which faced them. One of their number declared at a local society dinner that potatoes had, in his opinion, allowed small farmers to become 'lazy, idle and indolent'.[23] A number of landlords appeared to feel this way and seemed genuinely uninterested in the plight of the poor. From March 1846 to March 1847, for example, only 11 of the 32 Guardians attended more than half of the 54 meetings. Indeed, only three attended 40 meetings or more.[24] Such apathy offers an insight into possible reasons for the huge numbers of deaths in the workhouse between December 1846 and April 1847. As Dr Smith noted, the Guardians had no knowledge of the condition of the workhouse and paid little attention to the quality of food purchased. At a time when strict administration was of the utmost importance they were negligent in the extreme. An example of this was provided when Father O'Brien discovered a body which had lain in a ward for sixteen hours? The chaplain referred to this as a 'dereliction of duty' but it was a symptom of earlier problems.[25]

The Lurgan Union was not alone in its suffering, however, and on 6 January 1847 the *Belfast Vindicator* carried the following report:

> It is, unhappily, too evident that Ireland is now suffering under an awful calamity – famine, disease and premature death, prevailing in some degree everywhere. Accounts multiply of destitution and suffering and death in their most appalling forms; the cry of distress is becoming louder every day; the prospects for the future are very dark.[26]

With the workhouse full, the cry of distress in the union was met by the establishment of local relief committees. Such bodies had emerged in other parts of the country in response to the failure of 1845, but they had proved unnecessary in most of Ulster. However, in the worsening conditions of the winter of 1846, relief committees proved to be an essential component of attempts to counteract the effects of food scarcity. They also illustrated how the Poor Law, restricted to relief inside a workhouse, proved totally ineffective when dealing with widespread local distress.

By December such committees had been established in Lurgan, Portadown, Drumcree, Clonmacate and Moira. In January further groups emerged in Donacloney, Tullylish, Maralin, Ballinderry and Kernan.[27] From each area came harrowing reports of human suffering: in Drumcree the condition of the poor was described as being one of 'extreme deprivation and distress';[28] in Portadown there was 'great distress prevailing amongst our very numerous class of working people'[29] with Lord Gosford declaring the population to be 'very dense and in a most wretched state.';[30] in Donacloney there existed an 'awful want and destitution on the part of those applying for relief';[31] whilst in Moira comment was made on the 'destitute condition of the labouring classes in consequence of the failure of the potato'.[32]

For the most part, the catalyst for establishing the relief committees was the local clergy, both Catholic and Protestant, with the local landed gentry either participating at a minor level or solely through subscription. The most important aspect of the committees was their ability to purchase and distribute food – mainly meal and soup. Finance was raised by means of public subscription to a relief fund and any amount subscribed was supplemented by an equal amount from central government funds in Dublin. Most subscribers were clergymen, gentry or farmers although outside relief agencies did play an important part in augmenting local finance. Thus, the following agencies supported relief in the Lurgan Union: the Belfast Relief Fund; the Central Relief Committee of the Society of Friends; the National Club, London; the Ladies Dublin Association; the Durham Relief Association; the Irish Relief Association and the Calcutta Fund.[33]

Such external aid was all the more important when the evidence suggests that some landlords appeared indifferent to the suffering of their tenants. In letters to the local press, Rev. Clements of Tartaraghan complained bitterly about the obduracy of local landlords:

> There are only two resident landed proprietors within the parish ... The largest estate is under the administration of the Lord Chancellor for debt with no help whatsoever being obtained from it for its starving tenantry. A large portion of the parish is bog, the property of absent proprietors and upon it are located a large number of most wretched tenants who are not assisted by the landlord'.[34]

Indifference on the part of some members of the landed class was compounded by red tape and bureaucracy which meant that delay was encountered by committees when applying for financial assistance. A possible explanation is that the Relief Commission offices in Dublin would have been inundated with such requests. Nevertheless, on occasions the chairmen of local committees had to send two or three letters informing the authorities of the amount subscribed locally and enquiring as to when government money would be forthcoming. For example, on 28 March, William Morris, local postmaster and treasurer of the Lurgan Relief Fund, sent a letter to Dublin stating that £53 had been subscribed and asking for an equivalent amount; by April 17 he had not received a reply.[35] Similarly, in Ballinderry, the local treasurer, Miller, wrote to Dublin on 22 February; by the beginning of March he had heard nothing.[36]

Despite such problems local relief committees did manage to fulfil their purpose of selling or distributing food. In Lurgan, the Church of Ireland Rector, Rev. Oulton, was selling 'good substantial nourishing broth' together with a piece of bread, at one penny per quart;[37] while the Drumcree Fund was giving 'weekly aid to 450 destitute families, amounting to 2,300 people,'[38] with Babington, the secretary, commenting: 'I am prepared to state there is not a single family upon our relief list able to live without charitable assistance – without this, many would have perished from want.'[39]

In Ballinderry, relief consisted of sales of Indian meal at half-price (which was expressly forbidden by the Treasury) whilst in Donacloney, Kernan and Moira soup was being distributed through local kitchens with the latter committee supplying about 300 people.[40] One of the worst-affected areas was Tartaraghan where, as we have seen, Rev. Clements castigated what he termed the 'evil effects of absenteeism'.[41] A soup kitchen and meal fund were established to cater for over 1300 'destitute persons', a number which was 'expected daily to increase'.[42]

The following description of the level of distress in the locality was sent by Clements to the Commissioners in Dublin:

> Both weavers and labourers are daily becoming less equal to work and starvation is pictured in their countenances. Numbers are subsisting on less than one meal per diem and upon raw turnips and any herbs they can gather. Already one case of death from starvation has occurred ...and several have only just been preserved from it, while fever has attacked very many in the district. Within the last few days, parties of twenty to thirty famishing men have been traversing the county demanding assistance. In the absence of all public works of any kind, and when our poor houses are nearly filled, we hardly know where to turn for assistance.[43]

In the midst of such hopelessness it is perhaps not surprising to find that some resorted to obtaining food illegally. On 13 January, the police in Portadown reported that 'men to the number of five and twenty or thirty armed with flintlocks'[44] stole 50 bags of flour from a barge at Madden's Bridge. In the following weeks similar attacks were made on boats belonging to the Ulster Canal Company in which barrels of flour and Indian meal were taken.[45] At a subsequent meeting of the county magistrates, outrage was expressed at such developments with the gentleman believing the police to be 'totally inadequate in point of numbers to take the duty-keeping watch'.[46] In order to prevent a recurrence of such actions they recommended that 'a portion of Her Majesty's regular troops might be advantageously employed in this service as well as in protecting the boats laden with provisions on the Newry Canal'.[47]

However, the vast majority of people remained within the boundaries of the law and for many the only assistance available was at the local workhouse. In this institution, though, daily tragedy was becoming commonplace. In the first week of January there were 18 deaths recorded; in the second week the number was 36, and for the week ending 16 January the total reached 55 deaths.[48] The pages of the visiting chaplains' notebooks, previously occupied with details of 'divine services' and 'scripture readings', now told a sorry tale of multiple burials, with both the Catholic and Episcopalian chaplains performing interments on a daily basis.[49]

Concern was expressed by the Commissioners in Dublin and, on 16 January, they sent a letter to the Lurgan Guardians indicating their regret at what they termed the 'great mortality' in the workhouse and requiring a detailed report from Dr Bell on the reasons for the high number of deaths.[50] Perhaps, mindful of the report of Dr Stevens in May 1846, they also asked for a report on the sanitary conditions in the building.[51] In his communication Bell stated that many deaths had occurred because numerous people had entered the workhouse in a sick condition and had died shortly afterwards. Thus, 'mortality in the workhouse is much greater than under ordinary circumstances and it is a well-known fact that many dying persons are sent for admission merely that coffins may be thereby obtained for them at the expense of the union'.[52]

In relation to sanitation, he reported that as there were four times the usual numbers of inmates, the building was now overcrowded and consequently it had been impossible to provide dry bedding; thus 'sleeping upon damp beds has increased fever and bowel complaints which have in many cases proved fatal'.[53] However, the doctor concluded his report with optimism by arguing that the cause of such deaths would be largely eradicated with the purchase of new bedding and creation of a proper drying house.[54] Such a statement, whether to placate the Commissioners or not, was soon shown to be utopian as in subsequent weeks mortality levels, far from falling, actually increased. In the week ending 23 January 1847, 58 died, and the trend continued upwards. On 30 January there were 68 deaths, on 6 February, 95, and on 13 February, 67.[55]

Given that large numbers were dying throughout the country, the Lurgan figures may be thought to be representative of the time. However, on examining the general mortality levels, this belief proves to be ill-founded. For example, during the week ending 6 February, there were 95 deaths in the workhouse in Lurgan.[56] This was the highest figure in Ulster, representing slightly less than one fifth of the province's total mortality for that week – 529; the second highest was 30 deaths in Enniskillen workhouse. Nationally, the highest number was in the Cork Union where, with a workhouse population of 5,388, 128 deaths had occurred. In the province of Connacht the highest level was in Loughrea workhouse in Co. Galway where, with 524 inmates, 26 had died.[57]

Lurgan's total of 67 deaths in the following week was second in Ulster behind that of Glenties, Co. Donegal where, out of a total of 426 inmates, 69 had died. The highest figure was once again Cork where 164 paupers had died.[55] Glenties was later to be deemed as one of the 'distressed districts' by the British Relief Association – the only one in Ulster; as such, large-scale relief was required to stave off widespread poverty and hunger. At the same time, Cork had become synonymous with the horrors of famine and the existence of mass famine graves. So, in the early months of 1847, the Lurgan area, described by a local paper as a 'prosperous and thriving town'[59] was suffering a level of workhouse mortality on a par with the worst-affected areas in the country.

Dr Bell's explanation that many deaths had occurred from sleeping on wet beds does not appear to have been entirely satisfactory as members of staff, presumably enjoying better accommodation than the paupers, began to fall ill. By late January, the porter had dysentery and the assistant ward master, together with the schoolmaster, were ill with fever.[60] In February the assistant ward master died and the clerk was suffering from the 'high symptoms of dysentery'.[61] In a desperate effort to alleviate what the Guardians called 'this dreadful visitation', two remedies were attempted. [62] Firstly, all available space was to be utilised in order to avoid overcrowding; thus the aged and infirm women were moved to a room above the stairs and the women's day room was acquired for hospital purposes.[63] However, the Guardians felt that more drastic action was required and on 5 February they issued the following announcement: 'Notice is hereby given that in consequence of the present state of the workhouse and fever hospital, the Guardians have been obliged to close their doors for the present against all further admissions'.[64]

As a second measure, Lurgan Board of Guardians requested a visit by three 'eminent physicians' in order to remedy the 'unprecedented extension of disease and death'.[65] The doctors – Thompson, Cumming and Purden – recommended that a third medical officer, along with Doctors Bell and McVeagh, was essential to meet the current epidemic.[66] They also conveyed the opinion that the present paupers' diet was inadequate in that recently they had been receiving soup for dinner, and four ounces of rice for supper, instead of bread and buttermilk.[67] However, the doctors considered such a diet to be insufficient to meet the needs of the paupers and recommended the following regime: breakfast – three and a half ounces of meal and porridge, and one quarter pint of buttermilk; dinner – six ounces of bread and one pint broth; supper – three ounces of bread and one quarter pint of buttermilk. They also stipulated that the porridge was to be made entirely of oatmeal – not Indian corn-meal.[68]

The closure of the workhouse and visit of the doctors suggests that the authorities and medical staff were having severe problems coping with the numbers of destitute persons now prevailing in the Lurgan Union. Indeed, in a communication to the Relief Commissioners' Office in Dublin, John Hancock reported that of 313 cases on the books of the Lurgan Dispensary, 136 were suffering from fever and dysentery; for the same period in 1846 this total was 20.[69] The extent of the epidemic may be gauged by Hancock's enquiry as to whether the Central Board of Health could appoint a medical officer 'to provide food and medicines for diseased, destitute people at their own houses'.[70]

Unfortunately no reply to this letter remains, but its details illustrate both the alarming extent to which fever and its associated ailments had become endemic in the Lurgan area and the level of helplessness felt by concerned gentlemen such as Hancock. However, any belief that the disease was rampant and could not be blamed on the authorities was challenged by two devastating and condemnatory investigations – one from within the workhouse, the other from without – which cast huge doubts over the competence of both the medical and administrative staff in that institution.

The deaths in the workhouse eventually reached the ears of the press and under the headline 'Mortality in Lurgan Workhouse' the *Newry*

Telegraph reported on the 'frightful mortality' and the fact that many of the office-holders, as well as the paupers, had been, or were presently, ill.[71] *The Belfast Vindicator*, meanwhile, informed its readers that 'nearly 400 paupers have died in the Lurgan Workhouse during the last eight weeks.'[72] The Commissioners had been monitoring the situation and, obviously dissatisfied with the previous report of Dr Bell, they decided to send Dr Smith from the Central Board of Health to investigate workhouse conditions.[73] The fact that Smith only visited two other workhouses, Bantry and Cork, and then made a trip of 300 miles north illustrates both the urgency which the Commissioners attached to the situation and their determination to effect a remedy as soon as possible.

Dr Smith's report, completed on 17 February, concentrated on the standard of medical care in the workhouse but as a consequence it also offered an insight into the competence of the general administration therein. The most obvious feature of the institution was the level of overcrowding, and Smith reported that in the male and female infirmaries there was an average of two persons to each bed although three and four per bed was not uncommon.[74] The wards were found to be in a terrible condition:

> There are four wards in the idiot department that are without any flooring but the earth, and in two of them there are no bedsteads, so that the beds lie upon the wet ground. One of them – in which at the time of my visit two wretched creatures were dying – was in an exceedingly foul condition; in one corner a pile of old filthy clothes, shoes, etc.; in another a large heap of straw; in another place a quantity of coals scattered about; the ventilation was very imperfect.[75]

Further investigation found the floor and walls of the infirmary to be in a 'very discreditable condition with the windows almost 'universally closed, the atmosphere close and foul; the smell upon entering the rooms most offensive'.[76] Walls had not been white-washed, buckets, used as lavatories, were allowed to sit for hours without being emptied and medicines and drinks were served out on the floor where the boards were in a filthy state'.[77] A similar scenario was presented to the doctor in the fever sheds. However, the fever hospital, controlled by a full-time nurse, was found to contain comfortable beds, clean walls and floors, well-ventilated wards and well-attended patients.[78]

Due to general overcrowding it emerged that, as a result of an inadequate supply of garments, the clothes of those paupers who had died of fever or dysentery were used by other paupers without prior cleaning and drying.[79]

Another area of concern was that of pauper burials. Many paupers had been buried less than four yards from the fever hospital and in the centre of the burial ground was the well which supplied water to the workhouse. In fact, the graves had been dug so close to it that the water had become muddy and unfit for use.[80] Not surprisingly, in the light of what he had seen, Smith described the Lurgan workhouse as 'a picture of neglect and discomfort such as I have never seen in any other charitable institution'.[81] He recommended that the following measures be implemented as soon as possible:

1) All admissions to the workhouses to cease until fever and dysentery cases abate.
2) All rooms used by the sick to be properly fumigated and white-washed.
3) Movement of some patients from the infirmary to the workhouse where space was available.
4) Thorough whitewashing of the infirmary; cleansing of its floors and improvement of its ventilation
5) Daily inspection of the above recommendations to be carried out by the medical officer.[82]

Alongside such improvements, Smith felt it necessary to apportion blame for the terrible conditions which he had encountered, and remarked, 'It is not difficult to deduce the causes of the mortality which has lately devastated the Lurgan workhouse and which still continues'.[83] He believed that the problems stemmed from the death of the master, John Meason, in early November and the fact that three weeks passed before a successor was appointed. During this period overcrowding had developed and continued until the end of January. This, coupled with the fact that many subordinate officers had been ill at one time or another, meant that 'ventilation, whitewashing and cleanliness appear to have been neglected at the very time when the strictest attention to these important means of arresting the spreading of disease were most imperatively called for'.[84] He contended that, despite a heavy workload, 'a little more activity'[85] on the part of Dr Bell, together with a stricter surveillance by the Guardians, would have prevented much of the mortality, stating:

> It appeared to me that the Guardians had no knowledge of the state of the infirmary as regards cleanliness, ventilation, etc. either from personal observation or otherwise. The reports of the physicians informed them of

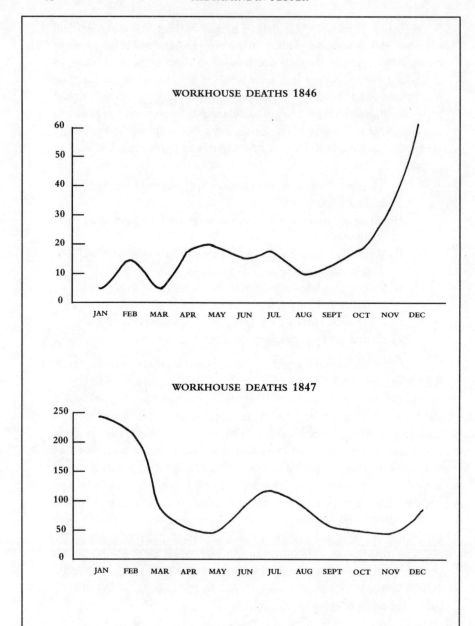

WORKHOUSE DEATHS 1846

WORKHOUSE DEATHS 1847

its overcrowded state and this was the only particular about it with which they seem to be acquainted.[86]

He concluded his report with the following indictment of the workhouse administration: 'I am of the opinion that the chief causes of evil in question are internal, and the result of defective management of the institution'.[87]

Such a wide-ranging report served to undermine the competence of those charged with caring for the paupers in the workhouse; but almost immediately after a letter from one of the chaplains illustrated that there was a degree of negligence and indifference of an almost incredible nature amongst both staff members and the Lurgan Board of Guardians. In a lengthy letter to Lord Lurgan, Rev. Oulton felt the need to draw his attention to the appalling standard of food being used in the workhouse: 'It is hardly to be wondered at that so much disease should be in the workhouse if the description of food has for any length of time been such as I saw there today'.[88] He said that the bread used for supper was dark-coloured, insufficiently baked, and sour, whilst the broth was so bad that many paupers could not eat it.[89] He described the meat as being 'of the worst description that could be got in Lurgan Street – more like the flesh of an animal that had died of disease than being killed for food'.[90] Further, he doubted whether the cooking utensils and kitchen were in an hygienic condition: 'It was once in a very bad state and might be so again'.[91] Oulton concluded his letter thus: 'I could not refrain from mentioning these matters to you which doubtless have had no inconsiderable share in producing the dreadful mortality which has sweeped our workhouse and I am sure you will take the earliest opportunity of investigating them to the utmost'.[92]

Almost immediately an internal enquiry was convened by the board involving many of the principal workhouse officials. The ward master, Thomas Lutton, said that the bread had been bad for over a week and believed it to be 'unfit for human food'.[93] He continued: 'Many of the sick paupers have complained to me that the bread was so bad that they could not eat it and I consider their complaints are well founded'.[94] He said the beef used for soup was of very poor quality and reported this to Mr Bullock. He said it had a very offensive smell but this soup was afterwards sent to the patients in the hospital.[95]

However, the stark contrast between the lives of the paupers and those of the officers is illustrated by Lutton's following revelation: 'The bread furnished to the officers cannot be complained of and is much superior to what is provided for the paupers'.[96] This point was corroborated by another ward master, William Fairly, who remarked: 'The baker, when he brings bread always has the officers' bread in a basket by itself'.[97]

Fairly also believed the paupers' bread to be unfit for human consumption[98] – a view shared by Dr Bell who believed the bread to have been of poor quality for almost two months.[99] Bell further remarked that the meat had been 'defective'[100] for a long time, though never as bad as now, and concluded: 'I have no hesitation in stating that the disease in the house would not have been so bad if we had a sufficient supply of wholesome bread and good beef such as was contracted for'.[101] Dr McVeagh concurred with this opinion, believing that the diarrhoea and dysentery now prevalent had been aided by the use of sub-standard bread, 'From my experience as a medical man I don't know a worse description of food for persons affected with diarrhoea and dysentery than sour bread'.[102]

The immediate consequence of the inquiry was the return of 200 lbs of bread to the contractor, Kennedy.[103] However, John Hancock, in a letter to the Commissioners, reported that only six lbs of meat had been deemed to be unsound.[104] He also offered as a possible explanation for the obvious chaos in the workhouse the fact that the master and matron both had fever and thus their duties were being undertaken by the schoolmaster and mistress who were 'doing their duty as well as can be expected under the present trying circumstances'.[105] Regardless of any such excuses for the conditions in the workhouse, the institution appears to be have gained a rather notorious reputation in the union which was reflected in the following comment from Henry Wynne, chairman of the Moira Relief Committee, that 'The mortality in the Poor House of Lurgan is such as would prevent our Guardians from sending any of our poor to the establishment at present'.[106]

Unfortunately, on examining the sources, the revelations of both enquiries do not come as a surprise. It is important to remember that in February 1846 a visiting committee from the Poor Law Commissioners had described the workhouse as being 'filthy and unclean'. Some months later Dr Stevens discovered conditions which, in his opinion, necessitated an immediate removal of the medical officer. On the whole, the Board of Guardians, together with some medical staff, appear to have shown a complete disregard for the paupers under their control. They made no attempt to ensure cleanliness and the application of proper medical facilities. It seems incredible that the clothes of disease-ridden inmates, who had perished, were then passed, unwashed, to incoming paupers. Equally, no attempt was made to ensure a decent standard of food for the paupers. Indeed, the use of unclean clothes together with supplies of bad bread and meat meant that instead of limiting the spread of fever and other diseases, those in charge through sheer incompetence, hastened its advance through the workhouse.

It is significant that Dr Smith pointed out that the lapse between the death of Mr Meason and the appointment of a new master came at a time when the workhouse numbers were rapidly rising. In fact, between May 1845 and May 1847 there were no less than seven masters in the workhouse. Such disruption would have done little to ensure the establishment of a smooth-running administration. However, this cannot excuse the inaction of other administrators. They appear to have had no idea as to what the conditions were in the workhouse and it took the reports of a visiting doctor together with the observations of a chaplain to bring the reality of the situation to their notice.

Consequently, it is surprising to find that no one was prepared to shoulder the blame for the deficiencies and in fact only one member of staff resigned – Dr Bell.[107] In doing so, he reported that overworking had resulted in a deterioration of his health. However, regardless of such an explanation, it is unlikely that Bell would have been able to continue as medical officer after the scathing reports which had cast serious doubts on his professional competence. Consequently, the only course open to him was that of offering his resignation, which was accepted. However, those charged with appointing both the medical and administrative staff and contracting for food did not feel the need to take similar action, nor did any member of Lurgan Board of Guardians resign.

Mortality and destitution did not prevail only in the workhouse and a local newspaper gave the following account of conditions in the Lurgan area: 'Sickness is spreading rapidly outside the workhouse, and unless government immediately send down a medical gentleman from Dublin, to investigate the cause of the distemper, and take measures to check it, it will make an awful havoc here'.[108] This prediction proved to be correct as shortly afterwards the fever claimed its most high-profile casualty, the landlord Lord Lurgan, who died of typhus fever in April. His sudden demise was lamented by the local press, with *The Newry Telegraph* declaring: 'He has ever been one of the most deservedly esteemed landlords in Ulster –

paternal care and consideration for his tenantry he unceasingly manifested'.[109] For its part, *The Armagh Guardian* printed the following eulogy:

> The death of one whose charity and benevolence shed happiness and comfort on the neighbourhood in which he so constantly resided must not be passed over in silence. Constantly residing at his baronial mansion, he united daily with all classes of the people, patiently lending a ready ear to their distress, and ever mindful to their welfare.[110]

However, *The Belfast Vindicator*, though regretting the late Lord's death, added a more sombre tone, when it stated, 'When the concomitants of famine prey upon such victims, it is high time for the mighty and the wealthy to make common cause with the poor, and close the door against pestilence by shutting out hunger'.[111]

Like all the mighty and wealthy of society, Lord Lurgan was afforded a stately burial attended by local and national dignitaries as well as thousands of others. His body was interred in the Brownlow family vault in Shankill parish graveyard.[112]

However, unlike the late Lord, those hundreds of paupers who perished in the workhouse and in the ditches, on the roads or in their pathetic mud-walled huts received no extravagant eulogies or burials. Lord Lurgan's death received more attention in the press than any of the terrible occurrences in the workhouse. The paupers in that institution died in such quantities that the only testament to their existence was their number in the Book of Deaths which was painted on a label and placed at the head of each grave.[113] As the following report illustrates, they did not even receive the dignity of an individual burial:

> In the graveyard attached to the house, a large grave is made which fills nearly full of water a short time after it is opened. To its verge are brought the coffins containing the dead bodies – these coffins frequently contain two and three each – they are then put into the grave, in which they usually float. One or two persons then stand on the coffins in the water until the mould is heaped upon them. There are frequently twenty bodies in the one grave.[114]

Such indignity was not confined to workhouse burials and a member of the Society of Friends, commenting on conditions in Tartaraghan, in the west of the union, observed that 'Last year, to have been buried without a hearse would have been a lasting stigma to a family; now hearses are almost laid aside'.[115]

The fact that death and disease were endemic in the Lurgan Union appears to have made little impact on the local press. In fact these papers, doubtless appealing to the middle and upper classes, appeared more interested in events in America, Europe and Africa than in the terrible occurrences much closer to home. Indeed, without the reports of various religious societies, and the occasional letter to the press one could easily be misled into believing that there was little distress in this area and that famine conditions were limited to Munster and Connacht. However, the fact that such correspondence, although limited, does exist offers a valuable insight into conditions in Lurgan during that terrible time.

The following letter to *The Belfast Newsletter*, although lengthy, conveys the suffering of the destitute in the area:

Sir,

Employed in administering the benevolence of Christian Friends in England, I have met with some deplorable cases which, I think, cannot be exceeded even in the south of Ireland. About the beginning of this month – April – on the old road leading to Portadown, I called on a family named McClean and found the house like a pig-sty. Having fled from the Lurgan Poor House, where fever and dysentery prevailed, they returned home only to encounter greater horrors. Want sent the poor man to bed and I gave him assistance, but he died a few days later. The wife, almost immediately after, met the same melancholy fate; and a daughter soon followed her parents to the grave.

On the Thursday after, I repeated my visit, and just within the door of the wretched habitation, I saw a young man, about twenty years old, sitting before a live coal, about the size of an egg, entirely naked; and another lad, about thirteen leaning against a post. On turning to the right, I saw a quantity of straw, which had become litter; the rest of the family reclining on this wretched bed, also naked, with an old rug for covering. The boy who stood against the post directed my attention to an object at my feet, which I had not seen before, and over which I nearly stumbled, the place being so dark – and oh! what a spectacle – a young man about fourteen or fifteen, on the cold damp floor, off the rubbish, dead!; without a single vestige of clothing, the eyes sunk, the mouth wide open, the flesh shrivelled up, the bones all visible, so small around the waist that I could span him with my hand. The corpse had been left in that situation for five successive days.[116]

The same writer visited the house the following week and was presented with further horrors:

I put my shoulder to the door, pushed it again, and saw the same heap of rubbish and rug, under which lay two boys and a girl together. The young man, whom I had seen sitting at the coal in my preceding visit, now was dead upon the floor – thrown off the bed, and with his head close to the that of the living one, his knees up to the face, the eyes and mouth wide extended. I asked the survivors how long had he been dead? In a hollow, sepulchral tone, they replied 'three days'. They seemed to be in a state of insensibility with respect to surrounding objects; and in this stupor I left them. Out of eight members of a family, three only survive, and I understand that the doctor who has visited them through the past week states that none of these will be any time alive. This famine is stalking through our land, and pestilence in her train is accomplishing the work of destruction.[117]

Such harrowing and heart-rending sights were by no means uncommon. In Tartaraghan, the Society of Friends reported that people had died of starvation and one member commented on seeing a four year-old girl, 'a few weeks ago a strong healthy girl, who was so emaciated as to be unable either to stand or move a limb'.[118] Such were the sights witnessed by the writer that he concluded, 'We are, in short, rapidly approaching, and if unassisted, must arrive at a state parallel to the worst pictures that have been presented to the public from the County of Cork'.[119]

However, conditions did not degenerate to such a level due largely to the fact the Board of Guardians, under scrutiny by the Commissioners, quite literally began to get their house in order. On appointing a new medical officer, Dr McLaughlin from Downpatrick,[120] they decided to revise and improve all aspects of workhouse administration. From now on, the medical officer had to attend each board meeting and present weekly reports of sickness, mortality, medical requirements and dietaries.[121] Further, the master was now required to have his books written up and given to the clerk each Tuesday morning for posting to the Commissioners that evening. He was also required to attend each board meeting 'with all the necessary books of the establishment under his control for the information of the Board'.[122]

Taking cognizance of Dr Smith's comments, sanitary improvements were implemented: the porter was ordered to burn the clothes of deceased paupers and to fumigate with brimstone and sulphur the clothes of those still alive; all ventilators were to be cleaned and improved and 'lids with hinges placed on all the night stools'.[123] On 24 March, Dr Phillips was informed that his services were no longer required[124] and, on Dr McLaughlin's orders, the board refused admission to any further cases of

fever and dysentery until further notice.[125] A significant event occurred
towards the end of March when the Assistant Poor Law Commissioner, Mr
Senior, witnessed men and women helping themselves to food in the kitchen,
unsupervised.[126] He accused the master of being negligent, adding that he
did not believe he would prove to be an efficient officer.[127] Not surprisingly
perhaps, the master, Mr Easton, resigned shortly afterwards.[128] His
replacement, Charles Hinde, was appointed and resigned within a week.[129]
He was, in turn, replaced by David Gillespie, who had previously been
assisting the medical officer.[130] Gillespie was appointed on a temporary
basis but was made permanent master a short time later.[131]

With the appointment of a new master and medical officer, together
with administrative and sanitary improvements, the workhouse began to
operate more efficiently and this was evidenced by a significant reduction
in the numbers dying.[132] In early April, the medical officer reported typhus
fever as being 'very much on the increase'[133] and on 1 May, the weekly
board meeting was held at the local courthouse.[134] Perhaps mindful of Lord
Lurgan's fate, the Lurgan Guardians preferred this building to that of the
workhouse where there was a 'prevalence of fever'.[135] Fever appeared to be
endemic, both inside and outside the workhouse, and following a letter
from Dr Hannay of the Lurgan Dispensary informing them of the situation
in Lurgan and Brownlowsderry, the Central Board of Health dispatched
tents to those areas from ordnance stores at Charlemont.[136]

On 22 May and 7 June, permission was granted for the erection of
temporary fever hospitals at Moira, Lurgan, Kernan and Portadown which
between them provided beds for 225 patients.[137] However, such
accommodation proved insufficient and, by 17 June, the medical officer
reported sickness 'prevailing to a great extent – the fever and dysenteric
apartments quite full and incapable of receiving more patients'.[138] Thus, as
a matter of urgency, further accommodation, by means of sheds and tents,
was provided with the establishment of fever hospitals on the Portadown
Road, Lurgan and in Portadown itself – both of which catered for 20
patients.[139]

Accommodation was further augmented by the renting of Greer's
distillery in Lurgan which, with a capacity of 400, virtually acted as an
auxiliary workhouse.[140] Thus, although there was distress in the winter of
1847-8, the authorities were in an much better position to provide relief
facilities for the many hundreds requiring them. Indeed, by March 1848

over 1500 people were being catered for. This increase in workhouse capacity meant that the disastrous, and ultimately fatal, overcrowding of the previous year was avoided.

Further testament to the general amelioration of destitution was the sale of fever tents and bedding which had been used in the temporary fever hospitals.[141] Numbers requiring relief did not remain high throughout 1848 but the following year witnessed a significant reduction in workhouse numbers and a gradual return to the pre-Famine levels of the early 1840s. Of major symbolic importance, however, was the fact that in September 1849 potatoes were reintroduced into the workhouse diet for the first time since 1845.[142] The Famine in Lurgan was over – but why, particularly in 1846-7, had it managed to bite so hard?

CONCLUSION

The levels of distress encountered in the Lurgan Union, particularly in 1847, may surprise those who had believed the area to have been an industrial heartland and, therefore, immune to problems caused by crop failure. However, it is important to note that the industrial sector was itself undergoing a period of transition.

In the years prior to the Famine the linen industry, the most prominent feature of the area's economy, was undergoing much change. Mechanisation of spinning had heralded the almost total demise of domestic spinning, rendering many weavers unemployed. Similarly, weavers had become much more reliant on supplies of yarn from large-scale manufactures, and their ability to negotiate prices had been restricted.

Further to this, the years 1847-48 witnessed a serious slump in the linen trade. The *Northern Whig* reported that many mills were only working half their normal hours with 'the working population ... thrown out of employment and left dependent on charity'.[143] The construction of new mills was halted in Belfast, whilst those which had just been built were not filled with machinery.

1847 also witnessed the flax crop being attacked by a vegetable distemper. This resulted in a smaller crop than usual with the consequence of much increased prices. Thus spinners, already impoverished, were unable to purchase any supplies. It has often been claimed that weavers' families, due to a decent income, were able to enjoy a more varied diet than that of labourers, one of the main constituents being oats. However, even this source of comfort was undermined in 1847 and an oats crop of less than 50 per cent of the average harvest meant that prices soared, in some cases to over 22 shillings per hundredweight, more than twice their usual price.

In circumstances such as these, the role played by the workhouse was of critical importance. Of course, such institutions were not built to cater for a calamity on the scale of that of the Famine. Nevertheless, the incompetence of the Lurgan Guardians and the officers appointed by them served only to exacerbate the problems of those for whom they were responsible. As Dr Smith observed, the Guardians had no knowledge of the condition of the workhouse and paid little attention to vital concerns, such as the condition of food that was purchased. At a time when strict administration was of the utmost importance, they were negligent in the extreme. Thus, it is hardly surprising to find that the Lurgan workhouse resembled a morgue in the months either side of Christmas 1846. The improvements made both to the administration and to the building itself only served to accentuate the point that proper handling of the situation in 1847 could have contributed to reducing the high number of deaths which subsequently developed.

Why then, was there a Famine in North Armagh? A combination of factors led to this outcome. Long-term structural change had undermined the position and earnings of weaving families, leaving them vulnerable. This precarious position was exacerbated by the unlikely combination of an economic downturn coupled with poor oats and flax harvests.

The Board of Guardians and the workhouse officials appeared indifferent, incompetent and negligent in their attempts to deal with the numbers presenting themselves for relief. These factors, together with failures of the potato crop in successive years, ensured that north Armagh suffered grievously during the Famine.

THE FAMINE
IN
COUNTY CAVAN

FR DAN GALLOGLY

Throughout the first half of the nineteenth century Cavan shared with
the rest of the country a population explosion. In 1841 it had a population
of 243,158, an increase of 24.7 per cent in 20 years. The greatest density of
population was in the baronies of south-east Cavan with significantly less
in the mountainous west.[1] The majority of the people were extremely poor,
never far removed from starvation, depending on their labour for a living
and increasingly on the potato as their main source of food. Local shortages
and outbreaks of fever were not unusual in Cavan in the 20 years before
the Famine. There were reports of famine and fever in the county in the
early 1820s and 1830s but recovery was generally immediate and they
were short-lived. Eighty-two per cent of the houses in the county were
designated in the 1841 census as third or fourth class. Fourth-class houses
were of mud-wall, thatched, with only one room while third-class houses
were scarcely better except that they had two or three rooms.[2] They were
devoid of any form of furnishing except a few stools, a table, a few tins to

drink from, and a pot in which to boil potatoes. Pierce Morton of Kilnacrott House, near Ballyjamesduff, a tireless famine relief worker, described the housing conditions in Crosserlough parish before the Famine as follows:

> The cabins are of stone, mud walls or sods, as happens to be most convenient, seldom glazed or plastered; badly thatched; the floor of clay, which, as well as the walls, is, for the greater part of winter, wet with rain falling through the roof; the family sleeping on some dried rushes or thrown on the floor in the chimney corner, as the warmest place in the house, with stools placed to keep the bed from taking fire; their own clothes thrown over them to assist the scanty bedclothes.

The parish priest of Annagh described his people as 'half naked'[4] and elsewhere the clothing of the peasantry is described as 'miserable in extreme'.[5]

Economically the county had not been spared the decline in agricultural prices in the aftermath of the Napoleonic wars. The supply of labour outstripped demand and wages were depressed, ten pence a day in summer and eight pence in winter, among the lowest in Ulster. More damaging still in the Cavan context was the virtual collapse from 1825 onwards of linen as a cottage industry in the face of competition from factory spinning, mainly in the Lagan valley. Large numbers of labourers and their families depended on spinning and weaving during the winter to augment their income, particularly in the centre and south – east of the county which was the flax and linen district centred around Cootehill and Bailieborough. More and more the labouring class and small farmers found themselves edged closer to destitution. They were also in the precarious position of being totally dependent on the potato. Consequently, when the potato crop failed in 1845 it had catastrophic consequences for both these classes.[6]

Blight was observed throughout Cavan in the summer of 1845 but it was not until the crop came to be harvested in October that the true extent of the failure was realised. Abraham Brush reported from the vicinity of Cavan town that the disease prevailed 'to an alarming extent'. A Bailieborough correspondent to the *Freeman's Journal* reported on 10 November that 'in many places one third and generally one fourth of the poor man's crop is damaged if not utterly ruined'. From Blacklion, in the extreme west of the county, it was reported on 11 October that the failure was not general but some complained of a quarter to one-sixth failure. From Belturbet in early December the rector in Derryheen estimated that one half had been lost and that there was a poor chance of the other half remaining sound. From the same district the *Freeman's Journal* of 6 December reported that carts laden with diseased potatoes were on their way to Dickson's distillery in Belturbet in an effort to get rid of them before it was too late.[7]

This partial failure of the potato crop in 1845 meant that by the late spring and summer of 1846 large sections of the people had no food. Food would have to be supplied to them free or employment provided for the labourer in the form of public works so that he could buy food; otherwise he would die of starvation. As early as February 1846 public meetings were held in Bailieborough and Ballyjamesduff and shortly afterwards relief committees began to function in these areas.[8] Relief committees were also established at Shercock and Killinkere in April and in May in Cavan, Stradone and Ballyhaise. Their aim was to collect money to buy food for the destitute and to select public works to be carried out with the aid of government loans and grants. Their membership consisted of local landed gentry who were resident in the county, better-off farmers, business and professional people in the towns and local clergy of all denominations. Pierce Morton of Kilnacrott near Ballyjamesduff was particularly active touring the county trying to set up relief committees.[9] A county infirmary in Cavan town and three workhouses, at Cavan, Cootehill and Bailieborough, which had been opened in 1842, were expected to cope with a catastrophe the seriousness of which was not realised until early in 1846. Cavan workhouse, the biggest of the three, had accommodation for 1,200 paupers, Bailieborough 600 and Cootehill 800. In addition another five unions from neighbouring counties had territory within the county. These were soon overcrowded and fever broke out in them. They were increasingly hampered in their efforts to cope with the crisis by want of funds caused by the inability of the guardians to collect the Poor Law rate.[10]

Reports were coming in of distress from different areas of the county from early 1846. James McKiernan wrote from Scrabby (Gowna) to Sir Robert Peel on 31 January 1846 describing the potato failure there as greater than in any part of Europe, that the supply was not expected to last beyond 1 April, that cattle had died from eating putrified potatoes, street paupers were numerous and in the last stage of positive misery and often afflicted with disease and, finally, that famine was staring the district in the face, immediate relief was necessary and that delay would mean 'the murder of

NOTICE.

CAVAN RELIEF COMMITTEE.

The Relief Committee have received numerous complaints of persons having obtained employment in the Public Works in this district, who do not come within the description laid down in the instructions issued by Government to the Relief Committees, that is " persons who are destitute of means of support, or for whose support such employment is actually necessary."

It is obvious that Pensioners at a shilling a day, Farmers (or their sons) possessing a cart and horse, and several cows, with stacks of oats in their haggard, cannot be included in this description ; and yet many such, it is stated to the Committee, are at present employed.

When such persons once take into consideration that, as employment obviously cannot be afforded to all, their obtaining it throws out of the work poor destitute and starving people, the Committee confidently trust they will voluntarily with draw and give up their tickets.

The Committee, however, will continue to receive complaints ; and if the party complained of does not withdraw of his own accord, he will be called upon to shew upon what grounds he claims to be employed on the Public Works.

The Committee will not recommend for employment Servants or Labourers who are actually engaged, or those who leave their employers without consent.

When any Gentleman or Farmer requires Labourers, to be paid at the same rate adopted in the Public Works, if he will notify to the Committee the names of those he wishes to hire, they shall be immediately struck off their Lists so long as they are thus required ; the Committee being authorised to afford employment to those alone who cannot obtain it elsewhere.

The Commitee are informed that Carts and Horses belonging to wealthy farmers are employed at the Public Works. This they consider quite unjustifiable.— There are persons holding little or no land, who keep a Cart and Horse entirely for hire, and actually live by it. Of such, a list might, without much difficulty, be made ; and the Committee think that such might fairly obtain employment at the usual wages, of 2s. 6d. per day, under the Board of Works, provided they cannot procure it elsewhere. But if it shall be found necessary to employ the Carts of persons not in want, the Committee recommend that they shall receive three men from the Public Works in exchange, or if they prefer it, two men, and the wages of the third in cash ; but that in no case, shall the wages of 2s. 6d. a day for man, cart, and horse be paid, unless to those included in the list before mentioned.

The Committee are of opinion that, for the future, Overseers and Check Clerks, as far as may be found practicable, should be selected from persons at present in the Public Works ; their merit might be judged from their conduct while employed, and if any should be found deserving of promotion, it would be a great incentive to others, and would also be a saving of the Public Money.

FARNHAM. *Chairman.*

November 10, 1846.

JOHNSTON, PRINTER, CAVAN,

(National Archives, Relief Commission Papers, Cavan).

thousands.' Reports in April and May spoke of how one family near Ballyjamesduff without food or means shut themselves up for two days to conceal their state; that farmers in Crossdoney who were comfortable in other times were now without a meal; near Cavan town many a decent farmer was reduced to one meal a day. Pierce Morton spoke of 'cases of deepest misery' in the Ballyjamesduff area and that 'the appalling reality was like a wound uncovered'. Patrick O'Reilly CC, Cavan, reported that in an area of 50 townlands around Cavan there were 250 families (1,131 individuals) unemployed and in a state rapidly approaching starvation. In the *environs* of the town there were another 229 families (560 individuals) all demanding bread. Mr Tatlow, agent to Mr Nesbitt, distributed a meal to his tenantry at Crossdoney.[11]

Extraordinary Presentment Sessions were held in April 1846 in each of the eight baronies in the county. Besides forming new parochial relief committees and regularising those already in existence, these sessions presented schemes valued at £11,000 (later increased to £25,000) to the Board of Works for approval and a subscription fund was set up to set against the government loan for these works. The relief works targeted three areas – road works which began in May and June, drainage and railway construction.

The biggest drainage project was the cutting of the Ballinamore and Ballyconnell canal (now the Shannon-Erne link) which by September employed 3,500 at 1s 8d a day per worker. Drainage work was also carried out on the Erne and on the Inny at Killin Crosserlough.[12] The suggestion to build a railway from Kells to Cavan, first made by the Railway Commissioners in 1838, failed to gain approval and was ultimately abandoned.[13]

On 15 August 1846 the government ordered that the relief committees cease operating and that all relief works cease at the same time in order to release the labourers for the harvest. There is no doubt the work of the relief committees and the public works went a long way in staving off starvation in the spring and summer of 1846, mainly by distributing Indian meal. A greater catastrophe, however, was to follow with the total destruction of the new crop.[14]

Blight struck again, this time devastatingly, in the first fortnight of July 1846 and by August it was reported that the entire crop was lost in the county. Reports in the local *Anglo-Celt* as early as 31 July summed up the situation throughout Cavan:

> The worst accounts continue to pour in to us from all quarters of the early
> potato crop in the county. There are great fears for the late crop which
> independently of the disease has missed in many places. Four acres of
> potatoes of Mr Rathborne of Virginia have been completely destroyed by
> the vegetable plague. Near Cavan we fear the case is hopeless... Around
> Belturbet the leaves and stalks were reported as all black. Last week we
> made a short tour through the barony of Castlerahan... the disease already
> exists to an alarming extent throughout the district'.

Within a matter of weeks, the dreadful spectre of renewed shortage was
confirmed: 'The potato cholera has made fearful strides in the
neighbourhood of Cootehill. The small farmers are quite alarmed... .'[15]
Panic set in among the labourers and cottiers in September. They marched
in large numbers on the homes of the landlords demanding employment or
else they would be forced to steal or die. The price of potatoes shot up from
6d a stone in May to one shilling in December and by January 1847 they
were unobtainable.[16] During the winter oatmeal cost 24 shillings per
hundredweight, at a time when the wage of a labourer was 10d a day or 5
shillings a week. There were also reports of black-marketing by smaller
retailers and millers, creating a scarcity in order to be able to increase the
prices. In Killeshandra oatmeal bought for £20 a tonne was sold at 2°d a
pound or £56 a tonne, a profit of 180 per cent. Indian meal was much
cheaper and a tonne of it would go as far as a tonne and a half of oatmeal. Rev.
J.J. Martin, Killeshandra, asked the government to step in and set up a depot
somewhere in the neighbourhood and supply them with 50 tonnes weekly at
a reasonable profit as the local providers were unable to meet the sudden demand
and were over-charging. Otherwise, he said, there would be famine.

The prospects hanging over the country cast a gloom over the high
society dinner in Virginia held in connection with the regatta on 9
September. The Marquess of Headford said he could think of nothing but
the starving labourers. Col. Saunderson of Castlesaunderson near Belturbet,
during one of his visits home, wrote in an open letter to the county on 8
September that 'an awful calamity seemed to be hanging over the people'
and advocated useful employment such as land improvement and not the
wasteful road works of the previous season. Matthew McQuaid, parish
priest of Killsherdany, near Cootehill, reported that the labouring class
was entirely destitute and on the verge of starvation: the small farmer could
carry on only for a month or two. He also recommended productive

employment be found immediately.[18]

Extraordinary Presentment Sessions held in the eight Cavan baronies in the last week of September 1846 voted a further £60,000 for public works. Delays in getting the public works off the ground, due to the fact that each project had to be presented to the Board of Works and sanctioned by the treasury, caused further distress.[19] Implementation of these public works were in the hands of two Board of Works engineers and district relief committees. There were 15 such relief committees in the county organised by October and local relief committees continued to function under them. By the end of October 2,000 labourers were employed on road works over the county, 9,000 by mid-November and by February 1847 the number had risen to 25,000 on about 4,000 work schemes. The public works over the winter of 1846-7 had a number of shortcomings. They were too slow in starting; they only catered for roughly 10 per cent of the labour force; the wages were too low, (an average of 4 shillings a week or enough to buy just a stone of oatmeal) and wages were paid irregularly. There was a near-riot in Cavan town the Saturday before Christmas 1846 when a rumour went around that no wages would be paid that day. There were complaints that there were too many overseers with nothing to do. George Shaw, agent of the Ballyhaise estate of Mr Humphrey, described the qualifications for an overseer as 'a good frieze coat, a strong hay rope to bind it round his waste (sic) and the sheltered side of a sunny bush for his back'. There were also complaints of alleged favouritism in the allocation of work. At the Upper Loughtee Presentment Sessions on 14 December Fr Charles O'Reilly asked Lord Farnham if it were right that a number of persons from Cavan and Denn, who were in comfortable circumstances, should be employed in Lavey while numbers of his parishioners were almost in a state of starvation.[20]

On 20 March 1847 an order from the Board of Works dismissed 20 per cent of those employed in public works in order to release man-power for the spring's work and to ease the way for their eventual closure. The selection of the 20 per cent to be made redundant was difficult. At one scheme in Kilnaleck lots were drawn and the report added that 'the wretched creatures on whom the lots fell raised a cry that still rings in my ears, it was like a sentence of death on them'.[21] At Ballinagh 406 women and children who were employed breaking stones were dismissed and in Ballymachugh one of the two men who were dismissed committed suicide and the other went insane and murdered his wife. By mid-June the numbers employed on public works had fallen to a little over 2,000 and then the works ceased altogether. The small farmers and labourers released for the spring cropping found themselves with little to do. They had no means of buying seed and only about one tenth of the potato crop was sown. This grim picture was brightened somewhat by the introduction of the soup kitchens.[22]

The local relief committees set up in autumn of 1846 continued to operate, raising subscriptions for local relief in the form of soup kitchens where soup was distributed free or at a small cost to the destitute. From time to time these local relief committees acknowledged help given them from external sources. Assistance came from the Society of Friends, John McDowel, a Cavan man living in Liverpool and later from the British Association, but their main source of funds was local. Mr Foster, agent of the Society of Friends, visited Cavan on 4 and 6 April 1847. He spoke of the need for clothing as well as food. Grants of food and clothing from the society are acknowledged in the *Anglo-Celt* in July and August 1847 from Stradone, Ballyjamesduff and Cavan infirmary. Archdeacon M.G. Beresford writing to the Society from Ballyhaise said 'your grants have saved many lives'.[23]

In March 1847 the government reluctantly passed the Temporary Relief Act or Soup Kitchen Act which reorganised relief committees on a Poor Law basis. In future each Poor Law electoral division would form a relief committee whose finances would be under the control of a finance committee of the Poor Law union which would authorise the local relief committee to issue rations free or at a small charge. The cost was to be met partly by local contributions but mainly by a government grant repayable through the poor rate. The Soup Kitchen Act linked relief of distress to the poor rate at a time when the Poor Law unions in the county were heavily in debt and were reluctant to strike a new rate while some of the previous rate was still outstanding. In all events food depots or soup kitchens were set up all over the county by the end of April. Boilers were secured, many from the Irish Relief Association in Dublin, supplies of oatmeal and bread were advertised for and the lists of applicants scrutinised. Bakeries producing cheap bread were established by private enterprise in Bailieborough and Cavan.[24] In June, at the height of its activities about a third of the population of each electoral division was in receipt of daily rations. In the various divisions of the Bailieborough Union 16,000 were being fed, in

Tullyvin and Ashfield division of the Cootehill Union 5,200 out of a total population of 10,000. Of these 2,660 were cottiers and 2,000 owning from a half acre to four acres. During the five months of the Act's operation Bailieborough Union spent £12,400 of which £5,000 was paid by the government and the remaining £7,400 had to be repaid by the union from the poor rate. Overall, 35 per cent of the population was in receipt of relief from April to September 1847. There is no doubt that by the time the soup kitchens ceased operation in August 1847 they had saved the lives of thousands.[25]

While starvation was being kept at bay to an extent by the soup kitchens a new terror struck in the form of fever. In February 1847 there were 200 cases in Cavan workhouse where there was already an overcrowding problem. It next appeared in Belturbet and by April the epidemic was widespread in the county. It abated during July only to reappear during the following winter and throughout most of 1848. Three types of fever afflicted the county – typhus, relapsing fever and dysentery, the latter doing greatest damage in the spring of 1847 due to the poor diet. Doctors in Cavan town estimated that about one fifth of the population caught fever and that the mortality rate, while under 5 per cent in the poorer class, was 66 per cent among the upper classes showing that fever was no respecter of class. More people died from fever and disease in Cavan during the Famine than from starvation, children being particularly vulnerable. A report from Cavan town contributed by Drs Halpin and Maise to the *Dublin Quarterly Journal of Medical Science* for the period February to May 1849 stated that there were 1,236 cases of fever treated within the town and a mile radius of it.[26] In April eight funerals per day were reported to Moybolgue cemetery near Bailieborough and workhouse mortality was alarming. For the year ending 30 November 1847, 633 deaths were recorded for Cavan workhouse, the worst period being April to June during which there were 240 deaths out of an average population of 1,500, or 16 per cent.[27] Drs Halpin and Mease made a systematic inspection of Cavan town and reported on 22 April 1847:

> We visited every house in the town. We found twelve cases of fever, 25 of dysentery, 6 of dropsy and 6 of other related ailments. In one fever case a girl of 14 lay at the gable end of a fallen house where she had lain in the open for twelve days and nights in a most deplorable state without shelter or covering... Throughout the entire Half Acre, Mudwall Row, Kinnypottle, Kilnavarra Lane and part of Lurganboy we found extreme wretchedness;

very few of the houses have bedsteads and in most of them there are three
or four or more families, very little straw for bedding, no bed clothing,
dung-heaps at every door.[28]

The fever hospital at Keadew near Cavan was overcrowded in May and
three to eight patients were being refused admission daily for want of
accommodation.[29] A temporary hospital was set up on 9 April to provide
extra accommodation for fever victims and from 1 May to 18 June two
large barns were also acquired from Mr James Fay for the same purpose.
The cabins of the poor around the town were whitewashed and cleaned and
fresh straw supplied for bedding. In May and June the practice began of
carting fever patients from the country into Cavan town where they were
abandoned by the roadside to be treated by the local Health Board. On 18
May an 11 year-old girl, Anna Magee, was carted in and abandoned. She
had lain at the back of a ditch for several days before in Scrabby (Gowna).
She died in the fever huts on 20 May. Dr Flemming reported from
Bailieborough in May that dysentery or fever was in one cabin of every two
in the rural area.[30]

Temporary fever hospitals were set up throughout the county to try and
cope with the epidemic. A temporary fever hospital set up by Dr Wade in
Belturbet had 77 patients on 3 July, Virginia fever hospital had 76, Cootehill
60 at the same time. There were also temporary fever hospitals in Ballyhaise
(July), Kingscourt (October), Shercock (December), Ballyjamesduff
(September), Ballinagh and Milltown. The total number of deaths from
fever in Cavan fever hospitals was 1,214 in 1847, 1,280 in 1848, 1,615 in
1849 and there were many more who never made it to the fever hospitals
but died at home or in the ditches. Most of the temporary fever hospitals
closed in summer 1848 when a new fever wing was added to Cavan
workhouse. There is evidence of some opposition to the opening of
temporary fever hospitals from local people as the following account from
Killeshandra in the *Anglo-Celt* in early July 1847 shows:

> In the neighbourhood and in the town itself poor stricken victims are to be
> seen lying in the lanes and ditches and in the very streets with no bed but
> the hard earth and no covering but the sky. Inside the arch of the market-
> house a woman and two children lie in fever for some days, a wisp of hay
> under her head. Opposite Finlay's Hotel, two other poor wretches lie on
> the site of a house that had been pulled down within a yard of the pathway
> and in full view. At the back of the street a boy has lain for nine days and
> nine nights under a currant bush, exposed to the rains of last week and the

sun of this week and is still alive. The Relief Committee had first tried to erect temporary fever sheds and establish a Board of Health, but the inhabitants met the proposal with the most determined opposition in fear of contagion, saying they would pull down every shed. Yet fever abounds.[31]

The temporary fever hospital opened in April 1847 by Dr Wade in Belturbet was maliciously burned down but eventually re-opened in June.[32] Fever also wrought havoc on the nurses, doctors and clergy in the workhouses. Patrick O'Reilly, CC, chaplain to Cavan workhouse caught fever and died on 12 April 1847. The same day James Smith CC, Cootehill, died. A month later, on 12 May, Fr Francis McKiernan died from fever in Cavan. On 10 November another Cavan curate Eugene McQuaid, chaplain to Cavan jail, died of fever. The Rev. Charles Beresford, Rector in Bailieborough, an active relief worker also died of fever. So also did the doctors in Killeshandra, Ballyjamesduff, Mountnugent, Cootehill and Cavan. Mrs Mitchell, matron of Cavan workhouse and her sister and successor Mrs Boyd both died from fever. So also did Mr Gormley, master of Cootehill workhouse.[33]

III

The potato crop in 1847 was not affected by blight as had been the case the previous year but the amount of potatoes planted was only one tenth of former years. The public works had been discontinued, the soup kitchens abolished and the relief of distress made the sole responsibility of the Poor Law Guardians and the workhouses under the Poor Law Extension Act of August 1847. In theory, the hungry and destitute were to be accommodated in the workhouses. If these were full outdoor relief could be given to the aged, infirm and widows with children but not to able-bodied men unless the Poor Law Commissioners at the request of the Board of Guardians sanctioned it. Outdoor relief was to be administered by local relieving officers at fixed depots. The whole cost was to come from the poor rates.

The Act caused a major problem for the Poor Law Guardians. The workhouse in Cavan was already overcrowded and heavily in debt, with much of the rate for the previous year still outstanding. It had 100 paupers over capacity and was in debt to the tune of £4,500 with £1,500 of the old rate uncollected. Understandably, the Guardians were reluctant to have the total responsibility for relief of distress assigned to them. It met with such opposition from them that in the end the Cavan Board of Guardians was dissolved in November and two vice-guardians appointed. The vice-guardians who continued to administer the affairs of Cavan Board of Guardians from December 1847 until March 1849.[24]

Cootehill was also in debt to the tune of £2,350 with much of the previous year's rate still outstanding and the workhouse full. Yet some progress towards implementing the Act was made. Relief officers were appointed and commenced distributing relief in December and extra workhouse accommodation was rented, bringing the total pauper accommodation in the union to 1,150 in January 1848. But there were complaints of failure by the guardians to relieve distress in Ashfield, Lara, and Kill. These culminated in the disbandment of Cavan Board of Guardians and responsibility for its affairs passing to the Cavan Vice-Guardians. Bailieborough Board of Guardians implemented the Act after some delay. Districts were defined, relieving officers appointed, depots hired, supplies made available and a rate of between 4 shillings and 1 shilling in the pound struck.

It was a principle of the Poor Law Extension Act that the able-bodied were to get relief only in the workhouse. This necessitated the extension of workhouse accommodation by renting houses throughout the union. In November 1848 the total accommodation for paupers in the Cavan Union was 3,000 – 1,300 in the original workhouse, 120 in the new fever hospital and 1,620 in the auxiliary workhouses in Killeshandra, Kildallan, Drumalee (Belturbet) and Swellan near Cavan. Six months later, in mid-June 1849, the highest number of paupers ever recorded in Cavan workhouse and its auxiliaries was 3,734 (including 1,955 children and 1,657 able-bodied adults). A similar extension of accommodation took place in Cootehill Union providing an extra 690 places and in Bailieborough Union 650 extra places were provided in five auxiliary workhouses.[36] By January 1848 relieving officers had been appointed and relief depots set up all over the county. In theory outdoor relief consisted of eight pence a week for adults and four pence for children but in practice it consisted of seven pounds of Indian meal per adult and three and a half per child. In March 1848 Cavan Union was giving relief to 9,000 paupers and continued at about 7-8,000 until August when the vice-guardians cut the number to 6,000 and, in September, to 1,500. The number in Cootehill Union was about 6,000 which was cut to 876 in September.[37]

The table below indicates the pressure under which the three principal workhouses which served the county continued to come under during the Famine years.

PAUPERS ADMITTED TO COUNTY CAVAN WORKHOUSES 1845-51

	1845	1846	1847	1848	1849	1850	1851
Cavan	991	2,146	3,141	4,970	12,820	4,002	2,366
Cootehill	983	1,585	2,029	3,583	9,768	4,379	2,167
Bailieborough	724	1,616	1,906	4,705	6,098	5,842	2,476
Total	2,698	5,437	7,076	13,258	28,686	14,223	7,009

(Based on reports of the Poor Law Commissioners 1845-52)

A report in the *Anglo-Celt* in March 1848 shows the rigid, inhumane way the Poor Law Extension Act was administered. A father, mother and eight children from the Cootehill area emigrated to Scotland in October 1847. The mother and seven of her children returned to Ireland in December and entered the Cootehill workhouse. In February 1848 she was told that she was a deserted wife and that she and her children must leave the workhouse for outdoor relief provided she signed an affidavit that she was deserted by her husband. When she refused she was turned out and two of her children died of starvation; the rest were saved by the generosity of the local parish priest, Matt McQuaid and the wife of the local minister.[38] Another disastrous consequence of the Act was the manner in which it brought pressure on the Poor Law rate causing it to be increased and the insistence of the Vice-Guardians that it be paid. In July the rate struck varied from 4s 6d to 3 shillings in the Cavan and Cootehill Unions and 7 shillings in the Bailieborough Union. One important result of this pressure was that some landlords, who were obliged to pay the rates of tenants holding land valued less than £4, were prompted to clear such tenants off their estates. This, combined with the inability of tenants to pay rent during the Famine and the enforcement of the clause in the Poor Law Extension Act which prohibited relief to anyone with a rood of land, led to estate clearances by landlords. In the latter case the unfortunate tenant had to abandon his holding so as to qualify for outdoor relief. As soon as he did the landlord had his cabin levelled to prevent re-occupation. John Kelly, a rate collector in the Milltown area outside Belturbet, wrote to the *Freeman's Journal* on 25 July 1848:

In the townland of Coragh there were 30 tenants, of whom three were in
jail for rent arrears, nine were dispossessed and their houses levelled and
that he had not the heart to distrain them for rates as their food would last
two days.[39]

In August 1848 P. O. Farrelly of Crossbane, Mullagh wrote an open
letter to absentee landlords:

It is impossible for landlords to expect rents while tenants are reduced to
the necessity of driving a load of turf to Navan (19 miles away) and sell it
there for eight pence with which they take one penny of bread, and a half
stone of Indian meal home to their families some of which number eight
persons. Look at seven pounds of meal for eight persons in 24 hours and
you will see the distress of your tenants.[40]

While there were reports of evictions throughout 1848 and 1849 no
precise statistics are available. Letters from three areas are worth quoting
in full as they paint a vivid picture of the inhumanity of the landlords and
the distress caused by the estate clearances. The first is from Tom Brady
CC, Drung, near Cootehill to the *Freeman's Journal*, 1 March 1848:

In this parish at present there are fifty farms vacant, 200 human beings
sent adrift in an inclement season to beg or die; many of them have since
died. As I met them on the high ways livid corpses raised, I can give but a
faint idea of their wretched appearance... wishing for the happy release of
death... The landlords exterminate right and left. I have attended a man in
fever with two children lying dead before the fire for four days. I fearlessly
accuse some Irish landlords in this parish of wanting in common humanity;
they deprive the tenant of his crop, prevent him from getting outdoor relief
until he has the certificate of the bailiff that he had previously tumbled his
wretched cabin... Some landlords in this parish applied the screw so tight
that they have at present the November rents in their pockets.[41]

On 29 December Fr Foy CC in Shercock wrote to the *Freeman's Journal*
in response to an accusation by Lord Farnham that some Catholic priests
were encouraging outrages:

It is hard to teach patience to a man who sees his father and mother or wife
and children driven from the houses of their ancestors to the bogs and
ditches to starvation and death.[42]

The final letter was from Matt McQuaid PP, Killsherdany on 19 January
1849.

There never was perhaps a more terrible persecution carried on against
the poor than at the present moment. There seems to be a hellish rivalry

among some agents as to who will banish the most. It is heart-rending to see some families ... emaciated and ragged after the last three years of unprecedented famine and misery during which they contrived by denying themselves and their poor children the very necessities of life to pay the landlord two years rack-rent now unmercifully turned out because they cannot pay a third years... It is not enough to drive out the mother and flock of children like a parcel of swine on a stormy winter's night, nor enough to tumble their cabin, wound their feelings and see their tears, but, it is said some of those monsters grinned at their victims' devotions and mocked them... Everyone knows that the mere Irish are being banished from some estates and Protestants substituted for them on long leases.[43]

Starvation and evictions continued in Cavan throughout 1849. In June 1849, James Browne, Catholic Bishop of Kilmore addressed the congregation in Cavan town on the wretched condition of the poor landholders who were, after the fourth year of famine, destitute of all necessities of life. He also appealed on behalf of 'the poor respectable inhabitants of the town, ashamed to beg but faced with the horror of a lingering death by starvation...'. As a result of his appeal a charitable relief committee was established in Cavan which helped 128 families or 751 people with Indian meal. Conditions were somewhat similar in Belturbet, Cootehill, Bailieborough and Killeshandra.[44]

Of those set adrift by estate clearances, some died, some ended in the workhouse, some emigrated, though not many would have had the means of doing so, others took to begging. In April 1848 the *Anglo-Celt* reported the nuisance of beggars in Cavan town and a daily influx of paupers into the town from the country. The newspaper called for the application of the Vagrancy Act. It returned to the topic in June describing Mudwall Row in Cavan town as the abode of vice, pestilence and starvation and that the influx of paupers had increased. The petty sessions dealt with a number of cases under the Vagrancy Act. Four small children trained by their father and sister to beg roamed the streets of Cavan for two months crying for food. They were lodged in the workhouse and the father given three months hard labour. In May, a man named Mulligan from Cootehill stole a chicken at Cullies, near Cavan and was lodged in Cavan gaol where he died of starvation the following day. A report from Arva stated that knots of destitute of children hid inside roofless old walls and cried at half-doors for food. There were many cases at the assizes of robbery of food and some of homicide or attempted homicide against people protecting their property against the destitute and starving.[45]

During the decade of the Famine the population of the county declined from 243,000 in 1841 to 174,000 in 1851, a reduction of 69,000 or 28.5 per cent. The decline differed from parish to parish and even within the same parish certain townlands actually experienced an increase in population. The decline was greatest in east and mid-Cavan where the following parishes showed a marked decline – Castleward 31.6 per cent, Inniskeen 36 per cent, Killsherdany 36.0 per cent, Knockbride 33.5 per cent, Mullagh 33 per cent, Drung 32 per cent, Drumlane 35 per cent. In the west of the county it was much lower – Templeport (which included Glangevlin) 19 per cent, Kinawley 14 per cent, Kildallan 23.7 per cent, Killinagh 21.8 per cent. In the west of the county, where there was a much lower density of population than in the east and surplus population could be accommodated by moving higher up on the mountain-side to eke out an existence by growing potatoes and some oats, the decline was much lower. There was a much greater density of population in the east of the county and no such room for expansion as land became scarcer. There was also a much greater labour force that hitherto depended on the linen industry to supplement their incomes but with its decline tenants were now forced back to total reliance on agricultural labour and on the potato.[46] (See Appendix 1 for an outline of population decline in Co. Cavan 1845-51.)

We have no way of determining how many died and how many emigrated. There are some references to assisted emigration although the Catholic church was opposed to this. Tom Maguire PP, Ballinamore, Co. Leitrim spoke of it as 'shovelling the people to Canada'. Mr Scott of Fort Frederick, Virginia assisted people to emigrate in 1847. In November and December 1848 about 60 female paupers from Cavan workhouse had their fares paid to emigrate by the union. We know from reports in the *Freeman's Journal* in 1848 that people were finding it hard to get the money to emigrate. A news item from Kells in the same paper on 25 October 1849 speaks of the daily passage of strangers through the town on their way to Drogheda and Dublin. For those who could raise the fare, by whatever means, emigration must have seemed to provide the only escape route from the rigours of the Famine in Co.Cavan.

APPENDIX 1

POPULATION DECLINE IN CAVAN 1841-1851 (ACCORDING TO PARISHES)

Parish	1841	1851	% change
Urney and Annageliff	10,272	9,290	-10.0%
Annagh	13,071	9,200	-29.6%
Castlerahan/Munterconnaught	10,756	8,300	-25.6%
Ballintemple	5,341	4,116	-22.8%
Ballymachugh	3,517	2,151	-38.8%
Castletara	6,813	4,655	-31.6%
Crosserlough	10,303	7,274	-29.3%
Denn	6,696	4,643	-30.6%
Drumgoon	12,575	10,008	-20.4%
Drumlane	9,438	6,121	-35.0%
Drumlomman	8,807	5,963	-32.0%
Drung	6,551	4,396	-32.8%
Glangevlin	12,100	9,788	-19.1%
Inniskeen	8,841	5,651	-36.0%
Kildallan and Tomregan	7,468	5,698	-23.7%
Killann/Bailieborough	12,528	9,308	-25.6%
Killeshandra	12,552	8,551	-31.8%
Killinagh	6,512	5,086	-21.8%
Killinkere	8,126	5,862	-27.8%
Kilbride	2,774	2,961	+7.0%
Kilmore	7,250	6,764	-6.7%
Kilsherdany	10,208	6,459	-36.0%
Kinawley (pt of)	3,593	3,057	-14.9%
Knockbride	10,603	7,042	-33.5%
Lara	8,558	5,970	-30.2%
Lavey	5,931	4,100	-30.8%
Lurgan/Loughan	8,407	5,794	-31.0%
Moybolgue (pt of)	1,631	1,040	-36.0%
Mullagh	6,526	4,427	-32.0%
Templeport/Corlough	6,526	4,427	-32.0%

THE FAMINE
IN
COUNTY DONEGAL

ANTHONY BEGLEY AND SOINBHE LALLY

> The County of Donegal is one of the largest, as well as the wildest and
> most mountainous counties in Ireland ... Notwithstanding the generally
> rugged aspect, there is much excellent and cultivable soil, and it has a
> population of nearly 300,000 persons, more than two-thirds of whom are
> solely engaged in agriculture, thinly spread over an area of 1,190,000 acres
> of which little more than one-third is reclaimed and cultivated.

Thus, James Hack Tuke of the Society of Friends described Donegal when
he visited the county in late 1846 and early 1847 to investigate reports of
distress in the county.[1]

Eleven years earlier a Royal Commission had attempted to gain some
insight into the extent of poverty in Ireland. Its findings in relation to
Ballyshannon were based on statements taken from local clergy and
landlords. Rev. Francis McDonnell P.P. reported that the needs of widows

with children were sometimes assisted by small farmers permitting them to erect huts on the skirts of bogs and on the side of public roads. There were an estimated 400 labourers in the area, of whom about 100 were in constant employment. Wages varied from eight pence a day to one shilling. Labourers' diet consisted of potatoes, herring, salt, stirabout and milk. Their clothes were for the most part 'coarse, bad, filthy and wretched.' Most labourers held conacre with rents varying from £2 to £3 *per annum* for a cabin and a few perches. Conditions in the labourers' cabins were miserable, with bad furnishings and the bedding was the worst imaginable, with smoky filthy straw beds on the ground which were removed during the day. Rev. J. Cummins said he was aware of about 60 cases of two families in one cabin.[2]

Nevertheless, Ballyshannon was prosperous in comparison with other parts of Donegal. It was part of the Connolly estate which comprised 26 townlands in south-west Donegal. Between 1830-44, Edward Connolly spent £21,000 on improving agriculture practices on his estate. He ended the Rundale system, encouraged enclosure of open fields and the setting up of separate holdings, gave grants for building houses and when tenants were placed on moorlands they were charged only a nominal rent for the first three years. Farm sizes ranged from three acres to 150 acres but over 60 per cent were under 30 acres in size. This resulted in a fairly efficient agricultural industry in the area and considerable quantities of wheat and grain and potatoes were exported from Ballyshannon harbour between 1835-44. In 1835 alone, grain exports from Ballyshannon were valued at £11,000.[3] This productivity is reflected in the increase of Connolly's rental from £8,000 to £14,000.

In contrast with Ballyshannon, the parish of Glencolumbkille during the first half of the nineteenth century is typical of the other Donegal, wild, inaccessible and impoverished. Rev. John Ewing, Church of Ireland rector, described the parish in 1824:

> There is not one tree in the parish ... There are no modern buildings towns, or inns. The roads are horribly bad, there is not a perch of good road in the parish ... People from the interior cannot come in here for flannel, butter or fish. The latter is abundant on the coasts but the natives have no encouragement to take them. Strangers cannot drive them off by land and there is no safe landing place for boats except at Teeling which is at the eastern boundary of the parish.[4]

By July 1844, when the Devon Commission sat in Donegal town, there was such pressure on land in Glencolumbkille that rents were ten times the average in the county. While the agent, William Hume, paid only £108 to Col. Connolly for several thousand acres, James McCunningham, Farranmacbride, who represented the tenant farmers of the parish of Glencolumbkille before the Commission, in spite of threats from the agent's bailiff that 'you will rue of it', said he was paying a rent of £21 for 20 acres. He stated to the Commission that:

> In general all the county is in that state that they have neither cow nor calf. It is not one out of a score that has a cow. They are not able to keep cows by reason of the extraordinary rent and lack of earnings ... If you go to market with a bit of flannel or a pig he will be with us the next day before we are at home to get the price from us.[5]

On 31 July 1838 the Act 'for the more effectual Relief of the Destitute Poor of Ireland' passed into law. Poor Law Unions were set up in Donegal and workhouses built. The fact that the Act permitted no outdoor relief 'seriously limited its capacity for dealing with the wholesale poverty prevailing in Ireland'.[6] John Mitchell rhetorically expressed the contemporary attitude to workhouses when he saw Glenties workhouse in 1845:

> a certain new building – the grandest by far that those Rosses people ever saw – rearing its accursed gables and pinnacles of Tudor barbarism, and staring boldly with its detestable mullioned windows as if to mock those wretches who still cling to liberty and mud cabins – seeming to them, in their perennial half-starvation, like a Temple erected to the Fates, or like the fortress of Giant Despair, wherinto he draws them one by one, and devours them there.[7]

The Poor Law workhouses could have done little to relieve poverty before 1845 as very few poor people were willing to enter their doors. In 1846 they struggled to cope with the crisis. The relatively inconsistent spread of the potato disease throughout the county is perhaps best monitored in the minutes of the meetings of guardians of the respective workhouses. As early as January 1846, Inishowen workhouse 'resolved that in consequence of the high price of potatoes, meal be substituted until further orders, say 8 ozs for dinner to adults and so on in proportion to the classes.[8] The Letterkenny Guardians only felt obliged to note 'the want of potatoes and the necessity of substituting meal, as late as mid-July 1846.[9] The

Glenties Union found itself in a particularly parlous position as the spread of potato disease inched its way throughout the county. The workhouse itself was not opened to receive paupers until May 1846.[10] As early as November 1845, the Guardians had met with Mr G.C. Otway, Assistant Poor Law Commissioner, and had voiced their fears about being able to cope with the emergency which was gradually unfolding:

> The Guardians of the Glenties Union, being now anxious to open the workhouse, ...and not to undergo the responsibility of the workhouse of their Union not being open to receive the destitute poor, should it please Providence to inflict on this part of the county a scarcity in the staple and almost only fruit of the poor by a spread of the disease in the potato crop.[11]

Within a matter of weeks of its eventual opening, the implications of the potato crop failure were becoming fully apparent in the union. In July the master was 'directed to strike off his previous account 60lbs of potatoes rendered unfit for use by the disease'.[12] By August the Guardians urged the Poor Law Commissioners 'to communicate with the Relief Commissioners on the urgent necessity of forwarding large quantities of Indian meal to the sea ports of Teelan, Killybegs, Portnoo and Rutland for the use of the poor of the union, for if some relief be not afforded a famine must ensue throughout the union.'[13]

This was the context of Tuke's fact-finding itinerary in the county in the late autumn of 1846, in which he describes the human misery he encountered in every part of the county, 'Nothing can indeed describe too strongly the dreadful condition of the people, many families were living on a single meal of čabbage, and even, as we were assured, upon a little seaweed.'[14] In Dunfanaghy, he deplored the lack of development of the fishing industry and left for the destitute a quantity of meal and a sum 'for their further support, and also for a little turf, without which in this severe weather many would be frozen to death.' In spite of the extreme destitution noted by Tuke, Dunfanaghy fared better than other districts during the critical winter of 1846-47 because the gentry on the local relief committees, led by Lord George Hill, defied regulations and sold Indian meal below cost price and sooner than directed, thus preventing the fatal delays which occurred in other areas.[15]

Tuke's visits to some workhouses are an indication of the sporadic effectiveness of the Poor Law system. Only in Dunfanaghy, Milford and Stranorlar did he find poor houses providing tolerable living conditions.

LINES

*Composed among the Mountains of Donegal
On The Scourge, Man of War being placed by Government
At the disposal of the Society of Friends*
For the purpose of conveying a supply of Food to the famishing districts
of the North-West of Ireland.

Mysterious law! The Over-ruling Hand,
By means inscrutable to human ken,
Doth work His purpose with the Sons of men;
While the red Angel stalketh through the land,
Famine and Pestilence beneath him ranged,
He sends his Messengers of Peace, and lo
The very War-ship hath its nature changed.
The "Scourge" with thunders fraught to overwhelm,
And scatter ruin round, and death, and woe
Now bears a freight to save and succour life
To feed the hungry, One doth guide the helm,
Whose untaught faith abjures all blood-red ships.
Ye Nations, read the sign! Henceforth be turned
Your swords to ploughshares at the Prophet's voice:
And by the smile of Heaven thus doubly earn'd,
With Plenty, bid once more the Poor Man's lot rejoice.

March 3rd 1847.

Samonds' Lithog.

(Courtesy of Ulster Museum)

In Dunfanaghy he records, 'we found the poor-house in excellent order and the inmates appeared to be in good health ... This is only a small poor-house and the numbers of inmates was 116'. Milford 'appeared in good order, and the inmates in good health; the admissions during the past week were 100.' Stranorlar 'contained 388 inmates, whose appearance and general health formed a pleasing contrast to many we had seen.'

In Glenties, Ballyshannon and Letterkenny, on the other hand, conditions in the workhouses were appalling. Tuke visited 'the poor house at Glenties which is in a dreadful state; the people were in fact half starved and only half clothed. The day before they had but one meal of oat meal and water and at the time of our visit had not sufficient food in the house for the day's supply ... Some were leaving the house, preferring to die in their own hovels rather than in the poor house'. In Letterkenny a diet consisting exclusively of Indian meal had caused scurvy among the inmates. Tuke found that 'one fourth of the inmates were in the infirmary, a large number of them children, who suffered excruciating pain from what the master termed 'epidemic cancer in the mouth', which had broken out suddenly in the house.'[16] In Ballyshannon, Tuke

> ...found the poor-house in about as bad a condition as any we have seen; it was not quite full, but further admissions were prevented by an order from the Poor Law Commissioners until the blankets and other needful articles could be procured, of which at present the house was almost destitute. There were near 500 inmates, and the deaths were indeed fearful. We saw two corpses carried to the grave-yard in an open cart, without ceremony or procession of any kind.

The parish of Glencolumbkille, in the Glenties Union, was too inaccessible for Tuke's party. However, when they were informed about the impoverishment of the area they sent relief by ship to Killybegs. According to oral tradition in Glencolumbkille parish, only one person in the parish died in the Famine, from an accidental fall while gathering seabirds' eggs.[17] However, the records suggest otherwise. Glencolumbkille was inaccessible and its two main landlords lived elsewhere. Firstly, the progressive Col. Connolly of Ballyshannon left his Glencolumbkille estate in the hands of agents, the Humes of Glen.[18] Secondly, there was the notorious Alexander Hamilton whose Famine evictions on his lands within the Ballyshannon Union are remembered in oral tradition thus: 'He had a record of stern harshness to poor tenants who could not pay their rent promptly and many evictions took place on his land.'[19]

The disparity in the numbers who sought refuge at different times in the county's workhouses is an indicator of the regional impact of the effects of the Famine on the population. Early in January 1847, while Ballyshannon had by then exceeded its accommodation limit, the Dunfanaghy, Donegal, Glenties and Inishowen workhouses all reported 'no pressure' or 'no great pressure' on their capacity.[20] Within a few weeks, however, the full effects of the scarcity of the 1846-7 winter saw large numbers flocking to Glenties workhouse. In April the Guardians, in response to this influx and to reports of typhus among the inmates, refused to admit more applicants... 'in consequence of the number now at the workhouse door...being upwards of 90, that the master be directed to admit up to the number 650...there being a general cessation of relief works; under the circumstances the Guardians are led, although reluctantly, to adopt such a course'.[21]

In May 1847, the poor rate for the Glenties Union rose from 6d to as high as 15 shillings in the pound in order to cope with the numbers dependent on relief, inside or outside the workhouse.[22] Elsewhere, demands for relief were less pressing. John Vandaleur Stewart, chairman of Letterkenny Guardians, attributed the Glenties problem partly to the management abilities of the Guardians and also, interestingly, to the value of resident over non-resident landlords. When giving evidence to the Select Committee on the Poor Law, he was asked to account for the fact that Glenties relieved 4535 of its population, while Dunfanaghy only 2668. He opined:

In Dunfanaghy, the Poor Law has been administered by a Board of Guardians carefully selected, with a £10 qualification, representing the property of the Union which has long been remarkable for its orderly and industrious habits and the mutual relations between landlord and tenant...Glenties, on the other hand, without resident proprietors, elected a Board of Guardians selected from that class who are little identified with property.[23]

Evidence of the extent of the destitution unfolding in a number of regions within the county was presented to the committee of the Belfast Ladies Association for the Relief of Destitution, one of a number of philanthropic responses to the rampant dearth which emerged to full effect in the terrible winter of 1846-7. Barry D. Hewetson, writing to the Association from Gweedore in February 1847, described what he had found as he moved among the population:

I have just returned after a day of painful exertion...in one house I found a
family of fourteen – the eldest fourteen years of age, the youngest nine
weeks – the mother unable to leave her bed since its birth. They had not a
morsel of food in the house...

...I went to another house to inquire about a young woman who had been
employed on the public works and had gone away ill during the severe
snow storm. On reaching home she complained of great coldness; her mother
and father made her go to their bed (the only one in the house); she fell
into a sleep from which she never woke. This day her poor mother died
also, and there are two of the children who, I am sure, will not be alive by
tomorrow, to such a state are they reduced from bad and insufficient food.

Lord George Hill is doing all that man can do... He is occupied from morning
till night...sparing himself neither trouble nor personal fatigue.[24]

Correspondents from Arranmore, Carrigart, Templecrone and
Glencolumbkille confirmed that the winter of 1846-7 was indeed black.
Rev. Henry Carre, writing from Killybegs in January 1847, thanked the
Committee for 'their liberal grant [which] enables me not only to feed the
hungry but to give useful employment to many a poor peasant.'[25]

In June 1848, 25 per cent of children in Glencolumbkille were receiving
relief from the British Relief Association who administered relief in schools.
This gave rise to an increased number of children in schools. Captain
O'Neill, visiting the area on behalf of the Relief Commissioners, reported:
'I found the numbers pressing for admission to the school-houses because
they have heard that there is gratuitous relief about to be administered,
fearful ... I have not as yet issued any gratuitous relief from the funds
placed at my disposal (by the British Association);..I think it better to have
correct lists of probable numbers that will require relief before any provisions
are issued; this will check fraud.'[26] His obsession with bureaucratic detail
is typical of the period. There was an overwhelming dread of allowing
money to be spent on anyone who was unentitled or undeserving. This
caused unnecessary, and often fatal, delays. The parish of Glencolumbkille
lost 17 per cent of its population during the Famine, through disease,
starvation and emigration.

Similar conditions prevailed in the Rosses where the population was in
excess of 10,000:

As road transport was almost unheard of in west Donegal, it became obvious
to those in authority that food would have to be brought to Donegal by ship

and then landed along the coastline later, making use of the facilities at Rathmullen, Downings, Rutland Harbour and Killybegs and thus it was that food – Indian meal, rice, biscuits, etc., was brought to Rutland Harbour in Government ships and later ferried across to Burtonport in small boats.[27]

The food store, previously the grain store of the absentee landlord, Conyngham, was guarded by police and armed coastguard personnel. This premises was subsequently used as a fever hospital. Dr George Frazer Brady gave his services voluntarily and a young girl named Sally Niece nursed the sick 'for the paltry sum of 4s.-6d per week'.[28]

The plight of the islanders of Arranmore is described by an American visitor, Asenath Nicholson, who visited the island in 1847:

> Not one family appeared to have a morsel of food – nothing but chickweed, bits of turnips and sea-weed, unless, by some lucky chance they had the good fortune to pick up some shell-fish. They didn't ask for anything; but when they held out their dishes, containing nothing but cold turnips ... no one spoke: a kind of insanity – a stupid despairing look was all that was to be manifested.[29]

The Inishowen Union, in the extreme north of Donegal, with a population of 43,569 and served by the Carndonagh workhouse, was among the first areas affected by blight. In the autumn of 1845, the crop was substantially destroyed in many areas. By the end of 1845 relief committees were already raising subscriptions which were matched by government. In February 1846, a Presbyterian minister, John Mackey, reported: 'A large proportion of 3400 souls in the parish is in great distress in Upper Fahan and the workhouse can offer no relief as it is already full'. The clergy of the parish of Donagh, in May, forwarded to the Poor Law Commissioners the numbers 'likely to suffer severely during the summer if relief be not afforded': He estimated that it would be Protestants 165-181; Presbyterians 120; Roman Catholics 140.[30]

Ballyshannon, situated at the most southerly point in Donegal, had been relatively unaffected by potato blight in 1845. In 1846, however, *The Ballyshannon Herald* observed:

> The weather continues extremely fine and the crops are stacking in good condition, with the exception of potatoes, which no one thinks of digging except to search through whole fields to make out a basketful which those who have no other employment do. The Indian meal which a few merchants have brought here from Sligo has been the means of keeping hundreds from starvation – but why don't the merchants get in cargoes of it as is done in Sligo and elsewhere?[31]

Workhouses were ill-equipped for the catastrophe which struck. On 12 September 1846, the Poor Law Commissioners called the attention of the Boards of Guardians of all unions to the great increase of poverty and distress due to the failure of the potato crop, asking them to make relief available 'to the utmost practicable extent'. They also warned them to base their estimates on the assumption that 'the whole accommodation which the workhouse affords will be placed in requisition during a considerable period.'[32]

At that date there were approximately 135 paupers in the Ballyshannon workhouse. It had been built to accommodate 500 inmates. By November the number of paupers stood at 255 and the cost of keeping a pauper had risen by fourpence farthing per week. On 14 November 1846 the Guardians were concerned at the 'vast increase in the number of paupers in the last week.' The following week, the pressure of numbers was so great that the Guardians decided that no pauper be admitted provisionally in the course of the next week. By 5 December 1846, the number of inmates was 511, rising to 596 by 27 March 1847. Numbers in the workhouse fell temporarily in the summer of 1847. On 2 October, possibly due to the relative generosity of soup kitchen relief, there were vacancies for 200 paupers in the house and the Guardians ruled that there should be no outdoor relief while there were vacancies in the house. However, on 30 October the master of the workhouse informed the board that there was no more accommodation available as numbers had risen to 540 in the house and asked, if there were to be any new admissions, 'How I am to manage respecting them?'

By 27 November, 1847, in spite of the onset of fever in the house, the numbers rose again to 561. On 1 January 1848, there were 769 inmates in the workhouse. By the following week, the number stood at 626, with many elderly and infirm paupers living on outdoor relief of 8d per week. Up to this point the Guardians refused admission to persons from other unions. However, on 8 January 1848, the Poor Law Commissioners gave instructions that all paupers from any union were to be admitted to the workhouse. The Guardians ordered 'provisional admission of all at gate'.

Before the failure of the potato crop, workhouse diet was frugal but wholesome, based on oatmeal porridge, potatoes and buttermilk. When potatoes became unobtainable, Indian meal was substituted. Its nutritional value was lower and the poor found it unpalatable. Early in 1847, the price of meal rose dramatically from £18 per ton to £27. There was also an increase in the price of oatmeal. While the increase in oatmeal may have been partly due to a general price rise in Europe, the price increase in Indian meal was principally due to profiteering by those involved in its transport and sale. Merchants tried to prevent government sales of cheap meal as this would have reduced their profits. The government succumbed to this pressure. Indian meal imported by the British government late in 1846 for distribution along the more impoverished regions of the west coast was, on the recommendation of Trevelyan, held in storage until all other sources of food should have failed. This meal was purchased at £13 per ton but for fear of undercutting the prices charged by local merchants it was sold at the government depots for £19 per ton at the end of December.[33]

When supplies of meal became totally unobtainable in Ballyshannon, the Board of Guardians applied to a Mr Hamilton to obtain meal for the workhouse. This was probably Mr John Hamilton of St. Ernan's who imported Indian meal and other provisions into Donegal town for distribution to his tenants. Mr Hamilton was described by James Hack Tuke as 'one who was devoting his whole energies to the service of the poor.' Tuke found that in Ballyshannon the gentry, far from being indifferent to the plight of the poor, were strenuously involved in relief efforts. Col. Connolly and his family, contrary to their custom, remained at their residence for the winter in order to provide relief.[34] When the Society of Friends offered 'money in proportion to the amount raised in the town for the establishment of a soup-kitchen,' Col. Connolly subscribed one third of the amount, £600, to the Ballyshannon Relief Committee. He also reduced his Donegal rents by 25 per cent.[35]

With the resumption of Indian meal as the staple food in the workhouse, the cost of keeping a pauper fell but a committee of the Board observed that there was 'great attenuation among the children' and it was proposed that each pauper be allowed 'a good and sufficient meal of rice and milk' daily. Dr Kelly, Medical Officer of the workhouse, recommended removing children under 12 to a separate house. This resulted in an improvement in the health of the children and a reduction in dysentery. Dr Kelly attributed deaths from dysentery to the diet of the house and the lack of clothing by men working in open sheds 'in this inclement weather'. The master reported that he was obliged to take the men from their work due to the extreme cold of their feet 'for want of shoes and stockings'.

Pestilence followed famine. In November 1846, the Ballyshannon Guardians received a letter from the Poor Law Commissioners calling attention to the danger which must arise 'from admitting into the Workhouse a greater number of inmates than the institution was intended to contain.'[36] The Board promptly resolved to admit no more paupers until those already in the house were provided with necessary clothing and accommodation.' By this time numbers had risen from 184 to 469 in the space of a month. *The Ballyshannon Herald* expressed alarm at the spread of fever in the workhouse and on 2 April 1847 reported as follows: 'We regret to state that the poorhouse of the Union is crowded to excess which has caused fever and dysentery to spread among the inmates to an alarming extent.'

In July 1847, a temporary fever ward was erected. It contained only 50 beds although there had already been 100 fever cases in June. The enormity of the crisis did not prevent petty bickering. Disagreement between the Ballyshannon Guardians and the Relief Committee centred on the question of financing and control of the temporary fever hospital. The Board queried the financial records of the Rev. I. McMenamin, treasurer of the Relief Committee, and in September refused to provide further funding. On 4 November 1847, Dr Barclay Sheil, a prominent Ballyshannon physician and relative of Dr Simon Sheil who had charge of the fever hospital, wrote to the Poor Law Commissioners to complain that the Ballyshannon Guardians refused to pay the expenses of the temporary fever hospital.[37] The Poor Law Commissioners found in favour of the Relief Committee. Deaths from fever in Ballyshannon continued in 1848 with 13 dying from fever in the last week of January. Dr Stephens, one of the dispensary doctors, himself contracted fever from a patient and died. The workhouse master caught fever in April but recovered. At this stage, epidemic was on the wane, falling from 66 cases in February to 13 in December.

In Inishowen fever had first made its appearance early in 1846. The secretary of the Moville Relief Committee reported 'Fever has set in, in many cases fatally.' Fever in Carndonagh workhouse was reported a year later in March 1847, with eight inmates affected. Although the Guardians segregated the sick, treatment was almost non-existent. The Guardians were ordered to treat the patients by giving them alcohol but the record shows that only one bottle of wine was actually purchased. An anonymous ballad comments:

Tis for the doctor he says he has skill
He'll push around the wards the law to fulfill
If a pauper be dying or ready to drop
He says hold out your tongue and there is not more than that.[38]

The burial of such large numbers of workhouse dead caused difficulties. In Ballyshannon workhouse the problem reached a crisis on 8 May 1847 when the master reported: 'Resistance has been offered to the interment of the dead at several burying grounds in the neighbourhood, the consequence of which is that an accumulation of dead bodies to the number of seven are at present in the deadhouse, one having died of spotted fever, the others of dysentery; some of these deaths occurred four days ago.' It was decided to locate a paupers' graveyard at Mullaghnashee in the town.

While a record of the number of dead is not available in Ballyshannon and some other unions for this period, the cost of coffins recorded in the Ballyshannon Board of Guardian minutes gives some indication of the rising number of dead and the use of two covered barrows in January 1848 for conveying the dead. There have been suggestions that coffins were dispensed with. An Act, 10 Vic., cap. 22, empowered the relief committees to make arrangements for 'the proper and decent interment' of the dead, and to defray the cost from their funds,[39] a euphemism for the burying of uncoffined dead in mass graves. A record of a payment by the Ballyshannon Board of Guardians of £13 15s, which was half of the amount demanded by Mr Flanagan for the conveyance of deceased paupers to the burial ground during the fever epidemic, indicates that Ballyshannon workhouse had adopted the new procedures permitted under the Act. Payment by the authorities for such burials was usually per corpse and, according to oral tradition in Tipperary, this was 'a shilling or so per body'.[40] If the Ballyshannon Guardians paid a similar rate, then the sum paid to Mr Flanagan indicates approximately 550 burials.

Water and sanitation were inadequate for the increased numbers in the workhouse. In September 1847, there is mention in the minutes of an overflowing cess pool outside the women's yard. This may well have been the source of the 'manure on Workhouse ground' which was ordered 'to be spread at front of House for cropping' in October 1847, the use of sewage as fertiliser being permitted by workhouse regulations.[41] In November Mr D'Arcy, the temporary Inspector, complained to the Poor Law Commissioners of 'the sewers leading from it without a sufficient discharging power: the smell arising from this cause is most offensive, and distinctly to be perceived through the house itself.'[42] The problem persisted and, in November 1847, the master reported that the sewage was backing into the water tank. Water was in short supply. Early in January 1848, the master reported that there was an insufficient supply of water in the well to supply the house. At the end of the month he reported that bedding and clothing had not been washed for three weeks due to water shortage. The Guardians ordered two casks with handles for carrying water from the river. Subsequently, a contract was accepted for water to be provided at 5d per puncheon.

The question of workhouse funding was regarded by the government as the responsibility of the ratepayers and any advances made from government resources were given grudgingly and on the understanding that they would be repaid. The Poor Law Commissioners circularized the unions in September 1846, recommending that 'the means of affording relief which the law has put at the disposal of the guardians, should be made available to the utmost practical extent.' On 24 October, the guardians were obliged to make an increase in union rates above that struck in July 'to provide for the increased pressure on the union due to the failure of the potato crop'. However, there was considerable difficulty in collecting the rate due to 'the great distress which prevails in the union.' In January, an appeal was made directly to the Lord Lieutenant for some assistance 'toward the support of the poor in the Ballyshannon workhouse, otherwise the House will have to be immediately closed for want of funds'. At the end of February 1847, the Poor Law Commissioners lent £60 to the Guardians who expressed 'surprise at the smallness of the sum'. These loans continued weekly during the year until the Poor Law Commissioners refused, in July, to pay any more advances. In addition, in March the Poor Law Commissioners agreed to lend £240 for paupers' clothing.

In June the Poor Law Commissioners urged guardians to collect rates before the harvest and not to depend on government. However, collection of rates continued to be difficult and there was considerable waiving of rates due to the fact that the houses in question were 'down' and no longer subject to payment, for example 'Mr. Kitson relieved of paying further rates in Division of Devenish in which houses Nos 2, 11, 16, 23 & 28 have been shown to be down'. Such applications indicate that evictions had been carried out on a not inconsiderable scale. One account of eviction in the Ballyshannon Union is preserved in oral tradition:

> The usual procedure after an eviction was to burn the thatched roof to prevent the tenant from entering the house again after the bailiff and his assistants had left the scene. A man named Diver who lived in this townland was among those who were evicted out of their homes. The landlord himself was present on this occasion and he offered the sum of one pound to anybody who would set fire to the house. Diver who was standing out on the street with a number of neighbours, stepped forward and said he would earn the money. He thereupon stepped into the kitchen where some turf was still smouldering on the hearth, brought them out on a shovel and placed them among the thatch of the roof. In a few moments it was ablaze, fanned by a strong south-westerly breeze and in a short time his home was gone ...When the landlord tendered Diver the money which he had thus so strangely earned, he coolly put it in his pocket, turned on his heel, nodded to the neighbours and disappeared from the scene.[43]

By 1847 ratepayers were violently resisting paying a rate. The Inspector, Mr D'Arcy, reported that 'all the collectors, without exception, stated that if the assistance of police was not afforded them in the wild districts, and where violence might be apprehended, they would under no circumstances be concerned in it. There is a feeling of general insecurity abroad, some of the ex-officio Guardians left the Boardroom early, not wishing to be out after dark.[44] Little of the outstanding rate was collected.

In spite of shortage of funds, the workhouse maintained provision for education and religion as required by legislation. Ballyshannon workhouse had two chaplains, one Catholic and one Protestant. The Protestant chaplain requested an increase in his £20 per annum salary because of the increase in his duties which required him to keep a horse. The growth in the numbers of Protestants in the workhouse is also reflected in the purchase of 18 small and 6 large Prayer Books, the same number of Bibles, and catechisms for the use of the Protestant children. Sacramental bread and wine was provided out of workhouse funds for the Protestant inmates and in August 1847 an additional 30 Prayer Books were purchased. For secular studies, there was a schoolmaster and a schoolmistress. The Superintendent of Workhouse National Schools reported on 16 January 1847 that 'the female teacher is well qualified to teach reading, spelling and sewing and that the male can teach reading, arithmetic and writing and that the moral character of both is good'. The male schoolroom was equipped in the course of the year with one desk and a set of tablets. The female school was provided with 12 Carpenters spelling books.

The staff, apart from the schoolteachers, included the master, matron, porter and clerk. Their annual salaries were, for the master £20, matron £15, porter £6. The gate porter was a newly-created position. A sentry box was erected for him and he was provided with a great coat and a pair of shoes, to be returned if he left the workhouse. There appears to have been hostility between the master and matron. While the workhouse was in crisis with overcrowding, food shortages and fever, the Ballyshannon Guardians and the Poor Law Commissioners were devoting their attention to allegations that the master had made a female pauper pregnant. The investigation into the affair resulted in the dismissal of Mrs Keenan, the matron, for her collusion in making what was deemed a false allegation. However, the Poor Law Commissioners found that the investigation had been conducted in an illegal manner.

An increase in disorderly behaviour in the workhouses was to be expected in view of the overcrowded conditions. Punishment for disorderly behaviour or breach of rules ranged from confinement or withholding of food to discharge from the house. The board discussed the behaviour of 'incorrigible boys who threw stones at the assistant master' and concluded that corporal punishment was 'not wholly prohibited by the regulations'.

There were continuous attempts in all the Donegal workhouses to keep able-bodied inmates employed since 'It was a fundamental rule of the workhouse system that no individual capable of exertion must ever be permitted to be idle in a workhouse and to allow none who are capable of employment to be idle at any time.[45] Consequently, the minutes of Boards of Guardians throughout the county record orders being placed for 'sledges, scrapers, picks and barrows'.[46] In Ballyshannon workhouse, each adult male was expected to break half a ton of stones per day. Women did domestic work and sprigging and spinning wheels were available in some workhouses.

In addition to Poor Law Relief, Relief Committees composed principally of gentry and clergy also administered relief. Some of the earliest of these committees came into existence in Inishowen in response to the failed potato harvest of 1846. By the end of the year, local relief committees were raising subscriptions which were matched by government contributions but, by that time, the numbers of starving and destitute had increased so dramatically that the finance available was inadequate. Only one fifth of those eligible were able to avail of employment. The wage was 9d per day. When funds ran out, causing 'great distress,' the roads were left 'in a totally impassible condition.'

Early in 1847 the Moville Famine Relief Fund reflected the growing powerlessness of local committees to cope with the increasing scarcity in its appeal to the government:

> Amongst the numerous cottier inhabitants of the interior, and in the densely peopled hamlets of our extensive sea-coast, destitution to an alarming extent exists, and is on the increase. With multitudes of our people, their supplies and resources are exhausted and they are hastening to the same awful consummation. The causes of destitution are too obvious to be questioned; the traces of it, on the countenances and in the persons of the poor, are too palpable not to be recognised. By the inscrutable will of an all-wise providence, all things seem, at the present crisis, conspiring against our Poor. Reduced to debt and want by the partial failure of the Potato Crop last year – this year the whole crop, upon which their subsistence depended, has been utterly lost; the fishing which at other times, would have been a fortunate resource, has, this season, become totally unproductive; and provisions stand at prices hitherto unprecedented.'

The Ballyshannon Relief Committee came into existence in October 1846 with the aim of soliciting donations and selling meal at cost price. They had a store in College Street and raised a large sum to purchase meal which was sold in November 1846 to the distressed poor. Public works were proposed by a Presentment Session held in September 1846 but these were hampered by bureaucratic delays and bad weather. Tuke was particularly dismayed by the conditions of workers on relief works: 'The severity of the weather and the deep snow add greatly to the sufferings of the poor, and we felt deeply for the poor creatures at work upon the roads (amongst whom were several women), who in their ragged, miserable garments, are totally unfitted for exposure to the cold.' Delays in paying wages caused further hardship and on arrival in Ballyshannon Tuke reports: 'We again heard complaints that the men employed on the public works were irregularly paid, they not having received any pay for ten days or a fortnight, although the money was waiting in the bank.' This type of incompetence is confirmed by oral tradition: 'Relief was slow in coming owing to the slow methods of transport and the long distance from Dublin from which relief methods were directed and money sent to pay the men on relief works, which largely consisted of road-making.'[47]

In January 1847, the Temporary Relief of Destitute Persons Act, otherwise known as the Soup Kitchen Act, came into operation. The distribution of meal or soup was in the hands of the local relief committees and was generally unwelcome. There was an appeal from Clonmany Relief Committee 'not to establish a soup kitchen in Clonmany' but instead 'to set up a depot for the sale of cheap meal to the destitute.' The soup kitchens proceeded, providing a thin gruel for the starving but in August the Poor Law Commissioners, assuming the potato blight to be ended, ordered that all boilers be returned to the Workhouse. They were subsequently sold. After this date, all relief was channelled through the newly amended Poor Law.

Large numbers emigrated from Donegal, principally to America and Canada from the ports of Derry and Sligo, Ballyshannon and Donegal town. A government scheme was organised by the Colonial Secretary, Earl Grey, to send orphan girls to Australia. It was availed of by most Donegal workhouses. In Ballyshannon, 16 female orphans were selected in 1847 for emigration to Australia. Lieutenant Henry, the Emigration Commissioners' agent, visited the workhouse and selected the 16 orphan girls aged between 14-18 whom he felt would be suited to employment in Australia. It was agreed that each girl should be equipped with six shifts, two flannel petticoats, six pairs of socks, two pairs of shoes and two gowns. It was envisaged that it would cost £5 per head to equip the girls and they were to have free passage from Plymouth to Sydney. The orphans from Ballyshannon set out on their long journey from Ballyshannon to Plymouth under the stewardship of Sergeant Healy, the assistant master of the workhouse. On Monday 30 October 1848, the 16 girls set sail from Plymouth on board *The Inchinan* in the company of 148 orphan girls from other Irish workhouses. They landed in Sydney on 13 January 1849.

The Ballyshannon orphans who sailed on *The Inchinan* were: Jane Carleton, Margaret Sweeney, Mary Maguire, Mary McCrea, Ellen Feely, Jane Carberry, Sally McDermott, Rose Reid, Ann McBride, Margaret McBride, Letty McCrea, Anne Rooney, Mary Anne McDermott, Mary Allingham, Sally Lennon and Biddy Smith. The Earl Grey scheme was short-lived and came to an end in 1850.[48]

Details of the dock-side procedures for emigrants can be found in the diary of William Allingham, Ballyshannon poet, who was appointed

Customs Officer to Donegal Town in 1846. He describes his official duties:

> Outdoors, there came the occasional visiting of vessels, measurements of logs and deals, and 'bread-stuffs' (chiefly maize) and – by far the most troublesome, but the most interesting – the examination of the fittings and provisions of emigrant ships, and the calling over, when ready for sea, of the lists of Passengers, who came forward one by one, men, women, and children, to pass the doctor and myself.[49]

Strangely, during this period, the poet was preoccupied not with the grim details of famine but with less worldly feelings. 'My inner mind was brimful of love and poetry,' he wrote, 'and usually, all external things appeared trivial save in their relations to it.' He complained of suffering from over-clouding anxieties arising from his 'longing for culture, conversation and opportunity'. However, he had the consolation of corresponding with Leigh Hunt to whom he wrote in February 1847: 'fuel as well as food is much harder to the poor in this unfortunate time.'[50] This is the only acknowledgment of the Famine to be found in Allingham's writings of the period, apart from a description of a workhouse inmate whom the poet met in Ballyshannon workhouse:

> November 30 1847: Visit Poorhouse, Tom Read, crazy man with small sharp black eyes; sometimes keeps a piece of iron on his head to do his brain good; plays on a fiddle, the first and second strings only packthread, "Ain kind Dearie," "Pandun O'Rafferty," grunting and groaning all the while and groaning fiercely when he struck a note out of tune. I promise him strings. "Does your Honour live far away?"[51]

From a reading of Allingham's letters and diary, there is little intimation that he is living in the midst of starvation and death or that the Allingham family were involved in all Relief Committees set up during the Famine and, despite the poet's apparent aloofness, played a practical role in famine relief.

Allingham is not alone in this literary denial of the reality of famine. Chris Morash, in his introduction to *The Hungry Voice,* discusses the failure of so many Irish poets to find expression for the experience of famine. He attributes their silence to the fact that there was no precedent in English literature for expression of such a catastrophe. Whereas the native Gaelic tradition 'embraced a long history of famine, exile and destitution,' there was no such tradition in English. 'Famine, perhaps more than any other agent of change, forces the poet to make difficult choices; for while the sight of so many of his fellow creatures driven to the limits of existence cries out for some sort of response, famine does not sit comfortably in any of the established poetic idioms of the English tradition ... Had the same number died in battle as died from hunger and disease, there would have been a tradition on which to draw ... Famine however left the poets of the 1840s abandoned by tradition.'[52] It took Allingham another 13 years to find expression for the tragedy in his narrative poem *Lawrence Bloomfield*, a widely acclaimed indictment of landlordism and eviction.

A Ballyshannon diarist, Mary Anne Sheil, however, was less reticent. She reported: 'The fever carries off all it attacks, it is most fatal' and detailed local disturbances, '21 April 1848 – A great confusion in the town this day about the arrest of some people called Ribbonmen,' and later in July 1848 – 'The markets are well stocked, so are the jails. I do not know what folly the people are going on with. I think they would do well to wait till times would mend'.[53] The unsettled state of the country resulted in the billeting of British officers at her husband's home at Willybrook in Ballyshannon.

A breakdown in social order was to be expected as a consequence of a catastrophic event such as the Famine. In many parts of Ireland serious crime increased dramatically during and after the Famine years. While Donegal experienced some increase in crime, this was on a relatively minor scale. James Hack Tuke wrote with admiration of the:

> patience and resignation of the simple peasantry of Donegal ... Never have I witnessed so much good feeling, patience and cheerfulness under privation, of the existence of which there can no longer be any doubt ... Out of the scores of families which we visited and the many poor people with whom we conversed in Donegal, I hardly remember an instance of their murmuring or begging, although they were at some time suffering from hunger and disease.[54]

Nevertheless, as the winter of 1846 drew in, distress in the Ballyshannon Union was evident in a series of crimes reported in *The Ballyshannon Herald:* two tons of meal taken from the Abbey Mill and conveyed across the Erne under cover of darkness; the severed head of a cow left in the chain where it had been tethered, the remainder carried off; meal stolen from the local Poor Relief Committee's meal store in College Lane; and, on Christmas Eve, an act of piracy when bacon and ham were taken from a schooner leased by Mr Chism, a Ballyshannon merchant, which was lying inside the river bar. Also reported was a pathetic procession of poor through Ballyshannon, led by a man carrying a loaf speared on a pole.[55]

The attempted collection of the poor rate from farmers who were already destitute led to violent resistance. In November 1847, the Poor Law Inspector at Ballyshannon forwarded a report from a rate collector stating, 'I have met with opposition, and a forcible rescue at Connanger, where the opposing party was armed with a scythe and a grape, from which I providentially escaped being killed.'[56] Nevertheless, serious crime, reflected in the numbers sentenced to transportation to Australia, fell to six during 1846. This compared favourably with the previous two years when the numbers were 17 and 21. The adjoining county Fermanagh, with a population which was half that of Donegal, had 24 references in the transportation records in 1846. During 1847 Donegal experienced a minor crime wave. Transportation sentences rose to 31 for crimes relating principally to theft, cow stealing, sheep stealing, larceny and receiving stolen goods. In Fermanagh in the same year, the number sentenced to transportation was 114. In 1848, there were 32 persons sentenced to transportation in Donegal, once again for thefts which in this year included food and clothing. Allingham witnessed one of these sentencings and allowed reality to intrude briefly into his diary, 'December 29 1848 : To Session Court: girl convicted of stealing a purse and sentenced to seven years' transportation; she is removed shrieking violently. It seems a severe sentence.' The Transportation archive also records the occasion: 'Surname: Raddins; Other names: Mary; Age: 17; Crime Description: Larceny; Sentence: Transportation 7 years.'[57]

While these figures indicate an increase in Donegal in what the courts chose to regard as serious crime, the figures compare favourably with adjoining counties, with the exception of Co. Sligo which also had a low rate of transportation. On the other hand, an examination of the records often reveals that 'serious crime' by 1849 included vagrancy which carried a seven-year transportation sentence. Five such sentences were handed down by Donegal courts in that year. Four of the convicted were female and the ages of the guilty parties ranged from 16 to 20 years.

Today, in Donegal, there are many Famine roads bearing names such as 'brachan road' or 'line'. The expression 'taking the soup' is remembered and also the term 'malebag' (meal-bag) which, applied to a family, expresses the same concept. These expressions are sometimes linked to speculation as to how families came into prosperity. There are many sites of paupers' graves and in 1995, in Ballyshannon, a monument was unveiled to mark the burial place of the town's Famine dead. The massive iron boilers provided for Famine soup and gruel are to be seen at many locations in the county. Donegal Historical Society has received, on permanent loan, a large gruel pot which was previously kept at Coolmore House, Rossnowlagh, once the home of the unpopular agent and landlord, Alexander Hamilton. During the Famine, the pot was installed for use at Brachan Bray, the highest point in the neighbourhood, a site chosen so that only those strong enough to climb the steep hill would be fed. This pot will now be placed on a site at the Franciscan Friary, Rossnowlagh, to commemorate the Famine. Dunfanaghy workhouse has already been restored as a museum and heritage centre while in Ballyshannon plans are afoot to restore one wing of the workhouse which has remained in a state of remarkable preservation, largely unaltered since famine times. These once-dreaded buildings should continue to stand as an accessible reminder of the long agony of our ancestors in Co. Donegal 150 years ago.

THE FAMINE
IN
COUNTY DOWN

TREVOR McCAVERY

It would be impossible to find more distressing cases, short of the horrors of Skibbereen, in any part of Ireland than those narrated by our reporter from the eastern divisions of Down ...There are many cases of suffering in the immediate neighbourhood of Belfast not less distressing than in any other part of Ireland.

This was the view of *The Banner of Ulster* newspaper in February 1847.[1] This opinion conflicts with the impression that one usually has of the impact of the Famine in this part of Ulster. In Ulster as a whole there was a reluctance to accept that there was any destitution at all because it would be a 'disgrace to the province' and would 'sully the credit of Ulster'. In Co. Down, considered by contemporaries as the 'most thriving and best conditioned quarter of Ireland', this pride was particularly marked. Lord Londonderry, who owned of much of north Down, resisted the very idea of relief committees and the Grand Jury of the county was determined for as long as possible not to appoint any extraordinary sessions.[2] Only three of Ireland's Poor Law Unions chose not to offer 'outdoor relief' under the Temporary Relief Act in the first half of 1847. These were Antrim, Belfast and Newtownards, the latter in Co. Down. This would suggest that the Newtownards Union did not suffer. The extent of the suffering, and the debates about the adequacy of famine relief provision, in the Newtownards Poor Law Union – a prosperous area that is assumed to have escaped the suffering – are the subjects of this essay.

I

The Newtownards Poor Law Union comprised an area of almost 94,000 acres and a population in 1841 of 60,285. Its electoral divisions were Newtownards, South Newtownards, Mount Stewart, Greyabbey, Kircubbin, Ballywalter, Ballyhalbert, Carrowdore, Bangor, Donaghadee, Comber, Ballygowan, Tullynakill, Ballymaglaff, Kilmood and Moneyreagh.[3]

The Londonderry family was the major landowner and granted the custom known as Tenant Right. This was generally the practice on adjacent estates. In the decade before the Famine, Lord Londonderry's agent, John Andrews of Comber,[4] claimed that the state of agriculture in the parish of Newtownards was 'rapidly improving', with farmers using a five-course crop rotation and applying cattle manure and lime. But although a few farms were almost 100 acres, the average size of farm was considerably less. In the parish of Newtownards most farms were about 10 to 14 acres. In Loughriscouse, for example, the average farm was less than 6 acres. The better land was able to produce 15 hundredweight of wheat per acre, [5] which was only slightly above the national average for the time.[6] Andrews was only too well aware in 1844 that the area had an 'excess of labourers' and that their position was not improving.[7]

The town of Newtownards had been founded in the thirteenth century by the Anglo-Normans, and re-founded at the time of the Ulster plantation. In 1845, the *Parliamentary Gazetteer of Ireland* described it as:

> ...one of the few first class towns in the county of Down, as to size and importance; and one of the most attractive towns in the north of Ireland, as to neatness, regularity, architecture and convenience... The weaving of

muslin employs a large number of the male population; and the embroidering of muslin, for the manufacturers of Glasgow, employs many of the female population.

In 1837 there were 600 looms at work and 1,000 women were busy with 'flowering', or embroidery. The town also served as retail and market centre for north Down and the Ards peninsula, markets being held each Saturday and fairs three times a year. The town hosted a manor court, court leet, petty sessions and quarter sessions.

But behind the impressive facade of its Market House, the largest in any provincial town in Ireland, and main, bustling, broad thoroughfares, lay small, crowded, unhealthy backstreets. Its population had virtually doubled in the 1830s to a total of 7,621. In 1841 Mark Street was described as 'nearly stopped up with dunghills', Anne Street had 'many dung heaps' and there were dirty open sewers in most streets.[8] The town had no dispensary although the *Ordnance Survey Memoirs* of the 1830s said that one was 'much wanted' as 'the town's inhabitants are in a very sickly state. Fever is very prevalent.' The workhouse was built in 1841 to accommodate 600 and contained, on average, about 200. Over 700 families in the town depended on their own unskilled manual labour. As a consequence there was a sizeable proportion of vulnerable people in the town and parish of Newtownards in the mid 1840s.

Up to 1821, the town and district had benefited considerably from the exertions of the Londonderrys. The third Marquess, however, was an absentee landlord. Charles William Stewart (born 1778) was the younger half-brother of the famous Viscount Castlereagh. He had earned a deserved reputation as a fearless cavalry officer in the Napoleonic wars and enjoyed a brief diplomatic career as Ambassador to Vienna from 1814-22. In 1819, he married the wealthy Durham heiress, Frances Anne Vane-Tempest. The Vane-Tempest fortune included extensive properties and coal mines in Co. Durham, as well as land from her mother, the Countess of Antrim, in Co. Antrim; it placed the couple among the wealthiest in the British Isles. Lord Londonderry preferred to live at Wynyard, Durham, or Holdernesse House in Park Lane, London, managing his English estates and developing the collieries.

The Marchioness of Londonderry's costume ball at Holdernesse House.
The Illustrated London News, 22 July 1848

II

It was at the end of 1846 that distress came to the area. In August 1846, the potato crop in the district was, in the words of the Newtownards Board of Guardians, 'a total failure'.[9] Usually, an 'immense quantity' of potatoes was exported to Scotland and England from Bangor, Donaghadee, Ballywalter, Kircubbin, Comber and Ardmillan but due to the failure of the crop no exports took place in 1845 and 1846 and, indeed, there was not even enough to feed the labourers at home. The *Northern Whig* reported, 'The labouring class in Newtownards are now abandoning the use of potatoes and resorting to an oatmeal diet... There is a five-fold demand for oatmeal from a class whose usual food was potatoes.'[10] In the Newtownards area, food prices rose, and the position of the labouring classes – never comfortable, and deteriorating in the previous decade – became critical. With the absence of potatoes, and the high prices of other food, the farmers could not afford to feed labourers. As a consequence, they laid them off, and extreme destitution occurred, as unemployment coincided with a rapid increase in the cost of living.[11]

In response to these conditions, many landlords in Co. Down announced general rent reductions. On 28 December 1846, the radical landlord, William Sharman Crawford of Crawfordsburn,[12] published a letter to his tenants, saying:

> I wish no man in order to make payment of his rent at this particular time to subject himself and his family to a deprivation of their usual means of subsistence. From tenants who represent themselves so circumstanced, I shall accept such portion of rent as they are able to pay. I shall then cause their condition to be inquired into, and shall make settlement with regard to the remainder as the industry and conduct of the tenant may, in my judgement entitle him to. If ...misfortune has assailed him, I shall not shrink from bearing my proportion of the loss.[13]

The spirit of Crawford's letter is in contrast to one from Lord Londonderry to his agent, and published on 17 November 1846 in the *Downpatrick Recorder*. He believed that landlords should be free to decide for themselves on rent reductions and thus trusted that others would afford him the same freedom. He was always open to make exceptions in individual cases, but he was opposed to sweeping rent reductions as 'dangerous and fatal' and continued:

> I am not afraid of the dissatisfaction or discontent of my own tenantry if I do not yield to a sweeping or general measure of reduction of rents. ... I am well persuaded they duly appreciate our relative position; that they know and feel that my scale of rents has been fixed with a due regard to bad seasons as well as good; that they are aware that the permanency of every social relation can only be maintained by mutual good faith and by the reciprocation of mutual benefits and they will duly consider that a landlord, by largely foregoing his income, is not merely undergoing personal inconvenience but he may possibly sacrifice the personal convenience of others which he is bound, in the first instance, to personally guard and superintend.[14]

Between these two positions was that taken by J.W. Maxwell. He allowed his tenants in the Groomsport and Downpatrick districts an abatement of 15 per cent on rents in the year 1 November 1847 to 1 November 1848.

This was extended the following year to 20 per cent.[2]

When the hardship first appeared, public works were organised in Newtownards, but financed by voluntary contributions. Some 25 years later an account of this period was provided in the *Newtownards Independent* newspaper:

> Gradually the Famine crept in upon the weavers. Food rose [in price]; work all but disappeared and they were compelled to seek the workhouse until it was overcrowded. Gentlemen met to devise means and it was proposed that funds should be raised and the weavers employed at something that would benefit the town. The proposition was carried out and the Windmill Row was cut, one shilling per day being given for the work done. Then, the burn at the head of the town was widened; but the shilling a day availed but little, food was so high. Oatmeal was 3/1 per stone, potatoes 10d, Indian meal was brought into requisition, then pea meal, then bean meal and even that had to mixed with turnips and potatoes to make what is known as 'boxtie bread'[16]

Men aged between 15 and 80 worked outside in the bad weather, many of them were infirm and weakened by hunger, and some died. When these schemes were completed, an unnamed local gentleman, who had an estate near the town, employed a number of men for the same amount to do odd jobs on his property, but there were too many seeking work to enable him to maintain this project.[17] Then more funds were raised and men were paid 2° d per day to break stones on the North Street hill (though this figure compares very unfavourably with the average rate of 7˘ d a day paid out on government-run public works schemes).[18]

Meanwhile, numbers entering the workhouse doubled between October 1846 and January 1847, and doubled again from January to July 1847.[3] In mid-December 1846 the number of inmates exceeded the figure of 600 for which the workhouse had been built. At this point, the Guardians threatened to discharge single, able-bodied paupers; they ordered the fumigation and preparation of the newly-built fever hospital to obtain additional space and instructed their architect to draw plans for additional sleeping galleries and the carpenter to build temporary beds in one of the boys' dormitories. The admissions policy was tightened up too. The Guardians would only admit paupers who had been in the workhouse in the last six months, unless they had special endorsement from the Guardians from their electoral division or were in bad health. At the same time, however, they wished to be placed on record 'their opinion that it is necessary to guard against a continuance of an overcrowded condition of the sleeping apartments from the apprehension that disease will be produced thereby, especially among the children.'[20]

Early in December 1846, Lady Londonderry arranged to have clothes distributed in the vicinity of her house at Mount Stewart. From 18-20 December Lord Londonderry, in a brief visit to the locality, organised work at Mount Stewart at increased wages, and augmented the number of workers.[21] A soup kitchen, financed by voluntary subscription, was suggested by Lady Londonderry. She provided a recipe for soup and Lord Londonderry donated £20, and his wife £10. The couple then left for their home at Wynyard, Co. Durham. But on 21 December a public meeting at the Market House concluded that a privately-financed soup kitchen was not the best method of relief. A deputation was appointed to write to the Guardians and they stated:

> ...that distress to an alarming extent now exists in the two electoral divisions of Newtownards, that the inmates at present in the workhouse considerably exceed the number it was originally built to accommodate, that in our opinion it would tend considerably to lessen the distress so generally prevalent, as well as diminish the number of applicants for admission, if one meal in the day could be given in the workhouse to persons who would be recommended by the wardens or otherwise approved of by the guardians, the expense of such relief to be charged to the said electoral divisions.[22]

The deputation consisted of the Rev. Townley Blackwood, parish minister, the Rev. Hugh Moore, minister of the Non-Subscribing Presbyterian congregation, Major F.D. Montgomery D.L., JP of Regent House, and five merchants in the town. This request for a form of unofficial 'outdoor relief' reflected a growing practice in other parts of Ireland. However, outdoor relief was believed by many to encourage dependency and apathy. It had also been expressly forbidden by the 1838 Poor Law Act. This was the view shared by John Andrews and Robert Gordon of Florida Manor, Kilmood.[23] Stalling for time, they proposed that the request be passed on to the Poor Law Commissioners, probably in the full knowledge that it would be flatly rejected, but a majority carried an amendment that they believed that this mode of relief was in fact 'practicable' and 'highly desirable in the present overcrowded state of the House'.

The Guardians were becoming alarmed and recorded the following resolution in the minutes of 30 December:

This Board deem it right to place on record the present crowded condition of the female wards from the want of space in the apartments for sleeping accommodation. From this cause it has been necessary to place female children three in one bed and sometimes seven in two beds conjoined. In one room 17x 14° feet there are 19 women and 10 children but the excessive closeness is in some degree relieved by its being open to the rafters. Other rooms are proportionally crowded and having low ceilings are more oppressive by the insufficient power of ventilation; that the nursery which is an apartment of about 30 x 14 feet is often crowded to the extent of more than 30 nurses with 40 children and the mothers occasionally visiting the children; that although disease has not yet been exhibited to any great extent, this House is not free from diarrhoea especially among the children; that this Board apprehend that increased sickness will arise from the state of things so described.

Andrews was becoming very concerned too. On 10 January 1847 he wrote to Lord Londonderry at Wynyard:

Matters, I lament to say, are getting daily worse. The importation of food, though considerable, does not seem to satisfy demands or prevent the progressive advance of price, and the sufferings of the poor are considerably increasing... Families who have no head to work for them are much distressed. Many such exist everywhere and they are too numerous in Newtownards. After various projects, visiting committees have been appointed and on Tuesday next something will be decided upon, most probably a soup kitchen. The want of potatoes causes an immense consumption of grain by the farmers, which diminishes the quantity available for the market and I regret to say diminishes the resources available for *rent* which I fear will be deficient at May to a larger extent than I had ventured to contemplate. We must however do our best.

His next letter, of 18 January 1847, sounded a note of increasing alarm, confirming that the Newtownards area was indeed in the throes of the crisis:

Since last I addressed your lordship the distress of the poor has been fearfully increasing. The condition of even the fully employed labourer cannot now be other than one of straits and difficulty; and it is much to be feared that of the small farmer, who is eating out of his produce, and has little to sell, will become very bad long before harvest. Seed corn must be extracted from our stocks. All this now becomes truly alarming...if the weaving should fail, I know not what would become of us. In Newtownards a good subscription has been got up and the soup kitchen will speedily be in operation.[24]

However, the weaving did fail, a victim of the general economic slump, which meant that there was no work for the town's hundreds of handloom weavers. The soup kitchen was in operation by the end of January 1847 and Lord Londonderry had raised his contribution to £50 and his wife's to £20. The *Northern Whig* of 6 February 1847 reported:

> We regret to learn that distress prevails to an alarming extent in the town of Newtownards. In order to alleviate the same, as much as possible, a soup kitchen has been established and rations of soup and bread have been dispensed from one till two o'clock to all who may be inclined to purchase; and from two to three o'clock to about 240 families who have been recommended by Visiting Committees as fit subjects for gratuitous relief. The Committee have published, as will be seen by our advertising columns, the names of the subscribers to the fund which has been raised to defray the expenses of the soup kitchen, for the double purpose of showing the charitable disposition of the parties to whom they have applied for assistance as well as that of their fellow townsmen, and of inviting others, who have not yet done so, to come forward and aid them in this charitable and necessary work. It will be seen that Lord Londonderry heads the subscription list with £50... We refer with peculiar pleasure to the liberal contributions already received from houses in Glasgow through their agents in Newtownards, particularly from Messrs S.R.&T. Brown [£25], Lewis & Charles Park [£20] and Ewing, Paul & Co. [£10.10][25]

A reporter from *The Banner of Ulster* shed further light on the operation of this soup kitchen. Accepting that it was 'exceedingly well managed', he criticised the fact that it was only after the 240 families were issued with tickets, that those who had neither the tickets nor the money to purchase received free soup. It appears that 2,000 individuals were fed from the soup kitchen and 100 gallons of soup were given away free each day, with some of the rural poor walking two miles into the town each day to obtain it.[26]

The scenes at the soup kitchen were recalled in the *Newtownards Independent* :

> Oh to see those emaciated and half famished souls surround the dog kennel where the soups was distributed, was a sight never to be forgotten. How to get a shawl, or cape or an old petticoat to envelop the head and fit to be seen, even at a dog kennel, was a question difficult to answer. And for the men to go with a can or jug was out of the question. Yet even they had to go when the females could not find a garment to cover their squalid wretchedness.

The soup kitchen had to stay open to midnight and at times there were unpleasant scenes of jostling, shouting and fighting.[27] On 2 February, Andrews admitted to Lord Londonderry, 'No doubt very considerable

privation is endured by all from the labouring classes down and exertion through many months will yet be necessary. Several of the needy are badly situated and ... my plan and object is to press those who are destitute of means to sell and emigrate.' On 5 February, he reported that the soup kitchen was '...much visited. I lament to say the poor destitute are pressing on the workhouse beyond its powers of reception... The future is veiled from the most penetrating human eye.'[28]

Meanwhile, in Comber, private charity was addressing a 'truly lamentable' situation. In January 1847, some ladies set up a committee and sold meal and coal at reduced prices and paid women and girls for knitting and sewing. Finally, on 4 February, after meetings of the concerned of the town, a soup kitchen was set up which also was 'much visited'. It supplied, each day, 230 families with free bread and soup, and to another 100 families soup was sold at a halfpenny a quart. The soup kitchen cost over £30 per month of which Lord Londonderry contributed £10.[29] These measures appeared to be effective.

In Bangor, a soup kitchen was set up in the town's hotel. It was open only to those who resided within the Corporation boundary. Some 600 of the town's population of 3,000 were given free soup and a small charge was made for bread. The kitchen cost £10 per week, with one third of the expenditure met by Robert Edward Ward, the local landlord, but apparently the operation was unable to feed all that wanted help and no more money was to be had. In the rural districts surrounding Bangor, Lord Dufferin of Clandeboye and Robert Perceval-Maxwell of Finnebrogue and Groomsport had made arrangements to buy soup from the Bangor soup kitchen and distribute it to the poor of their estates.[30]

How effective were these privately-financed soup kitchens and the workhouse in relieving distress in the union? A reporter commissioned by *The Banner of Ulster* newspaper made extensive visits to homes in the area. He was able to gain first-hand observation of the suffering, and his reports leave no doubt of the very real destitution experienced in February

1847. The worst cases were those who had no head of the house to work for them, either through earlier death or current illness, or where there was no work to be had. In every case detailed, families had sold all their furniture and possessions, had no fire in the hearth and had not eaten for several days. A number of families had shared a raw turnip or had only partial meals every few days which were purchased with the proceeds of 'flowering' work done by the girls or, in the case of Bangor, through work done by children at the cotton mills. In all cases, the families were considerably weak with hunger and were on the point of starvation.

Half of all labourers in the townlands west of Crawfordsburn – Ballymullan, Ballygilbert and Ballygrot – 'could not keep their families in sustenance, seed the ground and meet the landlord's claim... Dysentery is exceedingly prevalent.' It would have been much worse here had not some of the wealthier farmers been engaged in drainage work. Although the town of Comber was spared the worst of the suffering, the state of the poor outside the town was not good. According to *The Banner of Ulster* reporter:

> In Magherascouse, Carrickmannon, Ravara, Ballygowan and Ballycloghan dysentery is exceedingly prevalent, and I find in those localities scarcely anything to warrant me in stating the condition of the poor to be better than in any other rural district I have traversed. In the neighbourhood of Ballygowan especially, an epidemic of a devastating character has appeared and I was informed by a very respectable authority who lives close to the village that three and four funerals pass his house daily. A great many of the labourers have chosen Scotland as a place of refuge, but unfortunately for the families left behind, it is discovered that the sister country has plenty to do for the support of her own. Many of the small farmers here, as elsewhere, have not an ounce of seed for the ground and the labourers that remain in the country have little or nothing in the shape of employment as yet... and to them a meal in the day would be a boon.[31]

In the town of Newtownards the soup kitchen and the workhouse proved inadequate to prevent suffering:

> In thirty or forty visits which I made nine out of every ten had been, were ill, or were taking ill of dysentery arising from the want of the common necessaries of life... A large proportion of 'the Deed' were in a wretched state. They were all bowed down by the stroke of famine in the first place and in the second, of its constant attendant – disease.

In the townlands near Newtownards – Drumhirk, Ballyhinney, Loughriscouse and Ballyblack – he was 'struck very forcibly' by the fact that he 'scarcely saw a labourer working in the fields and through a tedious day's travel I did not observe half a dozen ploughs engaged in the usual labour of this season of the year.'[32] The annual ploughing match of the Ards Farming Society, held near Greyabbey, was a flop, one observer noting that labour was in a 'backward state' and recognising 'the disheartening apathy into which many have fallen from the state of the times.'[33] In April 1847, it was noted that around Newtownards 'the great majority of the stackyards were quite cleared of grain.'[34] *The Banner of Ulster* concluded 'that if an overwhelming amount of destitution exists largely in the South and West of Ireland it is largely participated in by the inhabitants of the North and I might say at our own doors.'[35]

Perhaps the plight of the poor in Newtownards could have been made easier had negotiations between Andrews, on behalf of Lord Londonderry, and the Belfast & County Down Railway Co. for the sale of land for the new line been concluded earlier. Negotiations to purchase land began on 18 January 1847 when the distress was at its worst. Naturally, Andrews was asking for as much as possible. He admitted privately that he was asking for a high price: 'The estimated rent I have laid on both town plots and farms is much beyond what could be had from any tenants, and 33 years purchase is a higher [sale?] than I have yet known to be paid'.[36] Negotiations dragged on for weeks as 'they cannot be pressed without weakening our position.'[37] By mid-May they were concluded and the railway company began work, employing 'the labourers whom the farmers from want of money and dearth of food have been throwing off.'[38] If these negotiations had been concluded earlier, and the poor employed, their suffering would undoubtedly have been lessened.

III

When the Famine was at its worst, a great controversy arose about the behaviour of the third Marquess of Londonderry in relation to the suffering. A withering article appeared in the *Londonderry Standard* of 8 January 1847 entitled 'The Three Marquesses'. Its anonymous author alleged that, when it came to charitable giving, the third Marquess 'had secured his breeches with one of Chubb's double bolters, at least as far as the town of Newtownards is concerned.' He said that Lord Londonderry had promised

to attend the public meeting in the town at the beginning of January but, at
the last moment, had returned to London leaving:

> ...his agent Mr Andrews, to herald his munificence to the said assemblage.
> The sum total of his lordship's subscription to the relief fund being no less
> than £20; and the Marchioness, as if to mesmerise the folk in that quarter
> with an awestruck feeling of aristocratic charity, actually added £10 to her
> husband's princely donation.

The article then alleged that Andrews had produced a 'set of resolutions,
cut and dry for the occasion', read them out, and that the others present
abruptly left the meeting in protest. The writer applauded this protest action:
'the folks there have yet to learn the alphabet of serfdom'. The Marquess
had made an outstanding 'blunder when he supposed the spirited gentry
merchants, and other inhabitants of Newtownards, would tamely allow
such conduct to pass without protest,' he asserted, and concluded with a
harsh attack on Lord Londonderry's lifestyle:

> Let him not wrap himself up in the vain delusion that he was sent into this
> world merely to revel on the sweat and toil of others, without any care or
> thought in his part as to how or under what circumstances of pinching
> economy his revenues are made up.

The writer went on to compare Londonderry's contribution with that of
the Marquess of Hertford and the Marquess of Downshire.[39]

Andrews replied on Lord Londonderry's behalf to the *Standard's* attack.
He denied that he had chaired the relief meeting, and accused the
Londonderry Standard of trying to 'disorganise the social relation between
Landlord and Tenant'. He accepted that the Londonderrys had given £30
towards a soup kitchen but maintained that this was a first instalment.[40]
Indeed Londonderry had raised his contribution to £50 and later gave
another £50.[41]

The controversy took a new twist when Andrews published another
reply, but this time in the rival newspaper, the conservative *Londonderry
Sentinel.*[5] He enclosed a letter from Lord Londonderry himself. Londonderry
maintained that he had not been asked for rent reductions in Co. Down. He
took advice that there was an 'admirable workhouse in Newtownards' and
that the poor were provided for. He pointed out that Lady Londonderry had
suggested setting up a soup kitchen and that more money was to be asked
for if required. He said: 'I am entirely willing to remain in the hands and
judgement of my tenantry and my town of Newtownards on this and every

other subject.' Londonderry outlined his philosophy on poor relief:

My object has been to increase that reliance on their own energies which our people have always demonstrated, and did not wish to encourage that erroneous system of looking abroad for relief... I decided at an early stage in our distress to adopt and inculcate on those around me, namely, 'to help themselves and heaven will help them'... My conscience acquits me of ever having acted wrong[ly] as a proprietor, a landlord or a Christian. Believe me, yours faithfully, VANE LONDONDERRY.[43]

The editor of the *Standard* claimed that Lord Londonderry had received no applications for rent reductions because, a few months before, he had published a statement saying that he had decided not to make any rent reductions despite the onset of famine. The editor again compared the amount of Lord Londonderry's donation with that of 'three or four insignificant muslin manufactures who beat your Lordship and Lady Londonderry hollow in the way of liberality to your own starving people.' Finally, the editor mocked Lord Londonderry's claim to have never 'acted wrong[ly] as a... Christian': 'His Lordship is then in a most enviable state of inward blessedness for we imagine that some of the Apostles themselves could scarcely have made such a declaration!'[44]

Andrews saw the controversy, which was played out on the pages of these Londonderry newspapers, in wider terms: . It was, he believed, part of an attack on the landlord class, stating, 'There is a warfare against property, and its possessors, scarcely concealed.'[45] The *Standard's*

only desire is to drag people into controversy which will excite the interest of those to whose passion they are pandering. The paper in question ... is despised by the higher class and seeks to make good its fooling with the lower by vilifying the other.... Everything disagreeable in every shape has been raked up and tortured and misrepresented to suit the palate of those who love to feast on the abuse and vilification of landlords.[46]

Indeed, the editor, Dr James McKnight, was formerly the editor of the *Belfast Newsletter* and the Presbyterian journal, *Banner of Ulster.* McKnight's views were well known as a radical champion of Tenant Right.[47] He might have been attempting to stir up disaffection on the otherwise contented Down estates.

In defence of Lord Londonderry, he did increase his contribution to the soup kitchen considerably when asked. The family also distributed clothes and his share of the Poor Law rates, which supported the workhouse, was almost £500 a year.[48] He set up links between his estates and his collieries in Durham, which provided jobs for some of the unemployed. He made money available for drainage schemes.[49] But he could also be extremely insensitive. In 1848 the family made 'extensive additions', costing £15,000, to their mansion at Mount Stewart. This created work, and may have been an attempt at relief, but it appeared to most as conspicuous consumption at a time of general want,[50] an impression that can hardly have been dispelled by its lavish opening in late November of that year. As the *Downpatrick Recorder* reported from Mount Stewart:

> On Monday evening the splendid suite of spacious apartments were thrown open to the reception of the nobility and gentry of the county who began to arrive soon after 9 o'clock. The band of the 13th regiment was in attendance and about 10 o'clock dancing commenced which was kept up with spirit and animation till 1 o'clock. When at the supper table, extending the entire length of the new dining room, prepared for reception of 100 guests, at the centre table with tables adjoining, the *coup d'oeil* exhibited a display of beauty and fashion seldom surpassed in the County of Down. The noble host and hostess were unceasing in their efforts to promote the comfort and enjoyments of their guests. After supper, dancing was resumed with renewed spirit and not discontinued till a very late hour in the morning.[51]

Perhaps the most important consideration, and one not appreciated by contemporaries, was that Lord Londonderry did not have access to his entire annual income of £200,000. About £175,000 was his wife's, and this was tied up in a Trust which he could not touch. He had to make his Irish estates self-sufficient. Although his gross rental from the Co. Down estates was £23,000 with a further £2,000 from Londonderry and Donegal, when salaries, subscriptions, arrears and interest payments were deducted, he ended up with a deficit of £2,000 per annum.[52] In June 1847, the Belfast Banking Company asked him to pay his debts of £2,500 or they would make Andrews liable for them.[53]

IV

No sooner had Andrews finished fielding these attacks, when a rift developed between the Newtownards Guardians about the principles of relief provision. This was less personal, but went straight to the heart of the debate surrounding Famine relief.

At the height of the crisis, some Guardians had not been confident that they were adequately equipped to discharge their obligations to the poor in the union. A group of them decided to act on the request of the deputation for outdoor relief, and take advantage of new legislation called the Temporary Relief Act or 'Soup Kitchens Act' of February 1847. This Act permitted guardians, from February to September, to give or sell soup from a soup kitchen without the poor having to come into the workhouse. New legislation also established a permanent outdoor relief system after September 1847 with the costs paid from the rates. On 17 February 1847, even before the first Bill was passed, the Newtownards Guardians sent a letter to the Relief Commissioners in Dublin informing them that the number of inmates was 832 and warning that:

> ...if the House becomes more crowded some malignant disease will almost certainly break out and the Guardians are of the opinion that to avoid such contingency the greater numbers of the electoral divisions of this Union will avail themselves of the provisions of the Bill for the Temporary Relief of Destitute persons now passing through Parliament.

On 3 March 1847 the board voted, by 19 votes to 11, that a petition should be submitted to the House of Commons requesting the widest possible interpretation of outdoor relief :

> It is most desirable that there should be an extension of the Irish Poor Law Act as would confer upon destitute persons, *permanently* disabled by age, or by mental or bodily infirmity, and upon such as may become *temporarily* disabled through sickness or accident, a right to relief and to medical attendance out of the workhouse....that emergencies may arise from workhouses being full, in which it would be desirable that Boards of Guardians should have the power of giving temporary out door relief *in food* to the able bodied poor.

They also petitioned for new legislation that would give them the right to transfer beggars to their place of origin, or else that the government grant additional national funds to provide for them. In addition, they sought to make it more difficult for mothers of illegitimate children to get into the workhouse, though they accepted that it would be proper that they should act as guardians for orphaned and deserted children, with power to control, apprentice and otherwise provide for them. They felt that the government must assist destitute able-bodied poor to emigrate to the colonies. Clearly, the Board of Guardians of Newtownards workhouse were encountering such problems, and were feeling unable to cope.[54] However, Andrews, who was in the minority of eleven when the Guardians voted on the petition said, 'I greatly dread the creation of a legal right to outdoor relief. It would immensely increase the number of claimants and might in the end generate all the evils of the old English Poor Laws.'[55]

Nevertheless, it was obvious that the crisis was deepening and in March, Andrews and the committee organised an additional round of subscriptions to the privately financed soup kitchen, with Lord Londonderry heading the new list, giving an additional £50.[56] Throughout the spring and early summer the fever hospital was filling up with paupers suffering from dysentery and it was arranged that the medical officer be given an assistant. A report from the medical officer admitted that 'a number' had died. The grave-digger must have been busy for he was reprimanded for not sinking the coffins at least two feet below the ground. The Guardians were forced to seek new ground for another cemetery. It was decided to rent some houses adjacent to the workhouse as additional accommodation for the fever hospital.[57]

Andrews was glad that the Temporary Relief, or Soup Kitchens Act, was optional. 'I thank God these views do not contemplate our locality. I trust they will leave to us the workhouse test and I trust we shall have the good sense to apply it.'[58] He hoped that Newtownards would not engage in outdoor relief, even though a majority of the Guardians had earlier petitioned for such legislation. Andrews had his way.[59] By 14 May 1847, Andrews was able to report, with pride, to Lord Londonderry that:

> The condition of the district happily maintains its distinguished pre-eminence. Your Lordship and Lord O'Neill form the exception in all Ireland to universal dependence on the relief afforded by the Temporary Relief Act. The Unions of Newtownards and Antrim are the only local Unions into which that has not been introduced. Belfast is the only town exempt. Our [voluntary] Soup Kitchens [in Comber and Newtownards] are so far adequate to relieve the distress which the workhouse cannot meet... and the trading in Newtownards is tolerably brisk so that, on the whole, our situation is comparatively an enviable one.

Yet, despite such optimism, the crisis had not yet fully passed. In May, Andrews admitted that, 'Our workhouse contains 750 in the body of the House and nearly 100 in the Fever Hospital. Very heavy rates are on the point of being again levied, and though suffering much less than others, there is much of gloom in future prospects.'[60]

The heavy importation of grain in the late spring and early summer eased the situation and so food prices dropped. The soup kitchen was closed down in August 1847. It had been in operation for about six months. This meant that the only provision for the distressed was the dreaded workhouse system although outdoor relief had been made legal. In August, Andrews informed Lord Londonderry: 'The potato crop seems to be in a very precarious position. The disease, though trifling as yet compared with last season, is spreading, and I see no chance of the small farmers, in the position in which they remain, being enabled to hold their ground.'[61]

The stringent application of the workhouse test was Andrews' preferred method of dealing with the suffering, albeit reduced, but nevertheless real. He disliked outdoor relief and was reluctant to allow it to be given. This now brought him, and those who agreed with him, into direct conflict with other guardians – and the law. The Poor Law Amendment Act, passed in July 1847, sought to pass the whole responsibility for relieving all poverty, whether in ordinary or extraordinary times, upon the locality where it occurred. Boards of Guardians now *had* to provide outdoor relief for those permanently disabled by old age or those temporarily disabled by sickness or accident, and guardians were ordered to appoint Relieving Officers to assess these cases. A controversy raged amongst the Newtownards Guardians for the next six months over the principle, and costs, of the new scheme, and many of the leading Guardians resigned over these issues.

The first shots in this battle were fired on 21 July 1847 at a meeting at which Edward Senior, the Assistant Poor Law Commissioner for east Ulster, was in attendance so that he could clarify the operation of the new legislation. When a resolution was proposed that the implementation of the new legislation be undertaken at their next meeting, an amendment was passed stating, '... we consider that it will be unnecessary and inexpedient to make provision for outdoor relief at present.' William Sharman Crawford, the chairman, had it placed on record that he dissented from this amendment because it was illegal, and also 'because although the accommodation of the workhouse has been extended by means of galleries in the sleeping room for the adults and sheds for infants, the House appears to me incapable of affording healthful accommodation to the number of inmates it now contains.' The following week, Crawford had the following personal statement entered in the minutes: 'The sleeping apartments for the adults in this Workhouse are in their present crowded state likely to endanger the health of the inmates and that the like objection exists to the sheds in which the infants and younger children are kept.'[62]

On 18 August, the Board received formal instructions from the Poor Law Commissioners to appoint Relieving Officers. On 1 September the full battle was drawn. Andrews pushed through a series of resolutions:

> We rely with hope and confidence on the protection of the Workhouse Test as a safeguard against abuse and imposition and as a barrier to the rapid spread of pauperism, while outdoor relief has ever been found a curse and promoter of greater social evil.... Under those convictions we are quite prepared, if and when it shall be found necessary, to extend our own workhouse accommodation so as to enable us to meet any emergency... we therefore strongly remonstrate against any attempt to enforce the appointment of Relieving Officers as an expense exceeding the amount at present paid in salaries to all the officers of the Workhouse, till an occasion arise demanding the services of these officers.

Within a few weeks William Sharman Crawford had resigned as chairman, and Guy Stone and Robert Nicholson resigned as vice-chairman and deputy vice-chairman respectively. Crawford protested that there were too many deaths in the workhouse and that these were the result of over-crowding, and the fact that people held out too long before resorting to workhouse charity, so that by the time many were admitted they were seriously under-nourished. He claimed that in these circumstances the workhouse test was 'an unjust, uncharitable and un-Christian law.'[63] Robert Nicholson calculated that a labourer's family of five could be fed and clothed at the most basic level in the workhouse for nine shillings a week only because everything was purchased by the guardians below the market rate.[64] It was impossible for that same family to live outside the workhouse because no labourer could earn nine shillings a week or could purchase articles at those rates: furthermore, he would still have to pay one shilling a week for the rent of his cottage. The situation was worse for those who were too sick or old to work. Therefore, he concluded, the number of those in destitution were much greater than those who applied to the workhouse but they did not wish to lose their freedom and dignity by entering it. He declared that:

> a law which treats poverty as a crime, and provides relief for the poor by forcing a man and his family into a workhouse, where confinement and restraint are nearly as great, and where the associates amongst whom he is thrown are almost as bad, as in our gaols or Houses of Correction, is, I do not hesitate to say, both unjust and oppressive; and, further, that it is unjust,

because it awards the same measures of relief or punishment, call it which you please, to the disorderly and profligate that it does to the honest and industrious.[10]

The majority of the Board disagreed and followed the lead given by Andrews. He insisted that giving out free food to any not prepared to come into the workhouse must be a matter of *private* charity. He was aware of the danger:

> ...of affording anything beyond the supply of the merest necessities from funds levied by compulsory assessment. Everything beyond that should be the offering of private charity... God and nature never could have intended that the channels of private charity should be closed. The line of separation between public and private charity is clearly defined. The State may, and perhaps should, provide that no person should necessarily perish of want. The recipients of the bounty of Providence should think of their responsibility to minister comforts to those to whom the Great Benefactor has given a claim to their benevolence.

In fact, the voluntary arrangements made in Andrews' area of Comber were considered as 'excellent' and of 'great service'. Reflecting the fashionable views of political economy, he believed that outdoor relief encouraged pauperism and a culture of dependency. His brother had just returned from Roscommon where no grain was being cultivated, rents were years in arrears and the poor rates were four shillings in the pound. The Young Irelanders, the O'Connell party and the Tenant Right party exploited the situation. He was confident that :

> the very best feeling exists among our people. They suffered much, more than I at first anticipated from the potato failure, but the great body of them do seem intent on making the best of their difficulties, and are anxious to do what they can. It is hard indeed that we should be subject to the same discipline [high poor rates to pay for outdoor relief].

Andrews accepted the two complaints that the poor were under-nourished and that there was overcrowding in the workhouse but pointed out: 'the mortality in the workhouse was very great, [between August and November], but where was it not very great?... Very many were reduced by insufficient food before they sought refuge in the workhouse.'

But he maintained little else could be done as prices were high and there was a food shortage. If people were under-nourished before they came into the workhouse 'it was the hand of God and not of man that did it. But man was not unemployed in endeavouring to alleviate the infliction.'

Referring to the soup kitchen, Andrews added:

> Voluntarily raised funds, economically applied in rendering soup and prepared food, of a character not generally in use ...[gave] relief to the most suffering in a manner much more safe, and not less efficient, than any Board [of Guardians], with funds compulsorily levied, would have effected, and when the urgent necessity of their effort passed away, it was wisely discontinued.

> The other cause of increased mortality assigned in Mr Crawford's letter of resignation was the crowded state of the workhouse. I neither admit or deny that this operated to the extent Mr Crawford supposes. If it did, I for one hold myself blameless. When the house began to be overcrowded, I proposed that a building, admirably adapted for the purpose, which we now have hired for the trifling rent of £20 per annum, should have been taken. The Board preferred, and the Commissioners sanctioned, the erection of additional sleeping galleries and of a wooden house in the yard... Greatly extended accommodation is now provided and will be provided beyond the probability of any future demand... We will build and build, and in the meantime hire and hire, but by some means we will protect ourselves against the inundation of outdoor relief.'[66]

However, should avoiding outdoor relief have been his major concern? Was private charity infinite? *The Banner of Ulster* considered the Newtownards soup kitchen as only 'satisfactory in a temporary sense, not calculated to meet the extreme pressure upon the charity of the charitable when viewed in the light of... permanency.'[67] Was it right that those in distress, because of unusual circumstances, be made to wait until they were destitute, and then be forced to enter an already overcrowded, unhealthy workhouse? Andrews could not deny that there was overcrowding and that this had led to deaths. He believed, however, that they were at an acceptable level. In fact, deaths in the workhouse were considered, by some contemporaries, as excessive. In November 1848, the Newtownards Guardians received complaints from the parish authorities that the parish graveyard was filling up with pauper dead from the workhouse. As a consequence, they had to purchase an acre of ground in the townland of Milecross from Lord Londonderry as a burial ground for the paupers.[68]

Interestingly, Andrews viewed the Famine as a mechanism which could operate to better civilise the country. This, according to J.S. Donnelly, 'was the common view among the landed elite.'[69] Andrews argued that the repeal of the Corn Laws would create a free trade in grain and there would need to be increased vigour from Irish farmers to compete:

We are approaching a new era when no encouragement should be given to idlers. One year more and permanent free trade in corn will require the full energies of our working population, instead of a lethargic leaning on Poor Rates. [70]

... I also trust we shall be enabled to employ our own population and to guard against the incursion of the hordes, which the potato has generated in the south and west, and that our progressive knowledge and industry may enable us to adapt our procedure to the altered circumstances which free trade incur, and general free trade will produce. *And if we shall have no more potatoes, which I almost wish, that we shall be enabled to feed our people with more nutritious food and elevate them in the scale of civilisation.* I sincerely hope therefore that few or none of the dreaded evils will fall upon us, and I trust that by some means the regeneration of all Ireland may be affected [emphasis added].[71]

He did not shrink from clearing the estate of small tenants. This could be voluntary or forced – 'My plan and object is to press those who are destitute of means to sell and emigrate'.[72] In August 1847 he observed:

I see no chance of the small farmers, in the position in which they remain, being enabled to hold their ground, and I fear that the removal of many of them will be inevitable and consequently that the difficulty of realising a rental during the period of transition will be greatly increased.[73]

... I have been preparing, with painful apprehension, for the measures which will soon I fear be inevitable. I have served many notices at May and after November. Some at least of the most backward and involved must be forced to sell out and depart. This must be concluded quickly and not too rapidly, lest public commotion should be the result.[74]

Indeed his only consideration was that if he threatened to evict for non-payment of rent, the tenants would start selling their cattle to raise cash, and this would devalue the estates – or, in his words, 'killing the goose that laid the golden egg'. He also, he believed that by failing to threaten eviction he might be open to criticism for being too indulgent!

The resignations from the Board of Guardians left Andrews free to direct the affairs of the union. In November, he informed Lord Londonderry:

At our Board of Guardians I have carried a resolution by an increased majority of 17:5 (the Crawfords, the Wards and Nicholson having absented themselves) proposing a compromise with the Commissioners on the terms suggested by Lord Clarendon...I have carried another resolution calling upon the [Poor Law] Commissioners to order their architect to supply plans for the enlargement of the workhouse that we may avoid the risk of being unable to afford adequate relief in the workhouse. Matters are certainly not so alarming as last year but even now our workhouse is very full and in all parts of the county they are filling.[75]

The first resolution was to appoint Relieving Officers from the Rate Collectors but give them no duties or extra salary, and the second was to extend the workhouse to accommodate an additional 300 paupers.

Andrews may have held sway at the workhouse but he could not continue flouting the law. In the end, in January 1848, Andrews and his followers had to submit to the new legislation. The Poor Law Commissioners would not sanction such a large extension and insisted on outdoor relief. This prompted a bitter resolution, carried by 14 votes to 8 against. The majority of the Guardians expected:

> that in these times of continued pressure and apprehended difficulty we would not have been thwarted by the Commissioners in our desire to avoid an unnecessary waste of the funds of the Union by an order to endow officers of whose services we have no need, nor in our anxiety to prevent the growth of that dangerous and embarrassing expectation of outdoor relief which the appointment of such officers would assuredly generate in that class whose great aim is to obtain the means of enjoying petty luxuries in their own filthy cabins, but who are unwilling to submit to the discipline, and even dislike the cleanliness of, the Workhouse.[76]

The Newtownards Board had been fairly evenly split on the introduction of outdoor relief.[77] The voting patterns suggest a geographic division in the union. For example, the Guardians for Bangor were in favour of outdoor relief, and at one stage they sought to have outdoor relief in the electoral division of Bangor alone, 'leaving the Poor Law Commissioners and the majority of this Board to settle between themselves their differences of opinion on the construction of the Poor Law'.[78] In some instances, however guardians from the same locality voted differently. An explanation which related votes to the degree of suffering in the area does not fully explain voting patterns on a number of key issues.

It is interesting to note that virtually all the *ex officio* Guardians were in favour of outdoor relief. These were the landowners. When Robert Gordon of Florida Manor, the only other *ex officio* Guardian with Andrews to oppose outdoor relief, was asked to take over as chairman of the Board he declined. He remarked on the fact that most of the landowners were in favour of outdoor relief:

> I wish to raise my voice in protest against any preliminary movement made
> with a view to introduce the administration of outdoor relief with its
> inseparable evils. In taking this course I cannot but regret my sentiments
> have placed me at issue with the majority of those who comprise the *ex
> officio* Guardians and landed proprietors in connection with the Board
> ...the withdrawal of whose services at the present crisis cannot fail to be
> accompanied with most embarrassing results. Under the circumstances to
> which I have averted, where so much conflict of opinion and collision of
> sentiment must inevitably ensue in the conduct of business, and where my
> views are opposed to an influential section of the Board, I must be permitted
> to decline entering this office.

Why were the majority of landowners in favour of outdoor relief? Were
they acting paternalistically to their tenants? Was this out of genuine
concern, as Crawford and Nicholson's letters of resignation maintained?
Or, were they concerned to prevent lawlessness, or incur gratitude, or spread
the cost of supporting the poor? The latter seems unlikely because if outdoor
relief was cheaper the majority of elected Guardians would have followed
them: outdoor relief was, in fact, more expensive as it entailed the
employment of Relieving Officers. Then could it be that those who were in
favour of outdoor relief were the only ones who could afford to be generous?
Then there are other questions. Why did Andrews and Gordon, themselves
representative of the landed interest, differ from the other landowners?
Did wider political issues separate them from the others? In the next few
years, the Londonderry interest and Robert Gordon were censured by the
Tenant Right organisation in which their opponents on relief, William
Sharman Crawford, Guy Stone and John McKittrick, took a leading part.

The crisis had passed by the spring of 1848. In the quarter April-July
1847 admissions to the Newtownards workhouse had peaked at 426; by
July 1848 it had fallen to 99, though the administration of outdoor relief
may help to explain the reduction. The Newtownards Guardians were
released from the burden of having to meet a local crisis. In 1848, their
attention shifted to the issue of having to pay for the 'great calamity' still
being enacted beyond their union and they tried to resist having to pay
rate-in-aid, a tax which had been introduced to enable the more solvent
unions to finance the poorest ones.

V

So far we have confined our attention to one part of Co. Down. It was thought to have been the most prosperous part of the county and yet, even in Newtownards, there was intense suffering. What, briefly, of other parts of the county?

If we take another area that was prosperous we find a similar story of distress. Banbridge, described as 'flourishing', and 'one of the most important linen manufacturing towns in Ireland,' and 'in the centre of a well cultivated and fertile district', according to Lewis's *Topographical Dictionary* (1837), also experienced considerable distress. Numbers in the workhouse rose from 259, in February 1845, to 1,017 in February 1847, and these high levels were maintained for another two years. It was at its worst in early 1848 when 1,495 were in the house and 23 died in the first week of 1848. The master was unable to admit all that sought admission and they refused to leave. The applicants were described as 'in a state of extreme destitution', 'exhibiting symptoms of starvation and some even of death'. He was instructed by the Guardians to call in the constabulary to disperse them but also to give them some food to enable them to make the journey to their homes. Banbridge Choral Society gave a dress concert in the Town Hall to raise money for a relief committee. A relief committee also operated in Loughbrickland.[79] However, not everyone was so charitable. A local landlord, John Joseph Whyte, evicted a large number of his tenants, who could not pay their rents, in the words of his agent J.P. Kelly, in order to 'make such changes in the landed property of the country as will meet the altered circumstances of the times.' Kelly encouraged remaining tenants to convert to pasture and root crops, and to facilitate this houses were levelled and farms enlarged. These evictions were 'the talk of the whole county'.[80] Between 1841-51 the population of the Banbridge Poor Law Union fell from 87,000 to 75,000.

The 'golden age' of Lecale was probably the turn of the nineteenth century when the Napoleonic wars had pushed agricultural prices high for the farmers in the barony. Decay had already set in when the Famine hit the area. Hugh Wallace, the seneschal of Downpatrick, at the request of the parish priest, the Very Rev. Bernard Mc Auley, convened a meeting of the town's inhabitants at which it was decided to provide free meal and soup. Four hundred families took advantage of this and soup kitchens were set up in every parish in the barony. For example, in Killyleagh between 30

and 50 women gave meals to the poor every day and in Killough soup was
provided from the end of 1846. In 1847, smallpox broke out in Downpatrick
and over 200 patients were admitted to the fever hospital and the workhouse.
In August 1849, cholera occurred in the town and half of the 50 patients
treated died.[81]

As might be expected it was the south of the county that suffered the
most. Captain Brereton, the Board of Works inspecting officer, cited
Rathfriland and the Mournes as the worst affected areas in the county. At
Castlewellan, by October 1846, women and children were described by a
local source as 'feeble and weak through sheer hunger'. He continued:

> Owing to the extraordinary wetness of the season, turf cannot be procured
> – coals are out of the question and the poor have thus the double pressure
> of hunger and cold to bear up with. ... The continual cry among the small
> farmers is, 'What in the world are we to do?' The rent is being called for,
> in some instances with merciless perseverance. Add the prospect of being
> turned out of their holdings, to that of depriving themselves of the means
> of sustenance and you will be able to form an opinion of their feelings of
> the poor farmers in the district. The bodings of the cottiers and day labourers
> are melancholy in the extreme: their accustomed food is gone, and no
> substitute forthcoming. Their usual wages would require to be trebled to
> be of any sufficient service whatever; it is provokingly barbarous to offer
> them 8d or 10d per day, and yet none of the farmer class is able to pay
> more.

Despite these conditions, the landlords of south Down did not turn up
at a relief meeting held in Castlewellan. They were criticised for preferring
to '"shab" away to England with their people's money in their pockets',
leaving them 'to the tender mercies of heartless, ignorant bog-bailiffs and
screwing agents whose pay depends on the amount wrung from the
unfortunate class committed to their cause.' All the meeting could do was
to petition the Lord Lieutenant to order an extraordinary Presentment
Sessions for the barony to levy a new rate to provide urgent relief.[82] On 30
December 1846 the Marquess of Downshire circulated a handbill objecting
to such sessions 'as a pretext for voting away other people's money for
useless jobs ... for the purpose of carrying on useless or injurious works.'
When the sessions did meet a few days later some 6,000 people, many
starving and ragged, crowded outside the courthouse in Castlewellan to
ensure that a rate would be struck. Captain Brereton only persuaded the
men of property to vote it with great difficulty. He noted 'the great desire of

the landed proprietors to hide the poverty of the people.'[83]

VI

What conclusions can be drawn from this study of the experience of the Famine in the Newtownards Poor Law Union? It would seem that the poor of this union were forced to wait by their social superiors until they were weakened in health, almost at starvation point, and then it was insisted that they come into an overcrowded workhouse where there was a real risk of death through fever (though the worst months had seen the operation of a privately-financed soup kitchen). These Famine relief policies were shaped by contemporary ideas of political economy, and were carried out by the wealthier tenant farmers led by Lord Londonderry's agent, John Andrews. The greater landlords of the area tried without success to have outdoor relief administered. Andrews hoped to force the smaller farmers to emigrate in order that agriculture become modernised to cope with the new situation after the repeal of the Corn Laws. This idea may have backfired for it was not necessarily the poor who emigrated, as *The Downpatrick Recorder* pointed out:

> We observe, with regret, that much of the wealth and comfort of this hitherto prosperous county is being transported to the shores of America, and other parts of the globe. It is a bad sign indeed of Ulster's prosperity when the Down peasantry are on the move to the far west. Lord John Russell's rate-in-aid scheme is driving some of our farmers out of the country. Within the last few weeks upwards of 2,000 individuals have left the districts of Newtownards, Lecale, and other parts of this county for emigration to America and these we can safely affirm did not leave the country with empty purses. In one emigrant ship alone, which sailed from Belfast the other day, more than three-fourths of the passengers were from the County of Down.

The combined effects of emigration and death reduced the area's population. It has not been possible to calculate how many people actually starved to death in the Newtownards Union during the potato Famine, but many of those weakened by under-nourishment, because of the high food prices, died of typhus, relapsing fever, dysentery or scurvy. The population of the Newtownards Poor Law Union in 1831 was calculated as 53,837; in

1841 it had risen to 60,285. One might expect the population to have increased to perhaps 63,000 by the time of the 1851 Census had the Famine not occurred. But it had fallen to 56,861. Between 1841 and 1851 the population in the parish of Newtownards fell by 14 per cent and in 12 of its townlands it fell by over 20 per cent.[84]

Inevitably, the controversies damaged landlord-tenant relationships. There is a direct connection between the Famine and the Tenant Right agitations which followed. In Newtownards, hostility was vented towards Londonderry at a meeting in the town. This hurt the third Marquess and Andrews wrote seeking to console him:

> I greatly lament that your lordship should be so wounded... and I think your lordship ought not to estimate the tenants generally by the indications of a meeting of the town of Newtownards where haughty spirits may have felt a gratification in exhibiting their independence. After all, my lord, we must not expect too much from weak and fallible and selfish men. Gratitude, it has been too truly said, has more regard to future expectation than to past favours and the multitude are proverbially fickle and unstable; but from my soul I do not believe that there is at present any default of affection or good feeling to your lordship. It has been the selfish few who may be disappointed that their rents were not now reduced.[85]

Other evidence contradicts Andrews' assessment. The obituary in the Newtownards Chronicle in 1893, of David McKean, refers to the very real danger of rioting. At the time of the Famine, McKean was a highly respected agent in the town for Messrs Brown, sewed muslin manufacturers of Glasgow, who contracted work out to local people. He eventually became assistant to Lord Londonderry's agents from 1862-87, and was an elder of the town's Second Presbyterian Church. His obituary 45 years later throws light on the mood of the town during the Famine:

> At the time of the potato blight, great distress prevailing here, as indeed everywhere throughout the country, threats of bread riots were heard. The late Mr John Andrews, the agent of the estate, dreading bad consequences from the assembling of the masses and the temper they manifested, solicited the intervention of Mr McKean as the most likely person to bring them to reason, which happily he succeeded in doing.[86]

In the general election of 1852, voters, concerned about the security of Tenant Right, but undoubtedly not forgetting the opposing positions taken up during the Famine, in an unprecedented act of defiance, refused to vote for Lord Londonderry's candidate, and voted instead for William Sharman

Crawford. Lord Londonderry responded by evicting 70 tenants who were in arrears and had voted against his wishes; he halved many of his subscriptions to charitable causes in the district. The Famine marked the beginning of the end of deference, an end of the moral economy.[87] In this connection, it is difficult to see how the building of the Londonderry Monument (or Scrabo Tower) in 1854 was inspired, as it is claimed, by a tenantry grateful for Lord Londonderry's generosity to them during the Famine. Indeed, a study of the subscription list would not support such a conclusion.

Other evidence confirms the strained relations in the town. The year 1848 was a time of revolutions and attempted coups all over Europe. In Ireland, the Young Irelanders sought a repeal of the Act of Union. The government solicited statements of loyalty to counteract their claims. In April 1848 Andrews suggested that Lord Londonderry prepare two, one each for the parishes of Newtownards and Comber, after which 'the principal inhabitants could then be invited to attach their signatures which are procured without the risk of inviting a public meeting.' [emphasis added]. Towards the end of April 1848 a private meeting took place of 'the most influential inhabitants of Newtownards' with this in mind. But Newtownards' nationalists, led by John McKittrick (a guardian and local draper), and the parish priest, had already seized the initiative and had submitted a petition declaring that Newtownards sought the repeal of the Act of Union. The meeting decided that a counter petition should be sent but, as Andrews said to Lord Londonderry, 'they desired me to request that your lordship would forego a public meeting which they feared might be disturbed as such meetings often been by the adverse party however small' [emphasis added].[88]

Apparently there were other consequences of a religious nature. According to The Newtownards Independent, which commented 25 years later:

> The weavers after the famine were not the same men they were before it. Saturday night squabbling had ceased; the public houses might as well have been closed for all the business done; prayer meetings were established in different localities, in out-of-the-way places where cock-fighting, dog-fighting and rat-hunting-on-Sunday characters lived; and a tone of seriousness pervaded the people. Many of them felt they had something else to live for than to eat, drink and be merry. Numbers of old Bibles, hymn books and Psalm books were fished up from all sorts of places.[89]

To apply a quotation from Austin Bourke, 'with such a change of heart, we might truly speak of a visitation of God.'[90]

THE FAMINE
IN
COUNTY FERMANAGH

JOHN CUNNINGHAM

Emigration.
FOR NEW YORK,

The New Iron Steam-ship,
SARAH SANDS,
To Sail the 18*th January.*

In the county of Fermanagh the population dropped from 156,481 to 116,047 between the years 1841 and 1851, according to the census figures.[1] This represents a decline of over 25 per cent and amounts to 40,434 persons missing, either through death, migration or emigration during the Famine decade. Of the eight baronies in Co. Fermanagh that of Magheraboy which runs from Enniskillen towards the west and takes in the villages of Derrygonnelly and Garrison was worst effected and lost 31 per cent of its population. Of the other baronies Clanawley and Clankelly lost about 30 per cent each while the nearby barony of Coole in the east of the county suffered the loss of 28 per cent of its people.

The barony of Lurg in the west which includes the villages of Belleek, Irvinestown, Kesh, Ederney and Lack declined in population by 27 per cent while those 'least' effected were the baronies of Magherasteffany, Knockinny and Tirkennedy which declined by 22 per cent, 20 per cent and 13 per cent respectively. Tirkennedy, which suffered the least decline, includes Enniskillen, the county town, and Tempo but this small decline may reflect migration from other parts of the county into Enniskillen plus the additional population of the chief workhouse in the county.[2] Part of this migration into Enniskillen was by tenants of Lord Belmore from Co. Cavan who came in search of any beneficence which their landlord might have been able to offer.

In some individual townlands the percentage population decline was even greater than this but there is no way of telling whether or not this was due to famine or the movement of people to other areas. In the Belleek area the village of Belleek grew in numbers during the Famine suggesting people had moved there from townlands nearby. Other townlands grew on account of evicted people moving to them. This emigration exodus was set in motion and today the continuing impact of the Famine on the county may be measured by the fact that Fermanagh has only about one third of the population it had in 1841.

In spite of the widely-held belief that the potato blight in Ulster was first detected in Co. Fermanagh,[3] the Famine only reached Fermanagh slowly and it was one of only four counties that did not need to have a relief committee established in 1845 when the first outbreaks of blight decimated the potato crop over a large part of the country. Three workhouses had, in the years immediately prior to 1845, been slowly, reluctantly and poorly built in Fermanagh in a line along the centre of the county: at Irvinestown in the west, Enniskillen in the centre and Lisnaskea in the east. Enniskillen workhouse, having been built in 1842, evidently had to wait until the autumn of 1845 before it was in effective operation.[4] At either end of the county, workhouses at Clones in Co. Monaghan and Ballyshannon in Co. Donegal served the extremities of the county.

After the initial scare of autumn of 1845, which did not seriously effect Fermanagh, something of the relief that the blight had not taken root in the county is evident in the letter from A. Graham, land steward on the Colebrooke estate, which was published in the local press in December 1845:

> I beg to leave to lay before you the following observations in connection with this neighbourhood. The tenantry on the Colebrooke property are, I am happy to say, nearly exempt from the disease; and, in reference, to my own experience I have to remark that I raised about 400 barrels in the domain. A considerable portion of them has been in pits for the past six weeks, and after a regular and minute examination of them up to this date, I have discovered no faulty potatoes.

I may remark that I made very narrow pits and only covered then with sods or scraws. Since Sir Arthur's [Brooke] return from England he was visited most of his tenantry, and has been diligent in impressing upon the necessity of securing sufficient seed for the coming spring, recommending above all things frequent turning and removal of any portion that may indicate signs of decay or taint, and repitting in narrow pits. I am also happy in being able to add that the neighbourhood all round Brookeborough is nearly as fortunate as ourselves.[5]

Other stories in the paper suggested that, elsewhere in the county, such confidence was misplaced. In November 1845 the *Enniskillen Chronicle and Erne Packet* berated farmers who exploited the poor by selling them unfit potatoes. Under the headline, OUR POTATO MARKET, the paper comments as follows:

We find it necessary, from several instances that have come under our observation, to call the attention of the local authorities to the state of our potato markets. At a time like the present, great caution should be exercised to prevent the sale or diseased of partly diseased potatoes. Farmers are, no doubt, solicitous to get rid of potatoes under decay; but the evil inflicted on the poor of the town should be strenuously guarded against.

Instances have lately occurred, in which the poor man or woman giving the only remaining shilling for potato food for a miserable family, have discovered that the potatoes when boiled and placed before their craving young could not be used – this is truly melancholy. And still more harrowing we have been creditably informed, that a poor woman, herself and two or three children recovering from fever, went the other day to the market with her only sixpence; purchased two stone of potatoes, which, when boiled, she found to her inexpressible grief, that scarcely one of them could be eaten.

This is scarcely a parallel for this distressing case: many are daily occurring; and surely it behoves those in authority, and those paid for such attention, to devote some energy for humanity sake. If necessity calls for it, we shall return to the subject with very strong remonstrance.[6]

Following the alarms over the potato crop in the autumn and winter of 1845 as relayed by newspapers in other parts of Ireland, Fermanagh awaited with some trepidation the harvest of the following year.

In general, however, the local newspapers carried remarkably few entries concerning the Famine. These accounts generally took the form of descriptions of conditions in the workhouses, the reduction of rents by landlords, instances of death and starvation seen in towns and villages and outrages committed when starving people broke into meal stores, or killed animals in the fields at night. The first meaningful impact of the potato blight began to be felt at the beginning of the autumn of 1846, particularly in the workhouses, where the diet of the inmates had been almost exclusively dependent on the potato. Enniskillen workhouse had continued to use potatoes, despite the rise in their cost, until July 1846, when oatmeal was substituted in the children's diet.[7] A month later potatoes were withdrawn from the adults' diet, when they were given 7° oz of oatmeal instead of their usual daily provision allowance of 3° lbs of potatoes.[8] At their meeting in mid-September 1846, the Guardians noted a letter from the Poor Law Commissioners 'concerning the general failure of the potato crop' and ordered that

> the following dietary be adopted from this day until further orders:
>
> Adult male and female – 7oz of oatmeal made into stirabout and 1 pint of buttermilk for breakfast; 7 oz oatmeal into stirabout and 1 pint buttermilk for dinner;
>
> Boys and girls 9-15: 5oz of oatmeal into stirabout and 1 pint buttermilk
>
> Boys and girls 2-9: 3oz of oatmeal and 3 noggins of buttermilk for breakfast.[9]

In Lowtherstown, potatoes remained similarly available until well into 1846: in January of that year, the Guardians had been admonished by the Poor Law Commissioners for giving the inmates three meals a day.[10]

By the end of 1846, a meeting was convened by the Lieutenant of the county to try to ascertain the degree of blight in the county and to dispense the best advice that could be given. The 14 November issue of the *Enniskillen Chronicle and Erne Packet* carried an account of the meeting:

POTATO DISEASE – PUBLIC MEETING IN ENNISKILLEN

> Tuesday last at 12 o'clock, there was a public meeting held in the Court-house of this town, convened by the Earl of Erne, Lieutenant of this county, for the purposes of considering the state of the potato crop in this county with the object of applying the best remedies for the preservation of the present sound part of the crop, and immediately converting the partly diseased into wholesome food.
>
> The noble Earl and a committee of gentlemen who sat the previous day (the fairday of the town) in the Grand Jury room, to receive the information of gentlemen and farmers, as to the extent of the failure in their respective

localities, that his lordship and the committee might thereby be enabled to lay properly authenticated information before the meeting.

His lordship then read a very able document, drawn up by the committee above alluded to, containing much sound advice to the Farmers and Peasantry of the county on the subject of the potato crop. FIRSTLY, as to the best manner of preserving untainted potatoes. SECOND, as to how to arrest the progress of the disease in potatoes already affected. THIRDLY, the most efficacious mode of converting the diseased potato into wholesome food. FOURTH, the best method of preserving sound seed.... Specimens of cake bread made from the starch of tainted potatoes were handed about through the meeting which appeared to be bread of an excellent description.

Dr Halpin of Cavan was then introduced to the meeting as a man who had studied the problem greatly. He is promoting a ventilating pit in which to store potatoes. He decries other advice being put forward at the time which included digging potatoes in wet weather rather than in dry weather, kiln-drying the potato crop or drying it over hurdles and immersing the potatoes in bog water to preserve them.[11]

Panic began to manifest itself during the autumn of 1846, when it became evident that the potato crop was again failing and on a gigantic scale. A meeting of tenants, landholders and landlords held in Lisbellaw in August 1846 was told that: 'Potatoes are nearly extinct and starvation stands at the threshold of nearly every door, especially the poor man's door.'[12] A meeting of 2,500 people in Brookeborough begged for relief and crowds of people in Derrygonnelly simply asked to be employed.[13] People began to flock into the workhouses which were mostly unfinished although they were open and providing relief. In addition the huge numbers entering put pressure on the immediate facilities, creating dangers of hygiene, cleanliness and the threat of the spread of fever.

As conditions worsened, papers carried critical reports. When the relief works began, the *Erne Packet* condemned the decision to grant relief by forcing the destitute to work on the relief works. It went on to make the point that Sir Robert Peel had at least made some effort to come to grips with the whole problem:

DEATH FROM STARVATION

On the morning of the 16th inst [December 1846] a man named James Roulston of Rohall in the neighbourhood of Lowtherstown was found dead in a field near his own house. On the previous morning he had left his family, six in number, to repair to the public works at Drumskool, a distance of about three quarters of a mile from his residence, where he was employed at 10 pence per diem and having wrought all day notwithstanding the severity of the weather and his pitiable state for want of food, it would appear that on his return home, at night, through the fields which were covered with snow, he sank from exhaustion. We have been creditably informed that, for many preceeding days, the only support that he had for himself, and family, was a few turnips and the stalks thereof together with the water in which they were boiled.

An inquest was held on the body by Dr Collum, of Enniskillen, on the 17th inst, and a verdict to the effect that 'James Rolston died of fatigue, and want of sufficient nourishment', was returned. The newspaper goes on: Gracious God! what a state of things have our rulers brought us to, preaching political economy to the people when they are dying of inaction, as if the verbiage of the temporizing commissary could satisfy the inane stomach while he leaves to usurious meal-mongers the providing of food, at a time when such unhappy circumstances afford them every opportunity of carrying on their usurious traffic, and which would require no uncommon foresight to suppose they would indulge in, even at the expense of human lives.

Surely it is too bad; and yet under the Russell administration we can scarcely conceive that things will mend. For the short time that the reins of government have been in his hands, what a fearful sacrifice of human life has been made! How many precious lives have been lost by his incapacity exclusively! We say by his incapacity EXCLUSIVELY, for we cannot for the life of us attribute it to any other source.

In the name of Heaven – in the name of suffering thousands – in the name of the hungry widow (whose husband has been sacrificed) and her famishing orphans we ask will the country tolerate this conduct much longer! Will they not hurl him from his eminence and reinstate the only man who is able to grasp with the difficulties which beset us – Sir Robert Peel – Let there be no delay. The country is being decimated at present; it will be doubly thinned before it can be wrested from their evil government.

In the neighbourhood of the death which we have above described, the utmost destitution prevails, and the poor creatures are without the means of purchasing even a pound of meal, while the poor-houses are being filled to overflowing around us. The workhouse in Irvinestown was forced to lease many other buildings in the town to hold the overflow of persons wishing to enter. Some of this crush was caused by the levelling of houses either through eviction or in order to stop people re-entering houses they had left.[14]

The following are some more of the reports from Co. Fermanagh at this time between September 1846 and May 1847 as they appear in the *Enniskillen Chronicle and Erne Packet....*

...Fever and famine are making havoc on human life in the heretofore healthy district of Ederney. On Sunday last a woman, named Walker, was to be seen in the street seeking charity, with two children, one dead on her back, and the other dying in her arms... At Rossory, within a mile of Enniskillen, a mother, unattended, carried the coffined body of her child and scraped a hole in which she covered it... .[15] We have it on good authority that two children, by the name of Philips, died in Enniskillen from starvation. They were unable to buy soup from the public soup kitchen....[16]

At Currin a woman lay dead for three days without burial. In the end she was carried like a dead hog, across a handbarrow, rolled in a mat, to Ballinamallard by two weak women where she was left exposed till the sexton interred her...[17]

In Garvery Wood, hundreds of corpses are buried, they were victims of cholera and their relatives were too weak to carry them to the graveyard...

A young girl died at Kinawley. Her friends, fearing the fever, put her on a bier at once and set out for the graveyard. On the way she sat up.[18]

By the end of 1846 potatoes were selling at one shilling a stone in Enniskillen and riots broke out in the market as forestallers tried to buy up supplies in the market and take them out of the area. Indian meal at 10 pence a stone and rice at 2 pence a pound were bought in preference to the dearer potatoes. Not only did the people in general detest these unfamiliar types of food but they added to their misery by being ill-informed as to how to cook them. Indian meal must be steeped overnight in water to make it palatable and failure to do this added intestinal illnesses to the burden of those dying of starvation.

In 1847 the government acknowledged the scale of the tragedy and endowed the Poor Law system with the main responsibilty of organising relief. Soup kitchens were established but already some people such as Roderick Grey, Fermanagh County Surveyor, and Captain Hancock had been organising this form of relief privately in Enniskillen and Lisbellaw. At first the people had to pay a penny for their portion but this was abandoned. By the summer of 1847 there were over 2,000 being fed by the Enniskillen soup kitchen, while in Maguiresbridge 2,700 were being fed.[19]

Doctors and clergy and members of the Boards of Guardians and

workhouse staff also perished and in truth no one was safe. In Enniskillen,
Drs Condon and Frith died of fever as did one of the Guardians. The stench
of the workhouse drove the Board of Guardians to hold their meetings in
the Townhall and anything up to 20 people died in Enniskillen workhouse
every day. Temporary fever hospitals sprung up in the villages of Fermanagh.
In mid-December 1847 there were 879 people in Enniskillen workhouse,
built to accommodate 1,000; by mid-January, the number of occupants was
1137, and by May of the following year this had risen to 1,433.[20]

The Enniskillen Guardians, at their 5 January 1847 meeting, directed
the master 'to admit no more paupers unless in cases of extreme
destitution...the workhouse now being crowded to excess'.[21] Not only did
the Enniskillen workhouse exceed its capacity of 1000, the staggering fact
is that in January of the previous year, 1846, it had no more than 144
inmates to shelter. The same story of tumultuous and sudden overcrowding
is apparent in the workhouses at Lisnaskea and Lowtherstown. In January
1847, Lisnaskea was coping with 581 paupers; the previous January it
held 186 paupers; and nowhere was the increase more dramatic than in
Lowtherstown. In January 1846 it had held 51 paupers; a year later, in
January 1847, it easily exceeded its limit with 453 inmates. Nevertheless
the weeks of 29 December 1846 and 12 January 1847 each saw over 160
paupers admitted to the Enniskillen workhouse, presumably because they
matched the criterion of 'extreme destitution' which the Guardians had
stipulated recently.[22] By 5 February, this figure had been drastically reduced
to five, as the problem of crowding mounted. The extent of the continuous
pressure that was, from later 1846, being increasingly felt by the three
workhouses which served the county is represented in the following table:[23]

WORKHOUSE	CAPACITY	DEC. 1846	DEC. 1847	DEC. 1848
Enniskillen	1000	892	1086	1667
Lisnaskea	500	551	767	821
Lowtherstown	400	403	600	593

It is worth noting from this table that the two workhouses at
Lowtherstown and Lisnaskea had, in fact, been filled to capacity from
December 1846. Enniskillen exceeded its capacity the following month.
By the end of 1847, not only did Enniskillen continue to exceed its limit
but the two smaller workhouses had become massively over-full. By the
end of the following year, 1848, the pressure had eased somewhat in the

Lowtherstown workhouse, though it was still at 150 per cent of its capacity. Lisnaskea and Enniskillen, however, were more overcrowded than ever: Lisnaskea had 321 more inmates that it could officially cope with and Enniskillen exceeded its limit by 667.[24]

As early as April, 1847, the conditions inside the workhouse in Enniskillen were giving great concern to Dr Nixon, the medical officer, who made the following report to the Guardians:

> The sewers were inadequate and flooded the laundry yard. The overflowing cesspool was causing disease. Refuse was dumped immediately beside the house and warm weather would make it extremely dangerous. The drying room had been converted into a nursery. There was no means of drying the straw used by those who slept on the floor. The interior of the Workhouse was not whitewashed and the floors were holed and never scrubbed. There was no ventilation. There was not enough clothes for everybody to get a suit. There were no facilities for inmates to wash themselves. Meals were irregular and inadequate. A new fever hospital was needed as 100 patients lay on thirty bedsteads in Hall's lane. Water supplies were hopeless. In the workhouse there were only 69 beds, the remainder of the inmates were lying on the floor. There were few other items of furniture. There were only two nurses for 312 patients.[25]

In addition to these near-insurmountable problems, the Enniskillen Guardians' position was exacerbated by their continuing financial difficulties. By May 1847 they were in debt by some £5,000. This, in turn, brought them into conflict with the Poor Law Commissioners. When they approached government for a loan of between £3,000 and £4,000 they were rewarded with a grant of £100 and told to collect, if necessary, an additional rate.[26] The Guardians were outraged and felt that the imposition of an additional rate on their ratepayers would bring... 'ruinous severity... and would thus cripple the means of employment and of production of our most fruitful men... The guardians believe that no system could be more dishonest in principle or more mischievous.'[27] Far from resolving the position, the conflicts between the Enniskillen Guardians and the Poor Law Commissioners continued until the Enniskillen board was dissolved at the end of 1847.[28]

Indeed, two of the three Co. Fermanagh workhouses were among only four Boards of Guardians in Ulster that were dissolved when responsibility for the administration of relief was handed to them. Lowtherstown Union also fell foul of the Poor Law Commissioners to the extent that it too was dissolved. As had been the case with their Enniskillen counterparts, the Lowtherstown Guardians (who were in fact the first board to be dissolved, in September 1847) felt that their local rate payers were being asked to bear an unfairly high financial burden. As was the case in many other unions, the amount raised from local rates proved insufficient to meet the demands being made. When the Poor Law became the principal relief agency, the additional burdens proved to be too much even though, as Christine Kinealy has pointed out, the burden of poor rates was not particularly high in the Lowtherstown Union.[29]

The Lowtherstown Guardians did not take their dismissal lying down. Even though Vice-Guardians were appointed in their place, and tried to levy a new rate, this was resisted, occasionally with the threat of violence against them, and the original Guardians were eventually restored in March 1849.[30] They were the first Board of Guardians to be dismissed and the first to be re-instated. True to form, when they resumed the reins of running the union they proceeded to heap abuse on the Vice-Guardians who had acted in their stead. They found the union as a whole... 'much demoralised, the poorer classes being impressed with the doctrine that, instead of finding employment it must be found for them and that the decree of the Almighty, 'that man must live by the sweat of his brow', is changed to the effect that 'man is to live by Act of Parliament'.[31]

Lowtherstown (later called Irvinestown) workhouse had been opened on 15 October 1845 after considerable animosity between the local landlord and the Board of Guardians and was built to serve most of west Fermanagh. Such was the local anger that an investigation was held into setting up of this workhouse.[32] The report lists their complaints as follows:

1 That the Commissioners fixed on a site, and gave an exorbitant price for it, before the Board was formed.
2 That the Commissioners allowed the Union to be imposed on by giving £150 for tenants' rights [which were never paid to the tenants]. The total price was £647-19-0.
3 That £878 was added to the contract without a second competition.
4 That a building with equal accommodation might have been built for less money.

Mr Justice Pennethorne, who investigated into the allegation of gross

AT A MEETING OF THE
Landlords & Cess-payers
OF THE
Barony of Magherastaphena
HELD AT LISNÁSKEA,

On Thursday, 17th day of September, 1846,

The EARL of ERNE in the Chair,

The following Resolutions were passed unanimously :—

I. RESOLVED—That we think it expedient to avail ourselves of the 9th and 10th Vic. chap. 101, as the most beneficial to the wants of our Barony, by which the employment of the Poor will be obtained, in improving the Land, which is to be assessed to the expense ; and the present visitation be made the means, under Providence, of conferring a benefit on those districts where privation is likely to prevail.

II. RESOLVED—That the requisite Memorials be forthwith filled up and forwarded by the Chairman to the Board of Works, to carry the above Resolution into effect, as soon as possible.

III. RESOLVED—That as the Line of Railway, laid down by the Engineer of the Newry and Enniskillen Railway Company, between Clones and Enniskillen, in the County of Fermanagh, has been settled by Act of Parliament to be the common Line of the Newry and Enniskillen, and of the Dundalk and Enniskillen Railways, which have obtained their Acts, and are now in progress of execution ; and as there is no doubt whatever but that this piece of Railway will be made in the course of a few years : that a Committee be now appointed to communicate with the Newry and Enniskillen Company, to see whether, and by what means, or for what terms, this piece of Railway would be put in progress of execution this Winter, so as to give work to the People.

IV. RESOLVED—That we strongly recommend to the Landlords and Tenants of this Barony THOROUGH DRAINING, as the best kind of re-productive employment, especially during the Winter Season, (when the Rivers are too flooded to be worked at,) and which can be begun in many instances by private arrangement between Landlord and Tenant, without the delay and expense of any Preliminary Surveys of the Government, and which will give employment to Women and Children as well as Men ; and we hope that the Resolutions of the undersigned Resident Landlords and Tenants, in this critical time, will draw the attention of the People strongly to this subject, which has been hitherto too much neglected in Fermanagh.

ERNE,
J. G. PORTER,
A. B. BROOKE.

V. RESOLVED—That the different Landlords, Farmers and occupiers of Land be earnestly requested to employ as many Labourers as possible, until the Drainage Act can be brought into operation in this Barony, and would suggest the utility of clearing the ground and preparing it for Grain Crops.

VI. RESOLVED—That the Relief Committee meet every Saturday at 10 o'Clock, commencing with Saturday the 26th Sept., instant, at Lisnaskea.

VII. RESOLVED—That the following Relief Committee be appointed for the Barony of Magherastaphena, to carry out the Resolutions which have been adopted at this meeting :—

Earl of Erne,
Richard Hall,
Henry Gresson,
Robert Graham,
Colonel Dixon,
William D'Arcy,
Charles Ovenden,
The Rev. A. Hurst,
The Rev. P. Maguire, P.P.,
The Rev. M. Fitzgerald,
James Fitzgerald,
John Patterson,
James Moore,
Alexander Beatty,

Sir A. B. Brooke,
George Brooke,
John E. Taylor,
The Rev. B. Brooke,
B. Leslie,
Paul Dane,
Rev. Sidney Smith,
The Rev. J. G. Porter,
John G. V. Porter,
The Rev. W. W. Watkin,
The Rev. Mr. Smith, P.P.,
James Armstrong, Brookeborough.

ERNE, Chairman.

Trimble, Printer, Enniskillen.

overpayment for the site of the workhouse, stated:-

> It appears to me that the only point on which I am empowered to given an opinion is the question, "Whether £697-19-0 was, or was not, an exorbitant price to be paid" for the sale. Whether Mr D'Arcy was paid £50 or £500 for the possession was of no importance to the Commissioners; they had only to give the true value of the fee of the land, without reference to the apportionment of the money.

> It does not appear by the documents that any person was consulted as to the value of the site. The Assistant Commissioner was incompetent, and so also was the assistant architect and they neither gave any opinion on the subject. Mr D'Arcy named his price; this is reported to the Commissioners, and they FORTHWITH, by their letter of January 28th, virtually agreed to the terms:- before their letter of March 2nd, and before they knew if a title could be made and before the question of expenses was settled, they had begun to build the house, thereby placing themselves at Mr D'Arcy's mercy; and were so compelled to pay his price.

PRICES PAID PER STATUTE ACRE FOR WORKHOUSE SITES:-

Lowtherstown	£139-0-0
Omagh	£125-0-0
Enniskillen	£113-0-0
Clones	£57-1-3
Lisnaskea	£51-16-8

The acrimonious manner in which the workhouse opened continued with complaints of mismanagement, among others, until in 1847 the Commissioners appointed two Vice-Commissioners, Mr Pierce Morton and Mr Bernard McManus. During their tenure the building was properly finished, the sewage system made to work and the paupers' graveyard prevented from sending its discharge into the workhouse yard. In the report of Denis Phelan, which led to the appointment of the Vice-Commissioners, he described the condition of this workhouse as the worst in the north of Ireland.[33]

Although it may have been the only Board of Guardians in the county not to have been dissolved, controversy nonetheless attended the deliberations of the Lisnaskea Guardians when they met to consider the government demand for an increased rate-in-aid in support of the administration of additional relief schemes in 1849. By this time, the accumulating consequences for society of successive failures in the potato crop – among them fever, disease, and homelessness – were becoming increasingly apparent. The minute of the board's discussion, and their subsequent letter to the Poor Law Commissioners, reveal a collectively vituperative outburst in which their resentment at being asked, as they saw it, to pay for relief in other parts in Ireland was expressed in divisive tones:

> ...it is with indignation we learn it is recommended...to impose a rate-in-aid on the peaceable and industrious inhabitants of the North of Ireland for the support of the lazy, vicious and indolent population of the south and west of the kingdom who neither fear God, honour the queen nor respect the laws of the land... That however we might have disapproved of the introduction of the Poor Law into this country, since it became the law of the land the Guardians of this Union have used all their endeavours to work out the law efficiently and give good effect to it... by giving shelter to the houseless and food to those who could neither work nor want...

> That the ratepayers of this Union, with that principle of honesty which so creditably distinguishes the inhabitants of the North of Ireland, have thro' a period of great and unparalled distress by suffering the greatest privations and with the most perservering industry paid their rates and discharged the public demands on them without the interposition of the law or any coercive means, while they see in other parts the military, the police and the magistrates set at defiance, the collection of the poor rate resisted and poor law rendered thereby inappropriate.

> That the Guardians...firmly believe [that] in expressing their own sentiments they express those of all the rate-payers of the Union as well as those of the Province of Ulster generally of the inequity and injustice of having their industry further taxed for the support of ratepayers who do not belong to them and they consider a rate-in-aid as a direct premium and encouragement to those who resist the payment of a rate for the support of their own poor in their own Union and the destitution they have been the great means of creating...if we did not use every constitutional means in our power to resist the collection of such an oppressive and unjustifiable tax which, along with others, is likely to reduce the majority of the rate-payers in this Union to the same destitute condition of those that it is intended to relieve.[34]

Of the first 440 entries to this workhouse, 221 were Roman Catholic and 219 were Protestant.[35] As time went on a greater proportion of the workhouse population was Roman Catholic and overall during this period of time approximately one third of the workhouse entry was Protestant.

The age profile of the workhouse was high in the lower age ranges and in the upper age ranges but low in those in those aged 20-40. In other words the workhouse was largely populated with children and old people. Overall the population of the workhouse was 60 per cent female and 40 per cent male and about 70 per cent of the total entry had addresses in the two electoral divisions closest to Irvinetown itself.[36]

Initially many came and went to the workhouse quite freely. One couple are recorded making seven short visits.[37] There are complaints of people selling their food down in the village and of others arriving and, having been kitted out in new clothing, immediately absconding over the wall. It is possible to see an influx of farm boys and girls entering in November after being told to do so by their employers who wished to have them fed by the workhouse in the least productive part of the farming year. In the worst months of the Famine in 1847, just under 80 per cent of those entering the workhouse in Irvinestown were under 15 years of age.[38]

The administration of the Enniskillen workhouse was equally riven with controversy. Perhaps the most unseemly instance was the proposition that, in acknowledgement of the financial difficulties the Guardians were experiencing, a new type of coffin be introduced to bury the mounting numbers of dead paupers. Mr Stewart Betty contended that a slip coffin – constructed with a mechanical spring and a false base – should be purchased: this would reduce the money spent on wood for coffins.[39] William Trimble, editor of the *Impartial Reporter*, voiced the feelings of many in the town when he wrote... 'oh forbid it, shades of our forefathers! that in Fermanagh – moral, Christian Fermanagh – men, women and children should be buried without coffins'.[40] In the end, the motion was not voted on and timber for the necessary Christian burials was purchased.

Within a short time of this case a more worrying burden was to perplex the Enniskillen Guardians. In January 1847 the increasing pressure on the workhouse accommodation had been acknowledged by the Enniskillen Guardians who directed the master 'to admit no more paupers unless in cases of extreme destitution...the workhouse being now crowded to excess'.[41] On 4 May 1847, as Joan Vincent has poignantly described, 351 men, women and children were admitted to the Enniskillen workhouse at the same time.[42] They had waited in the grounds of the workhouse all day and, during the Guardians' meeting, they had made their way inside, much to the consternation of the board. The *Impartial Reporter* recorded the scene:

Children appeared to be dying in the act of endeavouring to extract sustenance from the dried up breast of their parents, others more mature in years were propped up by some relative or acquaintance who was fast hastening to a similar state of weakness. The general appearance was truly sickening. An endeavour was made to enter the names when, some fearing they might be excluded, another rush was made and put *hors de combat* the guardians at the board. The horrors of the black hole of Calcutta were endured by them for a time – they rushed to the window and gasped for breath.[43]

In the event, all were admitted, as the 26 consecutive pages of the indoor admission register testify.[44] They included 163 adults – 67 male, 96 female, – and 188 children under 15 years, 101 male and 87 female. Joan Vincent's study has thrown up several significant factors in the aftermath of this episode. Most striking of all is the realisation that, of the 351 admitted on that day, 111 were dead within three months. By the end of May, 78 of the 4 May intake had passed away, including all the members of five entire families, four of them from Tempo. A further 33 deaths were recorded in June and ten in July. The great majority of these deaths was attributable to the contagion that was rife in the workhouse itself. The fever hospital attached to Enniskillen workhouse had been built to accommodate 120. By the beginning of 1847 it was full to overcrowding. Such was the vulnerability of the hordes of paupers who flocked to its gates during 1847, of which the 4 May incident was the most remarkable example, the workhouse was caring for up to 430 cases, 140 of whom were diagnosed as 'fever patients'.[45]

The first entry in the admission register of the workhouse which is preserved in the Public Record Office of Northern Ireland in Belfast was for John Porter. Quite an extensive amount of information was recorded about him, as for every other entrant to the workhouse, and this information can be illustrated in the record preserved for John. He was described as male, a mendicant or beggar, aged 75 and a Protestant. He had a wooden leg, he had no children and had been deserted by his wife. He was tolerably clean and healthy with no certain residence. With no fixed abode his upkeep rested as a burden on the union at large rather than on a particular area of the union. He entered the workhouse on 15 October and left 8 days later on 23rd.[46] He re-entered on 5 November of the same year and left again on the 7th. In all John Porter was admitted eight times to the workhouse in its first year of operation.[47]

Enniskillen's workhouse was, like Irvinestown's, a long-delayed project. Among other matters disagreed upon was the cost of the site, just as in the case of Irvinestown. The Earl of Enniskillen was the cause of a huge row

as he claimed after selling the site at a fixed price per acre that the acre
measure he understood he agreed to was the English acre rather than the
larger Irish acre.[48] This convenient 'oversight' by his Lordship succeeded
in doubling the cost of the site of the workhouse much to the annoyance of
the other Poor Law Guardians of Enniskillen who, like the other local
ratepayers, would have to pay this inflated price.

A row similar to that which had occurred in Irvinestown followed on
this and other issues and it was some years before the workhouse was opened
and the first poor admitted. Those who would have to pay the rate possibly
believed that they could postpone the opening of the workhouse indefinitely
but in the end pressure from the Irish Poor Law Commissioners forced
them to open. On Thursday 20 November 1845 the *Enniskillen Chronicle
and Erne Packet* reported the opening of the workhouse as follows:

> We rejoice to find that our Union Work House is at last about to be opened.
> Why it has been suffered to remain three years idle, since completed, we
> are at a loss to conjecture, except for a stubborn dislike to afford the poor
> of the district the benefit of a legislative provision. We can positively assert
> that our whole community (the Guardians excepted, which we must) would
> most gladly have, on the very first opportunity, paid the rate, and have
> seen the house in operation. Country gentlemen and farmers may imagine
> themselves to have so far escaped taxation; but assuredly our town has had
> to bear a heavy burden to prevent absolute starvation and the consequences
> of fever and contagion.
>
> Nothing can exceed the cheerfulness with which the inhabitants of
> Enniskillen, high and low, are paying the rate, both from motives of charity
> to the destitute, and as a relief from the far more severe oppression of
> elemosynary contributions. Three years of effectual good have been culpably
> allowed pass over – lives, no doubt, have been sacrified: but we hope the
> evil is at an end, and we shall not, therefore, further deal in complaints.[49]

Lisnaskea workhouse features least of all in the Fermanagh newspapers
of the period. It would seem to have been reasonably well run and did not
have an acrimonious beginning, unlike Fermanagh's other two workhouses.

A striking feature of the Co. Fermanagh workhouse population by 1848
was the extraordinary proportion of young people aged under 15 years they
housed. In December 1846, when there were 892 paupers in Enniskillen
workhouse, 385 (43 per cent) were under 15 years of age.[50] Within two
years, the house totalled 1667 inmates and the proportion of those aged
under 15 had increased to 48 per cent.[51] By this time – December 1848 –
the proportion of paupers under 15 was Lisnaskea was a remarkable 58 per
cent .[52] The ratio in Lowtherstown was 44 per cent.[53] From the guardians'

point of view, there was a realistic chance that these children for whom no means of support, particularly parents, could be found outside the workhouse, would become long-term drains on the rates as life-long inmates and, therefore, long-term charges for ratepayers. This fear had been shared by Edward Senior the Poor Law Inspector who, in turn, had conveyed his alarm to guardians elsewhere in Ulster.[54]

In these circumstances, it can come as no surprise to learn that there were some 107 female orphans sent by the Enniskillen Guardians, and 44 from Lisnaskea, in the scheme that took 4,000 other female orphans aged under 15 from workhouses throughout Ireland to Australia 1848-50.[55] The intention was to provide a better gender balance in the colony's male-dominated society, and at the same time it would serve to reduce the growing orphan problem in Ireland's workhouses. In point of fact, there was a greater preponderance of orphans in Ulster workhouses, where they amounted to 50 per cent of the total workhouse population, compared to the other provinces where the figure was closer to 40 per cent.[56]

On 11 January, 1849 the *Enniskillen Chronicle and Erne Packet* printed the following item. It is in the same optimistic vein as the news item of the autumn of 1845 telling everyone that blight was not really a threat if one followed the advanced practices of the Brooke estate. According to this report the Famine was over.

POTATO PLANTING – We are informed by a friend who visited Colebrooke on Monday last that the honourable proprietor (Sir A. B. Brooke, Bart) has determined upon trying what benefit may be derived from the early planting of this valuable esuculent, We understand, not withstanding the early season, and the probability of forthcoming frost, there is already laid down in the hon. baronet's precincts an area of seven or eight acres of the farinacious and prolific root. It is said that early planting is an effectual remedy for the potato blight, and we opine, that if they escape the influence of frost new potatoes will be no rarity in that quarter.[57]

This might well have announced that the potato blight in Fermanagh was over. The implications for the succeeding generations, however, of what had been a fearful tragedy for the county would only become clearer with the passage of time. And, of course, the Famine remained as a recurring theme in the county's folk traditions.

THE FAMINE
IN
COUNTY LONDONDERRY

TREVOR PARKHILL

I have reason to believe that there has not been so healthy and productive
a crop of potatoes for many years as the crop of this year. There has been
no disease in the crop that I have heard of, nor is it known to the farmers.[1]

The optimism of R.I.C. sub-Inspector Nesbitt's reply from Coleraine of
20 September 1845 to the Inspector-General's circular letter of some days
earlier, which had referred to reports that 'the potato crop of the present
year [having] totally failed',[2] was reflected in the summary report for the
county submitted by the County Inspector, George Fitzmaurice. He observed
'that the disease so much affecting the potato crop in some parts of the
country does not exist to any extent in this county except in the district of
Ballyrashane where ... much loss is likely to be sustained'.[3]

Their confidence, however, quickly turned out to be cruelly misplaced.
On 13 October, John H. Babington, medical officer to the Coleraine

workhouse, wrote to the Chief Secretary in foreboding terms...

> Reports in reference to disease of potatoes not by any means exaggerated.
> Whole fields looking last week most luxuriant and untainted unfit for man
> or beast. Such being the state of crops a great scarcity of food must be
> looked forward to, attended as a natural consequence by typhus fever or
> some other malignant pestilence.[4]

Within less than a month, further constabulary reports corroborated
Babington's gloomy prognosis, reporting (on 14 October) that 'the disease
alluded to is spreading very much in my district'[5] and (on 28th) 'the diseace
(sic) has got to an alarming extent'.[6] By 4 November 1845 the constabulary
relayed the news that ...

> ...the farmers in my district [Coleraine] have commenced digging their
> potatoes and on cautious inquiry in some parts nearly one half are deceased
> (sic) and in other parts one third...which has caused a great alarm among
> the poor class of people.[7]

In the southern part of the county, the shocking change from a healthy
to an infected crop had, if anything, been observed even earlier. Rev. Samuel
Montgomery, rector of Ballinascreen parish, recalled in a memoir inserted
the following year (1846) in his register ...'the entire crop that in the month
of July appeared so luxuriant about the 15th of August manifested only
blackened and withered stems. The whole atmosphere in the month of
September was tainted with the odour of the decaying potatoes'. Poignantly,
he added to his memoir, 'Increase the fruit of the earth by Thy heavenly
benediction'.[8] Indeed, the evidence of newspapers, Board of Guardian
minutes and parish registers indicate that the appearance of the potato
blight was widely reported throughout the county of Londonderry by mid-
October, particularly in four of the five unions which served the county –
at Londonderry, Coleraine, Magherafelt and Ballymoney.

The accelerating spread of the diseased crop was, by mid-October,
occupying the attention of the Guardians of the Derry and Coleraine
workhouses. (The latter had, in fact, been thoroughly alarmed by the death
of the workhouse porter of typhus fever in September 1845, in what had
turned out to be a singular case.)[9] On 18 October the Derry Guardians
'resolved that this Board is of the opinion that the Mayor should consult
with the merchants and inhabitants of Derry whether a Public Meeting
should be held to take into consideration the possibility of a large quantity

of food still being rescued from the failing crop of potatoes by inducing either the government or private individuals to take steps to have them converted into starch'.[10] On the same day (18 October) the Coleraine Guardians 'ordered that the Clerk do notify to the Guardians that the Board would on this day week take into consideration what steps should be adopted to meet the distress that is likely to follow the failure in the potato crop'.[11]

Something of the patchiness of the spread of the potato blight in the county, a feature which is generally characteristic of the first winter of the blight in the counties of Ulster, is evident in the one union – Limavady – which appears to have been spared the early traces of blight. A report from Newtownlimavady avowed that 'both corn and meal are abundant in the Union' and observed that 'large markets of sound potatoes are in Kilrea, Maghera and Magherafelt'.[12] In his own report, which he submitted to the Chief Secretary, the Lord Lieutenant of the county, Sir Robert Ferguson, chose to reflect this more measured and sanguine approach. He predicted that 'an absolute scarcity of food [was] not dreaded [but it] will be difficult for labourers to support their families'. He referred to the 'fair prospect of employment on railroads' and from other works such as the land reclamation on Lough Foyle. He trusted that 'the attention of government will be directed in the relief required' and rounds off his submission by anticipating that 'the landed proprietors will cordially co-operate with them on this emergency'.[13]

Christine Kinealy has drawn attention to the association of the landed classes with the work of the local relief committees as a general measurement of the landlords' collective response to the increasing privations of their tenantry, certainly in the early days when the crisis appeared to be manageable.[14] Indeed, the 'response' of the landed proprietors in Co. Londonderry which Sir Robert Ferguson had envisaged was evident in the formation of the 14 relief committees which began to form themselves throughout the county in the late winter and early spring of 1846, to cope with the mounting pressures commensurate with the partial failure of the potato crop.[15] They ranged from the fairly standard donation of £10, such as that offered by Marcus McCausland of Fruithill to the Newtownlimavady / Tamlaghtfinlagan Relief Committee,[16] to the more interventionist approach of the Clothworkers' Company. The *Coleraine Chronicle* was 'gratified to learn' that the Company 'have purchased a large quantity of meal which is being re-sold to the poor of their estates at reduced prices. From 1 – 200 families are now receiving relief from this fund'.[17] Generally, however, the approach seems to have been that noted in the Claudy Relief Committee's submission...'the landed proprietors have agreed to contribute...in proportion to the value of their respective properties, as rated under the Poor Law Valuation'.[18]

In time, 25 relief committees were formed throughout the county, of which 20 were to receive full grants from government, matching pound for pound the amounts raised locally. Londonderry Relief Committee, for example, raised £1290, that at Newtownlimavady / Tamlaghtfinlagan £341 and the Coleraine committee £322.[19] Initially, the need for undue generosity was not universally shared. At its inaugural meeting in Coleraine in April 1846, when it was proposed that they should 'open a subscription list on the spot and each person...should subscribe a little, several gentlemen expressed their dissent, as being premature'. This was symptomatic of a general reluctance to acknowledge that the situation was serious enough to merit remedial measures. When it was recounted 'that in the parish of Dunboe alone there were hundreds of persons living upon one scanty meal in the day', Mr C.J. Knox retorted saying 'there was not one in the room more willing to subscribe towards any fund for the relief of the poor than himself, but he had too great a respect for his native town to allow it to go abroad that they were in a worse state of distress than the very poorest classes in the south of Ireland'.[20] The second successive failure in the potato crop, however, was enough to elicit a more thoroughgoing approach to the mechanics of relief. Even the touchy Mr Knox was brought by this second successive winter of distress to revise his opinion of the need for relief. In February 1847, he wrote 'as treasurer of the Dunboe and Macosquin Parishes' requesting 'government aid for this very distressed district'.[21]

Perhaps the most striking example of generosity was the total raised by the Aghadowey Relief Committee – £709. In April 1846, the deputation from the Ironmongers' estate which visited the village of Aghadowey described the state of housing as 'most wretched'.[22] The reappearance of the potato blight found Aghadowey and many clustered settlements throughout the county in a parlous position from which to withstand shortage. The submission of the Aghadowey and Agivey Relief Committee, made by Alex. Barklie, contended that 'much relief has been given and extreme cases of destitution in some cases prevented'. However, he added that 'we trust that our having already done what we could will not operate against our claim for a share of the public money. Had we permitted the destitution to go on until deaths from hunger had occurred, a more urgent case perhaps be made out but since our successful efforts to prevent so awful a calamity deserve public assistance now when we require it so much'.[23]

The extent of the public response aroused by the early stages of the potato blight may be attributed to the condition of the tenantry in the years immediately prior to the Famine. For Londonderry had been just as seriously affected as any county by the series of reversals evident in the Irish economy in the crucial 30-year period between the end of the Napoleonic Wars and the onset of the Famine. The Ordnance Survey Memoirs and the Poor Law Inquiry in particular each bore testimony to the social consequences of the economic hardships provoked by the general fall in prices for agricultural produce. What had affected Co. Londonderry, and in particular villages such as Aghadowey, however, had been the serious and precipitate decline in income previously derived from the domestic spinning industry. The introduction of the wet-spinning process in mills throughout Ulster spelled poverty for many families. The Poor Law Commission of Inquiry had noted the increased extent of annual emigration and seasonal migration from the county in the years 1832-4 as being perhaps the strongest evidence of the change in families' fortunes arising from the consequent decline in incomes.[24]

The full extent of the crisis of the 1830s in the east of the province, which was particularly badly affected, is illustrated in a series of petitions addressed to the agents of the Drapers' Company lands in the south of the county, at Draperstown.[25] The Drapers' Company had repossessed its lands in 1817 with a view to introducing a more efficient system of estate management which would, above all, see the consolidation of farms and the arrest of the process of subdivision which abounded.[26] The London Companies, which had taken possession of the county of Coleraine in the early years of the seventeenth century, were absentee landlords in the most literal sense. Their agents were, however, if anything more 'improving' than many resident landlords. Their rigorous 'new broom' approach was, nonetheless, cushioned by a level of tolerance which became evident in their submissions to the company's London headquarters. They communicated a large number of cases of destitute or severely encumbered tenants throughout the 1830s, when the full effects of reduced incomes

from linen began to be felt. Their recommendations often encouraged the
granting of relief for tenants whose livelihood was in peril and who, like
Widow Jean Convey of Bracaghreilly, had fallen on hard times.

> Petitioner's husband died August 1831 and left 7 orphans of which 6...are
> helpless, that from the misfortune of the death of her husband, the cheapness
> of yarn, the scarcity of money and supporting a helpless family, Petitioner
> finds herself unable to fulfil contract or even to pay the annual rent.[27]

The agents continued to recommend the granting of relief to the many
petitioners who continued with their requests even before the full impact
of the Famine became fully apparent in the winter of 1846-7. As early as
November 1845 the agents obtained the company's permission to provide
meal to tenants in need.[28] In February 1846, they drew attention 'to the
probable distress that may take place in this district from the dearness of
provisions and want of employment for the poor'.[29] In a considerable number
of cases, the tenant's circumstances were articulated and the company
encouraged to fund their emigration. This was their purpose when writing
on behalf of Widow Bradley of Ballygrooby in the spring of 1847:

> For many years a widow...she had to part with a portion of her holding to
> enable her to bear up under the many difficulties...and this year of famine
> and distress compelled her to part with the remainder and...sending her
> family out to America she is now left with an idiot boy who is also
> dumb...{and} that the money realised from her farm was not sufficient to
> bring them all out.[30]

When approval for this course of action was not received, the agents
took up her case again in May 1848 on the grounds that 'the memorialist's
children had promised to send for her and her son but some of them having
taken fever in America they were unable to do so and memorialist is left
here without any means of support whatever. We still respectfully
recommend £10 to be given...to take herself and her son to America'.[31]

The company's agents, John and Rowley Miller, had earlier outlined
how they viewed assistance to tenants as an integral part of their plans to
improve the estate:

> ...if the Company were pleased to put at our disposal a few hundred pounds
> we could make a wonderful improvement on the estate. For instance, when
> a smallholder with a numerous family wishes to sell, after he pays...his
> debts and the rent he may owe, he has not the wherewithal to pay the
> passage money, which amounts to £4.10s....had we it in our power to aid
> such person or persons....we would enlarge many of the farms on the estate.

> There never was in the memory of man so good an opportunity of improving the estates in this country as at present, the small holders of land being frightened at the prospect of the potato about to become extinct....[32]

There are indications in this communication that the Drapers' Company subscribed to the political orthodoxy which held that the Famine was both a means and an opportunity of restoring the Irish economy and society to more manageable proportions. This, James S. Donnelly reminds us, 'was the common view of the landed elite'.[33]

One of the other main landholders in the south of the county, an area which began by the winter of 1846-7 to feel the pangs of want most sharply, was the 3rd Marquess of Londonderry's estate at Magherafelt. Both John Andrews, agent to the Co. Down estate, and Andrew Spottiswood, agent on the Derry estate, had left Lord Londonderry in no doubt about the state of the tenantry on the Magherafelt estate where 'the small tenants are said to be starving and where, at any sacrifice, employment to procure food must be given.'[34] Confirmation of this came in greater detail from the Magherafelt agent in January 1847. 'We are suffering severely both from sickness and destitution...and as the new Relief Act is not yet in operation and our poorhouse necessarily closed against the admission of paupers for the last six weeks, we are obliged to help about one hundred people dayly at that door'.[35] Trevor McCavery has discussed in his essay on Co. Down the opprobrium Lord Londonderry attracted in the press in January and February 1847 for his alleged neglect of the tenantry on his several Ulster estates. Significantly, perhaps, the attack on his apparent reluctance to contribute anything other than nominal support for his tenantry was first launched in the *Derry Standard*.[36] Lord Londondery's response, given that he was armed with this information, was little different from that adopted by the Drapers' Company, to provide practical assistance to the most needy and use the opportunity to improve the estate. Andrews assured Londonderry that his thinking was very much along the same lines:...'several of the needy are badly situated and, even before the receipt of your Lordship's letter...my plan is to press those who are destitute of means to sell and emigrate'.[37]

It was this Gradgrindish approach to the accumulating crisis that possibly provoked another Co. Londonderry landowner, George Dawson of Castledawson, to set down on record his own reaction to the destitution he had witnessed and which had, in truth, distressed him:

I can think of nothing else than the wretched condition of this wretched people. We are comparatively well off in this neighbourhood; there is no want of food but it is at such a price as to make it totally impossible for a poor man to support his family... I do not exaggerate when I tell you that from the moment I opened my door in the morning until dark I have a crowd of women and children crying out for something to save them from starving....so great is their distress that they actually faint on getting food into their stomachs.[38]

In addition to his evident horror at the destitution in his locale, Dawson's philanthropy was an acknowledgement of his concern later in the crisis that other landlords would not be moved to action as he has been:

Hearing but not knowing the tyranny of Irish landlords I have endeavoured to show my tenantry that I am disposed to encourage them...I established a large concern for making bricks...and I have given away above 100,000 bricks to the poorest tenants to make brick floors for their cottages (if I may call them so)... .[39]

Elsewhere in the county, the landlords' contribution to local relief chiefly took the form of subscribing to relief committees. In this respect, the London companies would appear to have led by example. The Clothworkers' Company contributed 'an equal amount' to the 'upwards of £100' collected by Dunboe and Macosquin Relief Committee.[40] The company also donated £125 of the £709 collected by the Aghadowey and Agivey subscription list.[41] Local contemporary criticism of the landlord response, however, was not unknown. Rev. Dr John Brown, the Church of Ireland minister at Aghadowey, who...'although most unwilling to give offence to any landlord and, most of all to one such as the Marquess of Waterford, nonetheless he thought that [the] meeting...should request him to attend to the poor on his estate. Whatever was the cause, there had accumulated a larger number of poor cottiers on his property than in any other part of the parish'.[42] This attack on Lord Waterford runs counter to the reputation he had already established as an 'improving' landlord (and had been mentioned approvingly as such in the report of the Devon Commission, just before the outbreak of Famine). In fact, Waterford appears to have been as responsive to this local criticism as Lord Londonderry was to the newspaper exposé and the Drapers' Company to the advice of its agents. On Christmas Day 1846, when the certainty of the second year's failure had been confirmed, he wrote to John Barre Beresford, his agent in Co. Londonderry, from his Waterford estate to say:

I have received your letter stating that you think £300 would be sufficient to give assistance to the poor on my property [in Co. Londonderry]. I have also had melancholy reports from many clergymen stating the necessity of immediate relief. I have established soup kitchens in this county [Waterford]...I wish you to set them up in the different parishes in which I have property.[43]

He ordered that either £2 or £3 per week, amounting to £21 per week, be used for the provision of soup kitchens in the nine parishes in which he had lands. 'My great object', he averred, 'is to support the destitute on my estate...I am sure the clergy will be willing to assist in these works...Write to the clergymen of the different parishes of my intentions'.[44]

It is somewhat ironic that, in spite of this vision of landed proprietors and clergymen working in harmony for the tenantry, any local dissatisfaction with the landlord performance continued to be voiced by clerics. Rev. J. Jackson, writing from Ballinderry Glebe to the Relief Commission in March 1847, lamented:

Every one of our landlords are non-resident and the remaining population consists of cottiers and small farmers. Under these circumstances, having no materials for the formation of any committee from which I could expect assistance in supplying the wants of our numerous poor, I in conjunction with the rector's family have been making great exertions since the commencement of the year both in the distribution of relief and in raising money among our friends...I cannot any longer forbear from supplying my parishioners with food.[45]

Rev. Mitchell Smyth had earlier written as chairman of Garvagh Relief Committee echoing Rev. Jackson's regrets at the absence of leadership which a resident landlord would have provided for a stricken area. He asked the Relief Commission for 'the necessary instructions as soon as possible, this neighbourhood being the poorest and most destitute in the county, having no resident landlords and no manufactures or public works to employ the people'.[46]

These and many of the other submissions on behalf of the relief committees provide an opportunity to evaluate not only the role of landlords but also of the respective clergy in the management of relief until the main responsibility passed to the unions in 1847. The subscription list of the committee established at Portstewart, for example, contained no less than eight named clerics, who between them contributed to the raising of some £80 in a total of £421.[47] A study of the personnel on the committees generally confirms the initial impression of an overall positive clerical contribution, often in the form of heartfelt pleas on behalf of their parishioners, exemplified in Rev. Jackson's description of his efforts for the poor in his Ballinderry Parish. Having received no reply from the Relief Commission, he followed up a week later begging them to ...'without any further delay give an increased and more adequate allowance of food to the poor in this district who are entirely destitute and are suffering both from privation and dysentery'.[48] Three weeks later, having still apparently received no reply, he pleaded...'last week a man and his wife died in one night (the neighbours assert of pure starvation)'.[49] Rev. William Hughes, Church of Ireland minister of Aghanloo Parish near Limavady, wrote in November 1846 of the 'very great distress...now beginning to be felt in this place by the labouring or cottier class'.[50] Rev John P. Hewitt of Moneymore referred to 'collections in the two meeting houses and the Roman Catholic chapel. The distress is increasing every day'. His balanced judgment that 'although such fearful distress does not prevail as in other places, yet the destitution is great and our need urgent' carries as much conviction as a more graphic account of privations. He refers to the soup kitchen dispensing '100 gallons of soup daily and [we] supply 228 families, consisting of upwards of 1100 individuals. The workhouse [at Magherafelt] has...more than it was constructed to receive'.[51]

The responses of the Presbyterian clergy, who were nonetheless active in the local relief measures, tended to comply mournfully with the will of God which they detected in the disaster.. Rev. Adam Boyle, minister at Bovedy near Kilrea, who recorded that he was 'in the 92nd year of [his] age and [have] a tremor in my hand', could see only the hand of God's wrath in the unfolding crisis...'a dereliction from duty is often followed even here with the visitations of judgement...united supplications at the throne of Grace may be better for our relief'.[52] At Castledawson, the Presbyterian clergyman, Rev. J. Radcliff, inserted a memoir in the Sessions minute book in September 1848 which recounted how the onset of the potato failure had affected his congregation:

> In the year 1846 occurred the great failure of the potato crop. For a number of years previous there had been evident symptoms of failure... There ensued a winter of the direst calamity. Hunger was visible in its [faintest?] aspects. The people, suddenly changed in their food, from potatoes to the Indian meal, were visited with a most wasting dysentery. To meet these things were established Relief Committees. These were composed of the resident

magistracy, the clergy of the three denominations, Episcopalians, Roman Catholic and Presbyterian...It was a wearisome thing to spend days after days at these Relief Committees and to come into contact with the hideous picture of misery which was then presented. It was more sorrowful still to look out and see the hungry look of the multitudes and to mark that all joy seemed to disappear from the human face.[53]

Hewitt's reference to the Magherafelt workhouse accommodation being full in March 1847, and Radcliff's description of the twelve-month period January 1847 – January 1848, are strong indications of the accelerating pace at which the disaster was taking shape. In early January none of the five workhouses serving the county's population was officially full. Both Coleraine and Magherafelt reported 'no great pressure' even though, in the case of the latter, over 250 paupers had been admitted in the previous month. Londonderry noted that 'additional buildings are now in course of erection'. Limavady recorded 'no pressure in the workhouse'. Only at Ballymoney was there any suggestion of not being able to cope...'the Commission has called the attention of the Guardians to their powers...and offers to co-operate with them in providing additional workhouse accommodation.[54] By the beginning of February, indeed, Ballymoney workhouse had exceeded its limit, as had Coleraine and Magherafelt by early March 1847. In the latter, the statistics show that over 400 had entered the workhouse in December and January, further evidence of the distress described by the local clergymen.[55]

As the winter wore on, overcrowding spread. By the beginning of March, Londonderry had only two spare places in its capacity of 800. Only Newtownlimavady continued to fall short of maximum capacity during this period of severity. The table below sets out the numbers in each workhouse from 5 December 1846 to 1 May 1847, by which time the numbers in all workhouses had started to drop, though Coleraine and Ballymoney remained officially overcrowded.[56]

WORKHOUSE	LIMIT	5 DEC '46	9 JAN '47	6 FEB	6 MAR	3 APR	1 MAY
Coleraine	700	482	563	671	784	842	722
Londonderry	800	576	691	715	798	764	779
Magherafelt	900	519	775	918	1000	825	699
N'limavady	600	267	404	438	486	539	499
Ballymoney	700	357	591	711	770	835	704

The crisis of the spring months of 1847 abated slowly, only to resume in the autumn with the third successive appearance of the potato blight. By December 1847 the numbers in the workhouses exceeded those of the corresponding months of 1846: Magherafelt increased by 25 per cent, to 908; Ballymoney by 26 per cent, to 706; Coleraine by 31 per cent, to 731; Newtownlimavady by 32 per cent; Londonderry's 914 inmates represented the highest rate of increase, 37 per cent, on the previous year's total.[57]

More worryingly, at the same time the spectre of famine fever began to manifest itself in the crowded workhouses. This was especially the case in 1848: by the autumn, there had been only a limited reduction in the numbers in the county's workhouses when compared with 1847.[58]

WORKHOUSE	LIMIT	DEC 1846	DEC 1847	DEC 1848
Coleraine	960	554	731	590
Londonderry	1100	665	914	820
Magherafelt	1240	724	908	729
N'limavady	890	393	518	453
Ballymoney	750	562	706	670

The numbers who fell victim to fever in sheds attached to Magherafelt workhouse began to assume serious proportions in the winter of 1847-8. Between July and September 1847, the total increased from 41 to 136, and peaked in late December of the same year at 171.[59] Rev. J. Radcliff represented something of the sense of additional fear arising from the spread of fever when he wrote:

> The winter which succeeded which was that of 1847 was a drearful one of fever. From January 1847 until January 1848 there died out of this congregation fifty-two persons, one every week. On two separate occasions I recorded three funerals meeting in the graveyard at the same time. On two other occasions I saw two coffins brought in together in the same cart. I hope God in his providence will spare the country from such a disaster in future and myself from ever witnessing anything similar.[60]

In addition to the prevalence of fever, one of the most striking features of the workhouse population in Ulster in the years 1847-8 was the disproportionately large number of children in them. Already evident by 1847, it continued so that, by May 1848 there were 16,349 children aged under 15 in Ulster workhouses, 49 per cent of a total population of 33,238 souls.[61] By July the proportion had climbed to over 52 per cent. By way of comparison, the percentage of children aged under 15 in Munster workhouses at the same time was 41 per cent, in Leinster 42.5 per cent and in Connacht 40 per cent.[62] This had begun to develop as a consequence of the social distress evident before the famine. The early signs had become apparent in cases such as that reported in the *Coleraine Chronicle* in September 1844, that 'Wm Thompson.. was brought up on a warrant for leaving his wife and children, thereby sending them as burdens to the Union workhouse'.[63]

The additional problems posed by the influx of parentless children had been noted by Edward Senior, the Poor Law Inspector in whose Northern District were all the county's workhouses, except for Londonderry city. His concern at the increasing tendency of parents to dump offspring in the workhouses was evident in March 1849 when he told the Select Committee on the Poor Law (Ireland) that

> ...the guardians in my district, by my advice, spare neither trouble nor expense in arresting persons who desert their families. They offer rewards and very often parties are arrested from great distances in Scotland and in England.[64]

The following month, April 1849, Senior circulated a letter to some unions, including Ballymoney, urging them... 'to send as emigrants...any of the able-bodied inmates...especially females...In this mode, some of the permanent deadweight...may be got rid of at a cost to the Electoral Division of about £5 or one year's cost of maintenance'.[65] The Guardians in Derry and Coleraine in particular addressed the problem by reconstituting parents with children and then arranging for their emigration as a family unit. Approval was received in 1849 by each of these boards of guardians for transporting to Canada of 64 paupers, in the case of Derry[66] and, in the case of Coleraine, of 56 emigrants to Quebec.[67]

The powers of Poor Law guardians to proceed with such schemes had been increased in 1849 by the Monsell amendment to the Poor Law Act. Thereafter the total of workhouse-assisted passages increased, for some years, though it never averaged more than 5,000 annually.[68] Indeed, more were assisted to emigrate by landlord initiatives than by Poor Law guardians.[69] Given the heightened awareness of the problems of orphan children in the workhouses it is slightly surprising that the five workhouses which served Co. Londonderry sent only 109 female orphans to Australia in the scheme which saw over 4100 parentless children from workhouses throughout Ireland sail to begin a new life in Australia.[70] The scheme was undertaken by the Poor Law Commission in close association with the Colonial Office in London which saw it as a means of improving the gender balance in the Australian colonies, where males outnumbered females by over three to one. The exercise, however, had to be abandoned in 1850, after only two years, in the wake of allegations about the licentious behaviour by orphans from Belfast workhouse on board the *Earl Grey*.[71] The workhouse records indicate that the Derry and Coleraine Guardians appeared fully mindful of the vulnerable position in which they were placing their girls by sending them on a ship with an all-male crew for 16-20 weeks. The Derry Guardians 'authorised that Letty Harper, a widow, be sent out with the girls as a chaperone/matron'.[72] The minute also recorded that 'the orphan girls now going to Australia were brought before the board in the clothing prepared for them. The chairman and vice-chairman severally addressed them with respect to their maintaining a suitable demeanour and conduct when going out, and on their arrival in the colony'.[73]

In this context, the initiatives of the Guardians at Coleraine and Londonderry in assisting the passages of orphans and their mothers was a means of addressing the problem not only of 'orphan' children but also an additional characteristic of the Ulster workhouse population. This was the preponderance of females among the adult population in the workhouses of Ulster, equally evident in Co. Londonderry. By the middle of 1848 the ratio of able-bodied adults in the workhouses of Ulster was nearing three females for every one male; the ratio in the three other provinces was generally closer to two females to one male. In November 1848, for example, the proportion of females in Ulster workhouses was 77 per cent of the able-bodied adult inmates, compared with 66 per cent in Munster, 67 per cent in Connaught and 72 per cent for Leinster.[74] The proportion of females in the workhouses of Co. Londonderry in the same period was 80 per cent, compared with 74 per cent in December 1846.[75] This preponderance of females may well have been associated with the phenomenon of chain migration that was characteristic of Ulster before and during the Famine which saw one member of a family, usually the man, migrate with a view to arranging for the rest of the family to join him.

The great majority of these emigrations was conducted through the port of Derry from which went direct sailings to North America, principally Philadelphia and New York. The passenger books of the emigration agents,

NOW IN PORT.

NOTICE TO PASSENGERS.

Those Persons who have taken their Passages by the First Class Coppered Ship

SUPERIOR,

CAPTAIN MASON,

FOR QUEBEC,

Are required to be in Derry on TUESDAY, the 13th of JULY pay the remainder of their Passage Money, and go on Board, as the Vessel will sail first fair wind after that date. A few more Passengers will be taken, on moderate terms, if immediate application is made to

Mr. DAVID MITCHELL, *Dungiven,* or the Owners,

J. & J. COOKE.

Derry, June 28, 1847.

☞ The Cargo of the SUPERIOR, just arrived, from *Philadelphia,* consisting of Indian Corn, Indian Meal, Flour, &c., for Sale, on moderate terms.

BUCHANAN, PRINTER.

Advertisement for an emigrant ship built for J&J Cooke of Derry in 1845 at a cost of £3,200 (PRONI T.1665).

J. & J. Cooke, which have survived provide ample evidence of the extent to which the port was used not only by emigrants from the county of Londonderry but from counties Tyrone, Antrim and, above all, Donegal.[76] When statistics measuring the flow of emigration more precisely began to be collected from May 1851, the annual average rate of emigration from the county of Londonderry in the five-year period 1851-55 could be calculated at 3168.[77] Something of the extent to which the port of Derry may be said to have served not only the county but a much wider hinterland is evident in the numbers of emigrants leaving from it. In one year, 1847, for example, some 12,385 passengers are calculated to have boarded 50 ships which sailed for Quebec, New York and Philadelphia.[78]

The relative safety, if not comfort, in which the emigrants were able to make the crossing was tempered by the realisation that the first case of typhus or cholera, a spectre of famine emigration dreaded by every ship's captain, was reported in the late summer of 1847. The ship *Superior*, with 360 passengers, arrived at Grosse Isle with many sick on board, having had to bury 60 at sea. Moreover, only one ship was lost, the chartered English ship *Exmouth*. This had foundered off the coast of Scotland with the loss of almost all of its 240 passengers.[79] The following year, 1848, there was also a case of another phenomenon generally associated with the spectre of the flight from famine in Ireland – the coffin ship, such as that exposed by Vere Foster MP when he travelled *incognito* on board the *Washington* and reported his findings to the House of Commons at Westminster in 1851.[80] The *Belfast Newsletter* and other local newspapers carried on 5 December 1848 headlines such as 'HORRIBLE CATASTROPHE – SEVENTY-TWO LIVES LOST BY SUFFOCATION IN A STEAMER'.[81] The *Londonderry*, sailing from Sligo to Liverpool, had put into the port of Derry to shelter from a storm. The word spread like wildfire that the steerage passengers, who had begun the journey on the open deck of this cargo ship, had suffered greatly when the crew had crammed them in to the hold when the storm blew up. The scene which greeted onlookers when the ship berthed in Derry was truly tragic:

> ...Alexander Lindsay, mayor, and several local magistrates were in attendance. The scene on entering the steerage of the steamer was perhaps as awful a sight or spectacle as could be witnessed. 72 dead bodies of men, women and children lay piled indiscriminately over each other, 4 deep, all presenting the ghastly appearance of persons who had died in the agonies of suffocation.[82]

The increased human and cargo traffic which was evident in the port of Derry during the Famine years was one of the means of employment which Sir Robert Ferguson had looked for when, as Lieutenant of the county, he first relayed to Dublin early reports of the potato failure. He had referred specifically to the railway construction and associated land reclamation that had been envisaged and was, in 1845, about to take shape, providing the means of internal transport from one end of the county to the other.[83] Indeed, shortly after this communication, Ferguson made it his business to apply discreet pressure to the Dublin & Enniskillen Railway Co.'s construction of the railway line between Londonderry and Enniskillen and Londonderry and Coleraine.[84] The company consequently informed the Relief Commission that...

> ...a very large number of men could be <u>immediately</u> employed on the two Derry lines which as you will see embrace a large district. The Coleraine line is well deserving of a mention as a vehicle not only for immediate but for constant employment as 22,000 acres of very fine land will be reclaimed [in the construction along the north Derry coastline of the line between Coleraine and Derry].[85]

The construction difficulties associated with the land reclamation provided employment until the line was opened in 1852-3, initially to Limavady and then to Coleraine. This was the first of a series of railway construction schemes which provided employment until the late 1850s, by which time a bridge had been built across the river Bann at Coleraine finally opening up the county to unbroken rail communication with Belfast and beyond.

There is apparently conflicting evidence for an answer to the question of when did the Famine end? Certainly in the southern parts of the county there are commentaries which support the established view that, after 1847, things began to improve. The Rev. Samuel Montgomery, Church of Ireland rector at Ballinascreen, recorded in his register in May 1848 that 'the crop of potatoes dug in the autumn [of 1847] was only diseased to a small extent...This spring of 1848 a great breadth of potatoes has been planted'.[86] George Dawson confirmed and elaborated on this assessment when, in writing to Sir Thomas Fremantle, chairman of the Board of Customs in November 1847, he relayed the news that...

> ...we have been blest with a most superabundant harvest in everything but potatoes...In fact, those [potatoes] that were sown were of the finest

quality...but ... they are beginning to show signs of not keeping. It is not
the disease of last year but more similar to that of 1846...I have not had a
call for charity at my door and I now can walk about unmolested and without
having my feeling wounded by the wretched pictures of misery which I
recollect too well last year.[87]

These expectations of better times were not wholly reflected in the
numbers applying for admission to the workhouses during 1848. In general
terms, the five workhouses serving the county remained under constant
pressure in the early months of 1848 with, significantly, scarcely the normal
seasonal drop-off in numbers by June as weather and employment
possibilities improved.[88]

The spread of fever amongst a population whose resistance had been
progressively weakened since the autumn of 1845 was one of the two main
post-blight consequences which Lord Londonderry's Magherafelt agent,
Andrew Spottiswood, adverted to in his October 1847 communication to
his lordship. The other was the decreasing ability of tenants on the estate
to pay off arrears of rent.

> I have been making every arrangement in my power to enforce payment
> but I regret to say that the failure of the potato crop has placed the
> smallholders on the estate in a very bad condition and this district has
> suffered very severely for some months from sickness and we have at present
> about one hundred and fifty cases of fever in the hospital sheds attached to
> the workhouse where our inmates are dayly increasing.[89]

There is no evidence to support a claim that any tenants on
Londonderry's Magherafelt estate were evicted (though there were evictions
on his other Ulster estates, notably in Co. Donegal and even in Co. Antrim
where arose the famous case, as Cahal Dallat has reported in the chapter
on Antrim, in which the agent of the Garron Tower estates, John Lanktree,
was removed from his holding). In fact, a fellow landlord, George Dawson,
commented in 1850 that 'the tenant leagues make very little way here and
excite no agitation...If it were not for Lord Londonderry's foolish and
mischievous letters we should have no trouble...but he continues...to make
his private concerns a subject of public agitation'.[90] In the same letter,
Dawson expressed the view that 'it is harder to keep a good tenant than to
eject him'. Nor is there any record of evictions on the Drapers' Co. estate.
The agents' letter books, however, continue to contain a litany of
'clearances' by means of assisted passages for emigration being granted to
families identified as being worthy of donations and whose removal would

contribute to the declared aim of improved estate management by the consolidation of farms. By 1849 the company had spent almost £950 in providing assistance for over 400 tenants to emigrate.[91] Of the other London companies who adopted this policy of clearance by stealth, the Fishmongers' estate at Ballykelly provided for some 60 tenants to emigrate with their families. The Grocers' estate nearby also contributed to the removal of 80 families in the period 1849-51 as a means of helping their policy of consolidation of farms.[92]

Recovery from such a deep-rooted blight which had produced mounting difficulties could only be, at best, halting. The numbers of paupers being given relief in the respective Co. Londonderry workhouses in the latter half of 1848 and well into 1849 indicate how painfully delayed was any overall improvement. The table below shows that all five workhouses had to cope with more inmates in June 1849 than had been the case in September 1848. A rise in their numbers during the winter months of late autumn 1848 to the spring of 1849 would have been expected. The very slight decrease in their populations from March to June 1849, a time when a bigger decline might have been anticipated, is a reliable indication that the effects of the blighted years were going to be more long-term than might have been supposed.[93]

WORKHOUSE	SEPT 48	DEC 48	MAR 49	JUNE 49
Ballymoney	532	662	693	671
Coleraine	438	577	602	557
L'derry	536	733	837	769
M'erafelt	598	719	774	741
N'limavady	303	443	471	446

George Dawson, who had earlier penned near panic-stricken accounts from his Castledawson demesne, was reluctant to read too much into the promise detected in the 1849 harvest, recalling the disappointment of the previous year's crop.

> I never saw the crops looking so luxuriant; the earth actually teems with produce...As yet there is not the slightest appearance of a taint in the potato but it is too early to speak with any confidence; last year [1848] the disease showed itself partially before this time but the fatal blight did not appear until the 3rd or 4th of August...if it again visits us, no one can tell the amount of human misery which will prevail.[94]

The cautiously expectant tone of the county's landlords was not echoed unequivocally by the tenantry. Henry Keenan, who held some 12 acres of average-quality land at Ballyscullion, on the Bruce estate, described his situation and his prospects in a letter he wrote that same month, July 1849, to his brother in Baltimore, Maryland. A dignified sense of hopelessness, the outcome of five successive years of dearth and want, is strikingly evident from a man who had not been entirely devoid of the means of supporting himself or his family but who now feared the worst.[95]

> I am well thank God, as also my wife and family. I was unwell from November to May but thank God I am recovered after my death being often despaired of.

> I have seven sons at the fireside with me yet. Times, indeed, are becoming worse every day here. There is no appearance of the potatoes recovering. I wish you to inform me in your next letter what trades I am to put my boys to in order to go or send them to that country. It is very difficult here to hold land at any price. If I could get anything for my land I would yet go myself and take my family. Taxes are so weighty, amount in all to a fair rent, that I do not consider [how] people can stand up here at all.

Ironically, perhaps, Keenan's solution – emigration – was that favoured by landlords in his locale, though for different reasons. When statistics measuring the flow of emigration more precisely began to be collected from May 1851, the annual average rate of emigration from the county in the five-year period 1851-5 was calculated at 3168.[96] By that time (1851) the population of the county had decreased by 13.5 per cent on its 1841 total, falling from 222,174 to 192,022 in 1851.[97] The most significant declines manifested themselves in the barony of Coleraine (particularly the parishes of Macosquin, Aghadowey and Tamlaght O'Crilly) and even more strikingly in the barony of Loughinsholin, where the parishes of Desertlyn, Tamlaght, Kilcronaghan, Arboe and Termoneeny all dropped by upwards of 25 per cent.[98]

Equally, it is as difficult to estimate how many people died in the county during the Famine as it is to arrive at a more meaningful figure for the entire country than Cormac Ó Gráda's 'one million excess deaths'.[99] The 1851 census recorded that there had been 25,883 deaths in the county since 1841. The annual average number of deaths in the years 1842-5, before the Famine took root, was 1762; by contrast, the annual average for the years 1846-50 was 2723.[100] The best estimate that the evidence allows, therefore, is that there were approximately 1,000 excess deaths per year 1846-50 in the county of Londonderry.

Regardless of the statistics, the evidence of the observers – the clergymen, the relief committee personnel, the tenants and indeed even the landlords themselves – which have been used to compile this account of Co. Londonderry during the Famine testify to the inexorable difficulties which the successive potato blights engendered for the greater number of the population.

THE FAMINE
IN
COUNTY MONAGHAN

PATRICK DUFFY

Well fed pigs nowhere suspended in fletches from their dingy rafters for
the purpose of kitchen to their vegetable diet. All are transported to make
up the rent and nothing remains but the light, gay and cheerful spirits of
the emaciated frames of a half-starved population...[1]

Ｃounty Monaghan's experience of the Great Famine reflected very much
its peripheral situation in south Ulster. Although, like most of Ulster, it
may not have suffered the extreme destitution of the west of Ireland, it was
one of the more seriously affected regions in the province. All the indicators
of the Famine's impact in the 1840s – inadequate though many are in
describing the effects of the crisis – show that Monaghan county occupied
a transitional location between Ulster and the rest of Ireland. In terms of
population loss, relief expenditure, rates, estimated emigration, and reports
of destitution and deaths from starvation, Monaghan shared more
experiences with the north midlands and north-west of Ireland than with

Ulster. The regional distinctiveness of its population's ordeal was presaged in many pre-famine indicators which showed that the south Ulster borderlands had particularly vulnerable rural economies, teetering on the edge of Malthusiasn disaster in the 1830s and '40s. Although it was Donegal in the early 1830s which prompted his outburst, John O'Donovan's was a typical assessment of rural Ireland's woe:

> when [the Irish peasant] finds himself the holder of as much land as will support himself and one other, he immediately becomes anti-Malthusian – he marries and contributes largely to the multiplication of the Celtic stock, still looking to the potato as the sole support! But woe when storms rush from the angry ocean destroying the stalk... Malthus will never succeed here. The present state of things must end in general destruction.[2]

This essay considers some general features of landscape and society in pre-famine Monaghan and describes the social and geographical repercussions of the crisis in the county.

I

As population was the most sensitive, certainly the most dramatic, indicator of the onset and consequences of famine anywhere, a variety of dimensions of the population problem will be used as a means of illustrating the impact of famine. Population can have implications for pressure on land, housing conditions, landholding circumstances, land-use and landscape patterns, and all of these can be described to show what conditions prevailed at local level in the 1840s.

South Ulster, Monaghan and Cavan, contained some of the most heavily populated rural areas in Ireland in 1841. Freeman's map of population density shows an extensive belt of countryside running from south Cavan through Monaghan into Armagh and the parishes of north Co. Louth which contained up to and over 400 persons per square mile – enormous numbers of people by any measure.[3] These densities were shared with narrow coastal belts along the west coast of Ireland. Monaghan thus entered the mid-nineteenth century with a rural population pressure comparable with that in the west of Ireland. The difference was that land quality in the western districts was considerably worse than in Monaghan, and was exacerbated by its remoteness. But in Co. Monaghan in 1841 were found some of the most extensively overpopulated districts in the country. Although 'overpopulation' is an elusive and much-abused term, it is useful in suggesting that the population-resource relationship had become unbalanced in Monaghan. The resources of the land clearly had become too fragmented, farms had become miniscule, there were too many people with limited or no access to the land, and fewer and fewer of these had access to non-farm incomes. The linen industry's spinning and weaving crafts were in rapid retreat in the north-east, leaving a huge population of landless underemployed rural dwellers stranded. And it was the geographical transition, as well as the industrialisation of the linen industry, which separated Monaghan's experience from Armagh's in the 1840s.

The population of Monaghan in 1841 was 200,442. Excluding the town populations, 185,000 lived in the countryside, representing an average rural density of 58 persons per 100 acres (370 persons per square mile). Within the county, the most pressured districts were in the south, east and middle (Fig. 1). The barony of Farney in the south had some of the most heavily-populated rural areas. The lowest densities were to be found in the mountainy lands of the north-west. Altogether, one quarter of the townlands in Monaghan had extremely high population densities of more than 76 persons per 100 acres; many of these townlands in the baronies of Farney and Dartrey had densities which,when converted, amounted to between from 600 and 1300 persons per square mile, surely among the most overcrowded countrysides in Europe.

At townland level, of course, there were local contrasts in population pressure, with densely-peopled townlands being juxtaposed with virtually empty districts, coinciding with demesnes and large farms. But such areas were comparatively rare in Monaghan. As an example of the reality of population density in the localities, parts of Magheracloone and Magheross parishes in the south of the county had the following populations:

TOWNLAND	ACRES	1841 POP.	(1985 POP.)
Aghinillard	179	199	(16)
Alts	129	92	(11)
Ardragh	469	309	(33)
Barndonagh	115	106	(11)
Carrickadooey	266	207	(7)
Clonsedy	297	191	(105)
Corcuilloge	244	296	(56)

Corlea	190	167	(10)
Drumbo	191	162	(19)
Drumbracken	219	216	(44)
Drumgoosat	196	177	(31)
Kilmactrasna	139	170	(20)

The population in 1985[4] is given for comparative purposes to provide a context to understanding the pre-famine data. The contrast in the situation then and now confirms the exceptional nature of rural conditions 150 years ago and to some extent perhaps helps to explain the extent of the crisis in the later 1840s.

In trying to understand the landscape and social parameters of these demographic conditions in 1841, which seemed destined to lead inevitably to disaster in a short space of time, two principal dimensions may be considered: first, the owners of land, holding estates both large and small and, secondly, the occupiers of the land – tenant farmers, cottiers and other humble inhabitants of the countryside.

The landowner estates represented areas over which some sort of 'management policy' operated, to a greater or lesser extent depending on the involvement of the owner in the running of his property. Manifested either by its absence or its application, management of sections of the landscape by proprietors in the pre-famine years was an important factor in understanding the nature of rural demographic and social problems. For larger properties, estate offices employing personnel such as agents, bailiffs and clerks applied a range of practices designed to make orderly and efficient use of the land with the ultimate objective of squeezing as much income out of it as possible. Farms were organised by means of leases and other contractual obligations imposed by right of ownership. Less-extensive properties may have had less managerial intervention, with the owner or a representative making occasional contributions, coinciding at long intervals perhaps with the sale of the property or its mortgage, when accounts and surveys of the land were undertaken.

At a general level therefore, in theory, the imposition of controls had the effect of managing the numbers of farms, the sale of farms and the passing on of farms to the next generation. In theory also the sub-letting of land to cottier tenants was controlled. In practice, however, the reality was more unregulated and in many cases management was haphazard or non-existent. In all cases it is obvious that the estate, which represented a segment

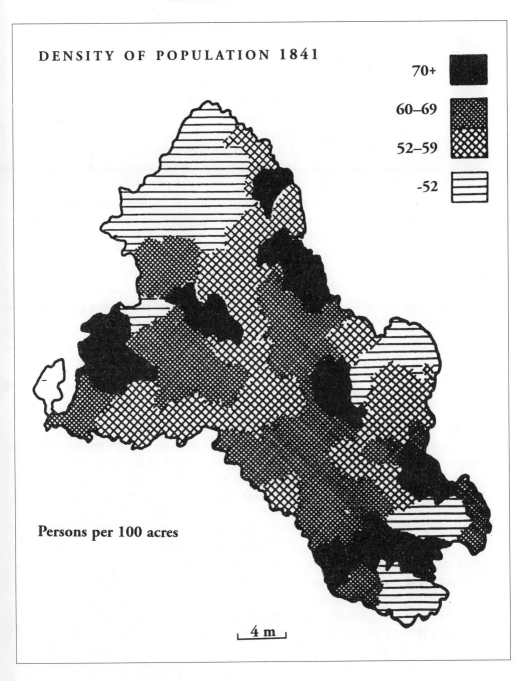

DENSITY OF POPULATION 1841

70+

60–69

52–59

-52

Persons per 100 acres

⌞ 4 m ⌟

of land in the county with a legal existence containing a group of occupiers with a variable legal relationship to the owner, provides an important, if sometimes tenuous, territorial context for the problems and prospects of Monaghan's population in the early and mid-nineteenth century.

The largest estates in Monaghan exceeding 2,000 acres are shown in Fig. 2.[5] Although this map is based on post-famine data, the general pattern was not affected very much by encumbered estate sales in the county. Estates like these had offices for example in Carrickmacross for the Shirley and Bath estates, in Glaslough for the Leslie estate; most were in the houses or demesnes of the landowner. These larger estates were generally located in the lowlands of the county; the hillier areas contained the smaller properties not detailed in Fig. 2. Most of these smaller properties were less than 500 acres. It is unlikely that they had a permanent administrative presence, beyond a solicitor's office in town in which transactions such as rent payments were carried out. It is notable that the majority of the smaller estates in mid-nineteenth century Monaghan had addresses outside the county. For example 88 out of 154 properties of 100-500 acres were owned by persons not resident in the county in 1858, but in neighbouring counties or in other counties ranging from Dublin to Derry. Of the 28 largest estates in the county, only seven were non-resident – Lord Bath lived in Wiltshire; Viscount Templetown lived in Down. Many of the residents, of course, like Shirley of Carrickmacross, lived for part of the year in England.

The occupiers of the land gave life to the census data. Their numbers make up the density ratios, they lived in the thousands of cabins scattered across the hills; it was they who carved up the farms and fields which webbed the landscape. They are essential in understanding the social and economic processes which went into the making of the problems and prospects of rural Monaghan in pre-famine decades. They certainly operated within the parameters of the estates.[6] The lease and rental records of the Shirley, Leslie and Dawson estates, for example, reflect this. On the Shirley estate, there was a census of cottiers taken before the Famine; there were notices about sub-division and sub-letting in 1843, regulations on the keeping of goats (which destroyed the young hedges). There were petitions from the tenants to the landowner on a wide variety of matters. But it would be a mistake to conclude from this that the pre-famine Monaghan landscape was a product of closely administered estate structures like Downshire's Hillsborough estate. The fact is that a great many estates were small and

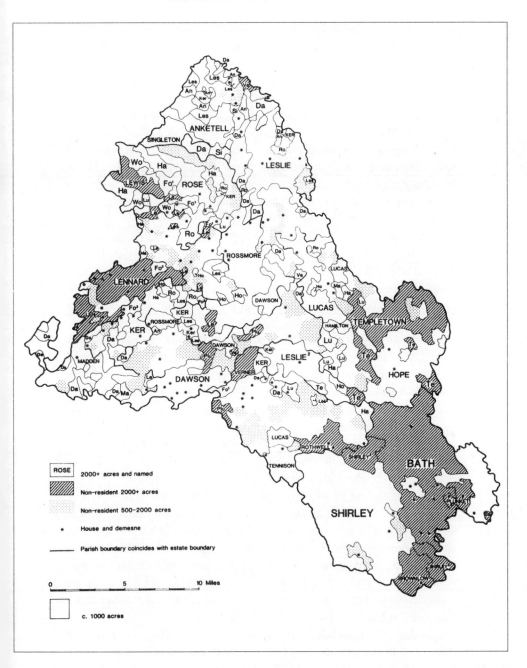

ROSE 2000+ acres and named

Non-resident 2000+ acres

Non-resident 500-2000 acres

* House and demesne

Parish boundary coincides with estate boundary

0   5   10 Miles

c. 1000 acres

scattered and had no discernible presence or policy beyond the twice-yearly rent collection. The occupiers of the land were left alone and in many cases the pressure areas in the mid-nineteenth century were the social and landscape consequences of this.

In the Devon Commission report in 1845, significant differences in the management of the bigger and smaller Monaghan estates emerged. Tenants agreed that landholding on larger estates was preferable, with rents and valuations generally more acceptable. Rents on larger estates were perceived to be closer to the Poor Law valuation of the land and in some cases below it, although the Shirley estate was exceptional with rents estimated to be 21 per cent above the official valuation. Smaller estates, often with a non-resident owner, were the least desirable areas from the tenants' point of view. One of the relatively few cases of pre-famine eviction in the county, reported to the commission, concerned a small holding owned by an absentee proprietor, Lord Wingfield: according to Patrick Murphy, the tenant, 'I could not know where the landlord or landlady was, I had a relation in Dublin and he called at Cork Abbey, but they were not there. I heard that the Colonel was over in Connaught, and the lady was from home...'[7]

The limited influence of a source such as the Devon Commission, which provides a fairly random view of the landholder system at a particular moment in time, should be acknowledged. The landholding structures which underlay the demographic dilemma of the 1840s were products of two or more generations of management or mismanagement and, while a broad picture of greater intervention on the larger properties does emerge, there are many exceptions. The new heir to the Rothwell estate of 2,300 acres in 1835 probably reaped the rewards of lack of attention to the property for many years when he had to evict 52 families, 'mere cottiers... with whom the landlord had no previty, and some of whom were not known even by name to Mr Rothwell or his agent'. They were variously characterised as 'undertenants of a house and garden', 'undertenant of a hovel', 'got in as a weekly tenant under a temporary tenant for a year', 'cottier from a neighbouring farm/adjoining estate', 'squatter from Farney', 'lived in gripe of ditch under road...never paid rent'.[8] In an illuminating dispute at the commission hearing, a tenant of the estate alleged that the owner had a "domain but had been there for many years" and lived in Nice. This was disputed by the agent who claimed that 'Mr Rothwell's usual residence from 1836-42 was well known to be in Co. Meath, with occasional temporary occupation of the mansion house on his estate in Monaghan...and his visit to Italy was not until 1842 – for health reasons'. The agent, who lived in Dublin, also claimed that he visited the Monaghan estate 'six to eight' times a year.[9]

The Lucas estate had 170 tenants in the mid-eighteenth century which rose to 570 in 1845 – a classic profile of land division and demographic expansion, which in this case was facilitated in the early years by the expansion of the linen industry. Flax growing, spinning and weaving in the later eighteenth century provided the larger landowners with the possibility of more stable rental income and encouraged occupiers to fragment their inheritance of land. From the late eighteenth century low-profile management policies caused a few problems during these periods of rural economic expansion. High prices for corn and textiles kept both tenant and proprietor happy; it was only as the prices declined into the 1830s that fearful Malthusian realities dawned for everyone.

The 26,000-acre Shirley estate, which the owner only occasionally visited until 1828, had a controversial management regime from the late eighteenth century. Tenants complained of unfair impositions by the various agents and indeed, in 1843, the newly-appointed agent William Steuart Trench supported their point of view. But in general there was little interference with the tenants' occupation of the land, in spite of regular warnings of a dangerous multiplication of holdings on the estate. In an survey as far back as 1789, it was pointed out that 'the tenants have increased in a very great and rapid degree in the last fifty years, and if they increase in the same proportion for the next fifty years the Produce of the Lands under their present mode of culture will be scarcely sufficient for their support'.[10] In 1814, another surveyor reported that it would not be profitable to 'make the best rental of the estate without entirely sweeping off the present population and replacing it by real farmers...an entire change of system should take place'.[11] The difficulty, he said, would be to find employment for the 'wretched occupiers who at present cling to the soil", and who of course had been permitted, even encouraged, to do so by previous managements. Policy did not change until the advent of the Poor Law; indeed Mitchell, whose agency finished in 1843, was openly encouraging sub-division of farms in 1839: he threatened to evict a tenant who refused to give a portion of his farm to his son.[12] When Steuart Trench took over in 1843, and tried to impose order on the affairs of the property, he became extremely unpopular by restricting fragmentation of farms and removing cottiers.

In general in the decades before the Famine one could talk of a balancing act, or a series of compromises, between a number of participants in the population-land relationship, which throws a light on the ultimate shape of things: the landowners, the tenants and, perhaps, the land agents. Agents, with other estate personnel, were powerful especially in situations where the owner was non-resident. They were also significant players on larger properties, where their advice and experience were essential to run the property on a day-to-day basis. Agents represented the interests of the landowner, but at the same time in many cases they also maximised their own personal opportunities through managing leases for favourites, and in the Shirley estate by imposing extra charges on the tenants. Tenants tried to outwit the agent, and the proprietor, often with a good deal of native cunning, by being carefully obsequious, for example, calling him, 'your honour'. Scally's study of the crown estates in Roscommon emphasises the extent of through-otherness on the property and the way the local tenantry played on the inability of the various agencies to comprehend the intricate local complexities in tenurial arrangements.[13] In 1847, there were 591 cottier families (2,647 people) on the Shirley estate, many of them tenants or undertenants of tenants.

II

The fourth-class house was the most inferior category of house occupied by the poorest classes in the country in 1841. It was usually one-roomed, often window-less, though the classification was frequently left to the discretion of the local constabulary. The poorest class of house in Aughnamullen parish in 1836 was 'beyond description...of a very low, open, ill-built kind, some built of sods, some of stones without mortar...ill-thatched, damp and smoky'.[14] In terms of house quality Monaghan fell into the median category nationally. It did not have the ubiquitous deprivation of the west, where many districts had from 60 to 80 per cent of their housing in this category. Monaghan generally was part of an extensive region extending from south Leinster to north-east Ulster with 20-40 per cent fourth class houses. Within the county, the poorest houses were concentrated in the southernmost parishes and in the north around Monaghan town, with more than one third in the fourth class.[15] Although the proportions are probably not very significant, many of the most densely populated areas in the county, such as Clontibret parish in the east and areas in the west, had less than a fifth of their houses in the fourth-class category. It is likely that the economic role played by the linen industry contributed to the paradox of population pressure and lower proportions of poorer housing.

The Devon Commission evidence from Monaghan does not contain as many reports of harrowing poverty as areas like Mayo or west Galway. Landless populations of cottiers were not as numerous in Monaghan which was emphatically a county of smallholders. There were, however, significant proportions of cottiers in some places – as in the west of Ireland. Unlike Leinster, where landless populations had a labour relationship with the farm population, the Monaghan cottier was in a very vulnerable situation. Some were undoubtedly linked to the larger farms in the Monaghan corridor area (which extended from Clones north-eastwards to Glaslough) and the southern extremities of the county, but their numbers were limited. The Devon Commission had noted that the largest farmers in Magheross parish had 40 acres: there were, however, only about ten of these in the entire parish, each having from four to six cottiers. Many of the cottier populations were legacies of an earlier, more vibrant, rural textile economy: in the Lucas estate in Castleshane there were eight mills, for example. Most were simply symbiotic extensions of the small tenant community, in many cases linked by kin. These cottiers were essential to the rent structure, as Smyth notes, for one estate in north Armagh where the rents paid to the tenant farmers by their cottiers, who occupied one twentieth of the land of the estate, amounted to one fifth of the rent of the estate.[16] The agent on the Lucas estate reported that often a labourer built his own house on a corner of a four- or five-acre farm, married the farmer's daughter and became his labourer. On Shirley's estate, Trench tried to break a well-established tradition for small farms to take cottiers. Owen Fitzpatrick pleaded in 1844 to be allowed to keep his labourer permitted by the previous agent: that he had built a house for him, 'roofed with timber before your honour prohibited'.[17]

In a county such as Monaghan, where small farming was dominant, employment opportunities for the landless population were very limited, with the cottier families subsisting on whatever work they could find at home, or abroad in some cases. According to the Ordnance Survey in 1835, there were in the south of the county 'few patches of ground where the utmost of cultivation has not been effected', so that undoubtedly Monaghan was a highly labour-intensive landscape. By 1845, however, a great many of the cottiers were two thirds of the year unemployed, according to the Devon Commission. In 1841, the linen industry was in serious decline in the county. By 1851 it was virtually eliminated from the rural economy, a development reflected in the disappearance during the famine of labourers in the industry. In the 1841 census, for instance, there were 24,687 women engaged in the industry, mostly in spinning, and 3,400 men, all mainly concentrated in the parishes of central and west Monaghan. By 1851, the corresponding figures were 2,331 and 1,283 respectively.

Small tillage holdings were the most characteristic feature of the rural landscape and demographic context in mid-nineteenth century Monaghan. Changes brought about by the Famine did not radically affect the overall pattern of small holdings. The greatest concentrations of the smallest holdings under 15 acres were to be found in the eastern districts of the county. More than a quarter of all farm holdings in much of Farney and around Monaghan and Clones towns were less than five acres. Well over three quarters of the holdings throughout most of Farney and Cremorne baronies were less than 15 acres, characterising them as decisively small-farm regions.

III

All these various pieces of data help to give some kind of picture of the general background to the socio-economic state of the county before the Famine. More direct evidence from contemporary observers of the poverty and destitution of sections of the population help to complete an overview of pre-famine Monaghan.

Trench's survey of the Shirley estate is a useful insight into conditions prevailing over a large section of the county. Trench, condemned in local folk memory, would not be the first to come mind as a humanitarian witness to the poverty of the people. His memoirs as a land agent were a source of popular outrage in the county.[18] His attitudes to the poorer sections of the Irish population generally ranged from contempt to racial arrogance. But the report he made to Shirley following his appointment in 1843 throws an interesting dispassionate light on living conditions on this large estate.[19] Having spent some months traversing the estate and visiting the tenants' houses and premises, he was quite candid in his reaction to what he saw: 'even in Ireland it has never fallen my lot to witness destitution to the same degree and over such a large extent as I have seen it on this property'. He noted that there were 'many tenants' houses where there are neither windows, bedsteads, tables nor chairs, and hundreds destitute of one or more of these comforts...'. He emphasised particularly the connection between the economic depression and falling agricultural prices and the serious problems for the tenantry, with some hard questions directed at the landlord:

> the Tenants generally speaking on this Estate, and I might perhaps add, on most subdivided estates in Ireland, are in a state of poverty and depression which would make it wise in point of interest, and just and humane in point of morality, that the landlord should consent to share with them the burthens by which they are unavoidably overwhelmed. Upon what principle of justice the Tenant should be called upon to bear the entire loss consequent upon bad seasons, depressed prices, and an altered tariff, I confess I cannot understand.

The petitioning system which was used on the same estate has left some harrowing accounts of the reality of life for many desperate people in south Monaghan in the years prior to the famine.[20] The number and range of the petitions are not only a reflection of the escalating crisis but also illustrate the welfare role which the estate played in the lives of the people in the mid-nineteenth century. From the early 1840s a great many sought relief in the form of concessions on rent arrears, for example, or help in times of sickness. One common request was for blankets, a reflection of particularly extreme poverty and a universal indicator of want, especially among the landless in wintertime.

The detail of many of the petitions was harrowing: Henry Magill of Carrickmaclim in January 1844 'lives a cottier with John Reburn and a family comprising a wife and four children, that it has pleased God to afflict him with an ulcerous leg which incapacitates him from labouring... has no means but what he receives from the charitable and humane...supplicates your Honour to given him a blanket which he stands much in need of...'. Anne McEneaney, whose pigs had died, held two acres near Carrickmacross in February 1844 and sought a blanket for her son lying 'on his deathbed'. Francis McCabe of Peaste in December 1844 lived on his aunt's farm and was 'put to the expense of burying her ...the death of pigs destroyed him...by going to the English harvest he got the means to clear arrears of rent...between himself, his wife and two children they have not one pound of day or night woollen covering and are nearly famished with cold'. Widows, like Catherine Martin of Corbane, were particularly vulnerable in distress: in January 1845, she petitioned that the blanket under which her husband lay dying and which was the only one in the house was nearly useless and expressed the 'hope that your honour will give her some covering to shade her feeble bones from the acute cold of the present season'.

The smallholders and the cottiers were in severe difficulties in the early 1840s. Trench in his report in 1843 paid particular attention to the way the estate had pressurised the smaller tenants by imposing a 'watching system' on them to make sure they paid their rents on time. 'Keepers' constantly monitored all possessions and transactions on their farms: 'the Tenant sooner than have this Keeper upon him... would make any sacrifices, or sell his pig or his crop at any loss, to get rid of him. Thus rents were kept up, little or no arrears accumulated, but the Tenant as times grew worse (pigs and corn being not much more than half their former value) was rapidly becoming poorer and poorer, his capital going to keep up the rent...' Peter Mohan, farming three acres in Magheracloone parish, might be selected as representative of the struggles of a whole category of society in Monaghan on the eve of the Famine. He told the Devon Commission:

> When I had my land cheap, and myself a youth, I was a good workman, and did work by the loom, and I would be mowing in the summer season, and earn a good deal, and make a little store for me, which was stood by me. I buy some oats and make a little meal out of it, and I take money in that way. It was not by my land I was paying my rent, but from other sources.... The people in my townland have ten acres among them all [eleven households in 1841]. You see my condition. I am the best man that can pay the rent in the townland and this is the best suit of clothes I wear...[21]

Peter's tiny plot of land did not pay his rent – it grew his potatoes to feed him and his family. In spite of the hardship of famine, however, he survived and the presence of a Peter Mohan in this same townland on 11 acres in Griffith's Valuation in 1858 is a reflection of the ability of this class to survive. The cottier population, however, had nothing: they were more transient, and only fleeting glimpses of them appear in the pages of the Devon Commission, wandering around looking for a place to settle: 'whenever sickness attacks the labourer, he is almost invariably obliged to leave his cabin, and his family become beggars or go into the workhouse'.[22] Of the 52 cottiers who were evicted from the Rothwell estate in the late 1830s, by the time of the Devon Commission some had gone to America, some were begging and some were cottiers elsewhere.

The critical nature of the social structure in rural Monaghan was exposed fairly suddenly by the introduction of the Poor Law Act in 1838. This had a catalytic effect in highlighting the imbalances in the territorial ratios of land to people, and the irregularities in the property management in the previous half century in the face of a dislocated economy. The effect of the Poor Law was to re-define emphatically large sections of the peasant and cottier population as surplus – a huge stratum of people whose property was at or below £4 valuation and who in times of increasing crisis would be maintained by a new property tax. This alarmed landowners particularly: properties with a limited number of poorer classes – potential 'paupers' – anxiously contrived to have the Poor Law electoral divisions, which would be responsible for paying the rates in support of their paupers, correspond with their properties. In Monaghan, for example, the boundary of the Bath estate with a smaller cottier problem than the Shirley estate coincided clearly with the Poor Law divisions. Elsewhere, the Leslie, Rossmore, Dawson, Blayney and Anketell estates all matched the boundaries of the new Poor Law unions and electoral divisions. Those with large numbers of poor tenants and cottiers set about trying to resolve their looming problem fairly quickly. The Shirley estate was typical and the new policies introduced by Trench in 1843, ranging from prohibition of subdivision and subletting through assisted emigration ultimately to eviction, were all designed to reduce the rates burden on the estate. Shirley's comprehensive survey of cottiers on the estate between 1840 and 1847 was unmistakably aimed at reducing his taxation liability.[23]

The potato blight first appeared in the north of the county in 1845. Obviously our retrospective characterisation of the next few years as the 'great Famine' colours our approach to the times. To contemporary farmers, cottiers and landowners it may have seemed like simply another crisis for the rural community.[24] However, many observers in this pre-industrial society quickly realised the potential for catastrophe. The *Northern Standard* of 1 Nov. 1845 echoed national apprehensions in editorialising on the 'calamities which seem certain to be entailed upon the land by the loss of the potato crop'.

Although the agricultural data are not very reliable (several districts not returning any data in 1847 due to the 'disturbed conditions'), it is possible to get some indirect idea of the extent of potato failure in the county by relating the acreage of potatoes in 1847 to what it had returned to in 1851, when a semblance of normality set in. The relative extent of cultivated crops in 1847 and 1851 was not very different due to increased grain growing in 1847. It was obviously, therefore, the potato acreage which changed substantially. Although the statistics do not indicate the proportion of the crop which was affected by blight, they do indirectly suggest failure. A high loss in potatoes in 1845 and '46 would result in a lower planting next season due to shortage of seed. Thus the 1847 acreage of potatoes in Scotstown, for example, was only 14 per cent of what it was destined to be in 1851; the acreage in Carrickaslane (near Castleblayney) on the other hand was 50 per cent. The greatest 'failures' in potatoes occurred, it would seem, in the north-eastern districts, in west Dartrey and in the northern hills of Farney, although as Ó Mórdha notes, the absence of a single mention of potatoes as food in a coroner's report for 1846 and 1847 would suggest that failure was total everywhere.[25]

Potatoes were widely cultivated in those areas where the smallholders and cottiers where most numerous. At the first hint of failure, the larger farmers would cease to plant, while the poorer classes had little alternative but to try again. Thus there were comparatively large areas planted in the small farm regions in 1847 in the east of the county and around Carrickmacross. Where the 1847 acreage was low and where there were substantial numbers of smallholders, as in the east of Farney and around Monaghan town, there was probably a high degree of failure in 1846 with no seed left to plant.[26] These areas must have been particularly distressed. Great distress which ultimately caused huge population losses also occurred in west Dartrey and the north-eastern districts where there were large numbers of landless labourers and where the potato apparently failed comprehensively.

Population loss was the inevitable consequence of the Famine disaster. Co. Monaghan had some of the most severe losses in the country which certainly made it exceptional in Ulster. Indeed the rate of population decline between 1841 and 1851 in south Ulster generally reflected its transitional demographic status between Ulster and the north-west. Monaghan's population fell from more than 200,000 in 1841 to 141,000 in 1851. When one excludes the towns, Monaghan and Cavan counties experienced some of the heaviest rural declines in Ireland.

COUNTIES WHICH LOST MORE THAN 25% OF THEIR RURAL POPULATIONS
1841-51

	%
Roscommon	31.6
Mayo	29.4
Monaghan	29.2
Sligo	29.0
Longford	28.7
Cavan	28.4
Leitrim	27.9
Laois	27.5
Galway	26.9
Clare	25.9
Fermanagh	25.8
Kilkenny	25.6

Counties Antrim, Down, Derry, Donegal and Armagh take up the bottom of the table with declines below 16 per cent; Tyrone lost 18 per cent of its population.

Within the county, 25 of the 65 electoral divisions had losses of more than 35 per cent, 11 of these losing more than 40 per cent of their populations in the decade. The heaviest losses were concentrated in the western regions of the county in some of the most densely populated districts bordering on Cavan and Fermanagh. With some exceptions, the small farm districts in the eastern part of the county had comparatively smaller declines. Bragan in the north-west mountainy area must have been one of a small number of areas in Ireland with a one per cent decline in its population. Half the townlands in Shirley's estate in Farney lost more than half their populations. Magheracloone parish population fell from 9,012 to 5,141 between 1841 and 1851; Magheross from 11,447 to 6,419. The decline in house numbers is perhaps a more dramatic reflection of the sweeping nature of the changes across the countryside. Aghnamullen parish lost more than 1,000 houses in the decade. Some townlands on the outskirts of towns had extraordinary declines, like Mullanary outside Carrickmacross whose house numbers fell from 133 in 1841 to 4 in 1851.

V

A number of factors can be examined to help in understanding these population losses. Destitution was reflected in the level of rates in each Poor Law Union, which was related to the proportions of poor in the area, mainly comprised the landless, cottier or small holder population with property less than £4 valuation. Of the population which held land, over one tenth in Monaghan Union was under £4 in contrast to between one quarter and one third in Clones in Carrickmacross Unions. As the crisis deepened in the late 1840s pressure on the rates increased. This had many repercussions. Tenants in arrears and unable to pay rents were increasingly evicted by landowners in the hopes of reducing the burden on the rates; this in turn often put more pressures on the rates as the growing numbers of destitute went to the workhouses. Shirley and other landowners tried to encourage cottier tenants to emigrate.

In Monaghan, as a result of its predominantly small farm structure a great proportion of its tenantry were themselves put under enormous pressure by the rates. Their small farms were classified just above the £4 level where they were expected to contribute to the Poor Law rates. In Castleblayney Union there were large numbers of tenants with farms valued at £4-5 who were under great pressure in 1847 with rates over 3s in the £.[27] In January the rate collectors found it impossible to collect the rate. In May the Board tried to lower the level of qualification for outdoor relief to below £4 to assist the great numbers in trouble. In November the military were called to help in the collection of rates. Many sold their crops and fled. Holdings between £4 and £5 valuation in Monaghan were broadly in the 5-15 acre category. It is evident from an examination of the districts of population loss that there is a correspondence between the areas with significant numbers of 5-15 acre holdings in 1848 and areas of heavy population decline, as for example in the western districts of the county where more than half of all the holdings were in this vulnerable range. Many of these areas also contained large numbers of landless cottiers, renting land from the small holders.

In contrast, many areas with significant numbers of very small holdings (i.e. under five acres) did not experience as high a rate of population loss. Over one quarter of all holdings in the eastern and southern parishes of Farney, for instance, in Clontibret and in Donagh parishes were less than five acres. In general these small holders may not have had the resources to leave during the famine. In the north-west of the county where population loss in the decade 1841-51 was also low, farms were large but low in value, and there too the population was characterised by inability to emigrate. Possessing small farms, like Peter Mohan of Magheracloone, they sat out the Famine.

The desperation of smallholders being pressed by the potato failure on the one hand and rent and rate demands on the other is reflected in the appeal of Thomas and Mary Marron to Shirley's agent in February 1848:

> extent yr honour...our forefathers for centuryes past were tenants to Mr Shirley and always paid his rent punctually... The emergency of the present crysis and the expense of the Burial of our parents which we had to encounter left us inadequate to pay...bear with us until harvest as we have a good promise of a wheat crop...together with oats which we are about to sow, our friends will help us in putting our crops in... .

Although the agricultural census returns, begun in 1847, are almost certainly unreliable – for some districts they show increases in all categories of holding between 1847 and 1851, for other districts there were no returns – they do serve to give an idea of broad trends in farms and population in the famine years. By examining the decline in holdings of less than 15 acres, it is possible to illustrate the nature of the population decline. The greatest losses in small holdings between 1848 and 1851 occurred in the Monaghan corridor and the hills immediately to the south of it, five electoral divisions where almost 500 holdings disappeared, more than half the total decline in the 20 divisions in north Monaghan. The most important conclusion from an examination of the agricultural returns on holdings, however, is not the changes which occurred but the stability and comparatively small declines in holdings in the light of the massive social and demographic upheaval that was taking place.

DECLINE IN HOLDINGS UNDER 15 ACRES 1848-1851

RD	1-5 ACRES		5-15 ACRES		RATIO OF HOLDINGS
	TOTAL	LOSS	TOTAL	LOSS	LOST TO POPULATION
	1848	48-51	1848	48-51	LOSS 1841-51
Monaghan	1403	352	2750	585	1:23
Castleblayney	1029	277	2494	510	1:12
Carrickmacross	1390	410	2881	724	1:12
Clones (incomplete)	632	280	1790	632	1:10

Holdings under 15 acres declined by one quarter, amounting to 3,770 holdings at a time when the rural areas of the county lost 60,000 people. Therefore the massive famine reductions in population bore heaviest on those with no land. The ratios of holdings to population loss show a variable connection. The average household size in Monaghan in 1841 was 5.2 persons. Where the ratio of holdings to population loss is closest to 1:5 one can assume that small holders accounted for significant proportion of the decline. It could also reflect attrition of family members – but it is generally agreed that migration of whole families was more significant during crises like the Famine.

In Monaghan, as in the west of Ireland, the class which was most at risk as the Famine decade progressed was the landless cottier class. This was especially the case following the second potato failure: they were in absolute destitution. Most of the coroners' reports on sudden death at this time relate to landless families who spent the winter begging. This class, therefore, was seriously depopulated by death and emigration. It is impossible to accurately distinguish the effects of either; death rates were certainly very high for the landless class but emigration was also an option in the face of desperate circumstances. Ó Gráda has noted that a very high proportion of the emigrants to the United States were classed as labourers.[28] Unlike the far west of the country, Monaghan's walking distance to the ports of Dundalk and Newry made the trip to Liverpool less daunting. The Shirley emigration records for this period suggest that migrants from south Monaghan passed back and forth to Liverpool fairly regularly.

There had also been traditionally a strong seasonal harvest migration out of Monaghan into the midlands and England. In the 1835 Inquiry, hundreds of labourers were reported to go annually to the English harvest, from Aghnamullen, Clontibret, Tehallen and the parishes of Farney in the south.[29] Not as many appear to have left from the west and north of the county, which had significant numbers of landless labourers. In the 1831 census, for example over one third of all males aged 20 and over in the northern and western parishes of the county were landless labourers. These districts, however, had some of the highest population declines during the Famine period, suggesting that much of this loss was accounted for by high rates of mortality and/or migration among the landless people.

The decline in fourth-class houses, inhabited by the poorest sections of the population, is indicative of the social impact of the Famine. The fourth-class house was virtually eliminated in Monaghan county by 1851. Almost every parish experienced reductions of more than 70% in this house type. In the parishes of Drumsnat, Kilmore, Donagh, Aghnamullen, Tullycorbet, and Muckno where there over 80 per cent declines, nearly all the house losses between 1841 and 1851 were accounted for by the fourth class. In Iniskeen and Killanny in the south of the county the other house classes increased in numbers in the face of huge losses in the poorest house category. While it is possible that some of these changes are attributable to some houses being reclassified in the 1851 census, the elimination of the fourth class category reflects the reduction in the landless labourer class particularly.

It is likely, however, that many of the poorest classes in the western parishes of Ematris, Aghabog and Drumully, which experienced some of the heaviest population declines in the 1840s, lived in third-class houses either due to their being differently classified in the census or to fact that their houses were marginally better in quality. Table 3 shows the changes in the house numbers in townlands in Ematris parish which were most densely populated in 1841. It shows the catastrophic reduction in houses which occurred in this region after the Famine and, by implication, the character of changes in much of rural Monaghan.

CHANGES IN HOUSE NUMBERS IN EMATRIS PARISH

TOWNLAND	OS (1835)	1841	1851	GRIFFITH'S VALUATION (1858)
Drumgole	20	23	14	11(2)*
Drumcall	14	27	18	12
Cornawall	20	21	9	8
Cordressigo	8-10	16	8	5
Dundrannan	13-14	16	8	5

Crosslea	7-9	12	8	4(1)
Dernamoyle	28-32	49	21	12(3)
Annaghybane	17-18	18	9	8
Derrylossett	15	16	8	4(2)
Kinduff	20-26	29	19	12
Derrykinard	16	17	8	5
Drumintin	24	22	7	4
Corranewy	21-25	25	14	13
Corragarry	18	20	11	10
Drumlona	12	11	4	4
Aghadrumkeen	15-17	22	9	5
Claraghy	13-16	19	6	6
Drumulla	23-27	34	7	5(1)
Lislynchahan	12	14	6	4
TOTAL	316-345	411	194	145(10)

(*houses in brackets were landless in 1858)

(Source: Ordnance Survey maps, census of Ireland 1851, Griffith's Valuation)

Figures are given for houses as they seemed to appear in the first edition of the six-inch Ordnance Survey (1835). These are unreliable estimates as it is impossible to distinguish between dwellings and outhouses on the map. Where there are small groups of buildings, a range from the lowest to the highest number of projected houses is given. By using the information on houses and holdings in Griffith's Valuation, farmhouses and landless houses in 1858 can be fairly certainly identified for 1835; the 1835 estimates can also be checked against the Tithe Applotment Books. Thus in Dernamoyle townland, at least ten farmhouses can be identified on the six-inch map. There were also three landless houses in Griffith's Valuation, which were in Dernamoyle in 1835. The vast majority of the remaining houses in 1835 (from 14-18) were probably landless houses. Table 3 shows a 20-30 per cent increase in houses in the area in the six years between 1835 and 1841 between the lowest and the highest house count for 1835. There were 411 houses in the 19 townlands in 1841 and 194 in 1851- a decline of 53 per cent. There was a further reduction of a quarter between 1851 and 1858, so that in less than 20 years this small area in west Monaghan had undergone a radical transformation in population and settlement.

The significant aspect of the Ematris parish data appears to be that the overwhelming majority of the houses in 1841 were cottier houses. In Griffith's Valuation there were only six instances of holdings comprising more than one allotment, suggesting that farms had been divided very little in the preceding two decades. Thus farms and farmhouses maintained a considerable degree of stability since 1841. It is possible to pick out the farmhouses on the six-inch map by reference to the later valuation map. From the valuation it appears there were only ten landless houses in 1858. There was, for example, one left in the townland of Drumulla – the huge decline in this townland from 34 to seven houses between 1841 and 1851 consisted mainly of cottiers' houses on the outskirts of the village of Rockcorry. Overall in this parish, the 53 per cent reduction in houses in the high density townlands – compared with 33 per cent for the whole parish – and the continuity in farms apparent in Griffith's Valuation, suggest that the vast majority of houses which disappeared were cottier dwellings.

The Ordnance Survey Memoirs for Ematris parish described the type of dwellings occupied by the poorest people in 1835:

> The mud houses, divided into three apartments, seldom exceed 1 storey high, furnished occasionally with small glass windows, but often without them, an earthen floor with no ceiling and universally thatched with straw. One extremity appropriated as a bedroom for the family, the opposite end for the cattle and the centre a kitchen and dining room for the whole household. Comfort and cleanliness little observed... Nothing can surpass the filth and dirtiness of these cabins and the enclosures around them... Families are numerous and the children swarm around the cabins.[30]

The huge house numbers and pre-famine population density in these western parts of the county – and their catastrophic collapse – were connected to the rise and fall of the linen industry in the county. This was one of the strongest flax-growing areas in Monaghan, with soil that was deep and damp. In 1835, the ruins of extensive bleachfields around the district were still in evidence. Before the decline in the industry, 'spinning wheels and looms occupied a large space in every dwelling and produced by their activity and occupation not only the full amount of the yearly rent of the holding but a considerable surplus of income...'.[31]

The fate of many of the weakest landless people is captured in the inquest on Mary Ann McDermott of Killeevan in March 1847. Her daughter aged 11 testified that her mother (who charged her children never to go to the 'poorhouse')...

had no mode of living but by begging... During the past fortnight deceased had no food whatever for herself and two children save a little gruel at night, the meal to make which she collected during the day, save the past two days on which they got a quart of broth each day at Ballinure soup kitchen... While returning from Clones on Friday deceased took suddenly ill near the house of Barney Greenan.... [Doctor Hurst] found in the stomach some greens of a coarse or bad kind; in the bowels a quantity of raw turnips, probably the rind of the turnips... .[32]

The distressed world of a Monaghan cottier is described in the inquest on Patt Murphy from the parish of Clontibret in February 1847. He had little except for

some money saved at harvest work in Co Dublin and the price of a pig sold about a month ago...the bed clothes of deceased was an old single blanket and when the weather was wet the rain fell on them when lying in bed... Often their diet was boiled turnips with meal and water... there were two days in which they had one meal of food...when there was much down-rain deceased would lie on some straw on the floor. Witness [his daughter] lay on a little straw but had no bedclothes'.[33]

Coroners' reports only occurred in cases of sudden or unusual death; during the Famine there was little that was unusual about the large numbers of deaths which were occurring from starvation and fever – or destitution as it was generally officially called. In Magheracloone in March 1847, a local curate insisted on having an inquest on the death of a cottier, whose family had been living at the back of a ditch, and he gave evidence that 'many persons have met with sudden deaths in this parish which he believes to have originated in want and destitution; the number of deaths in this parish average at present between seven and eight each day'.[34] The incidental evidence given in this inquest suggests that the deaths of many of these completely destitute people were occurring almost unnoticed by the more fortunate inhabitants. Some days earlier the dead man and his family had been 'obliged to move from where they at the time were stopping which was not a house but the shelter of a ditch'; he had been seen taking one of his ill daughters to the fever hospital; was refused admission to the workhouse. The dead man lay uncovered in an open field; a short distance away sat his wife and child 'exposed to the inclemency of the weather'. Witnesses in the field said that the family had been exposed like this for three days and nights.

VI

The profile of population decline in the barony of Farney is clearly reflective of contrasting living conditions and estate policies in the region. The Bath estate appears to have adopted comparatively stringent controls on leases as it entered the nineteenth century[35] and although it contained as crowded a countryside as the Shirley estate, it did not appear to have the latter's cottier problem. When the rates were charged on the Union of Carrickmacross in the later of 1840s, there was considerable opposition from the tenants on the Bath estate, who resented having to support what were perceived to be the Shirley paupers.[36] Shirley's estate contained over 18,000 people in 1841, about 16 per cent of them cottiers. As early as May 1838, when the Poor Law was being introduced, a letter from Lord Lismore mentioned Shirley's anxiety about his huge number of poor tenants and his proposal to set up a 'sinking fund' to buy out and provide for the useless tenantry.[37] Nothing of the sort happened, however, until Trench was appointed in 1843 when he embarked on a policy of restricting any further subdivision of the holdings of the estate. Laurence Levins was a cottier who felt the effects of the new approach. In March 1845 he was looking for permission to settle somewhere: 'is now cast on the benevolence of the world without a cabin to shelter him, his cousin George with your honour's permission offers him a spot to build on...humbly hopes that your honour will take his distressed state into consideration and generously please to grant permission.'

However, Trench's principal policy, which had significant implications for the population of the estate in the 1840s and later, was his policy of assisted emigration. He proposed to pay the passages of the poorest tenants to America and so reduce the burden on the estate. In July 1843, for example, Francis Segreff pleaded that he was a 'cottier these many years behaved honestly and quickly for which Mr Mitchell promised him a cut away bog in Bocks adjoining the road to build a small house on it for shelter for himself and helpless family...hoping your humanity will be good and kind enough to give him the same liberty'. The request was refused by Trench, but an offer of assistance to America was made. Between 1843 and the end of the Famine the estate directly assisted more than 1,500 to emigrate. Although this was a controversial undertaking in Ireland generally, it was obviously supported by the landed establishment. Their local newspaper in Monaghan, *The Northern Standard*, was greatly in favour of it, commenting on 27 March 1847 that 'emigration is the great safety valve...If we have a population that we cannot feed it is in our interests to provide them with means to go to those countries where there is a field for their exertions'.

Shirley's emigrants were given passage money and in many cases were provisioned and outfitted for the journey.[38] It is likely that many more were indirectly assisted by having their rent arrears written off on surrendering their holdings and destroying their cabins. Shirley's emigration, therefore, preceded the Famine by some years, but it intensified at the peak of the crisis. During the years 1847 and 1849 hundreds were assisted off the estate, including about 150 who were sent to South Australia in 1849. Although there is evidence in the petitions to the estate of a growing keenness on the part of the tenantry to go, many were also reluctant to leave, much to the annoyance of the agent. During the Famine years, the urgency of the crisis changed the emphasis from cajolement to outright eviction and the *Nation* newspaper reported on September 1849 that Shirley had 'served notice of his intention to execute 245 evictions, and the Guardians of Carrickmacross Union are already making preparations for the accommodation of Mr Shirley's 1225 paupers'.[39] No doubt most of the 1700 paupers in Carrick workhouse in 1851, treble the number in the other county workhouses, belonged to the Shirley estate.

Although a great many were assisted to emigrate, many more went without receiving assistance. The essential difference between those who were helped to go and those who went independently is that the subsidy assisted those tenants who were 'broken down' in the words of Trench in 1843, tenants who would have had no resources to emigrate. Altogether, the population on Shirley's estate fell by over 8,000 between 1841 and 1851; approximately 18 per cent of this decline, therefore, is attributable to the emigration subsidy. It is likely that the repercussions of the estate's assistance went far beyond the actual number who left, however. The assisted emigrants represented the creation of a pool of overseas contacts who almost certainly contributed to the establishment of chain migration from these districts. There is, therefore, little doubt that the extensive decline in population which distinguished the Shirley estate from the Bath estate in the 1840s was largely attributable to the effects of the subsidised emigration scheme. In this context, it is significant that in the following decade, when Trench was appointed to the Bath estate and assisted even more emigrants from this area, the rate of population loss here was more than treble that in the Shirley districts.

VII

The experience of the Famine in Monaghan and south Ulster had more in common with the north-west of Ireland than it had with much of the rest of Ulster. Yet in spite of the loss of 60,000 from the county's population in a few years – more than the population decline in the province of Munster, Ulster or Connacht in the 1950s – like the rest of Ireland, it has left no trace in the collective memory. Even in the 1938 Irish Folklore Commission's schools' survey, less than a century after the Famine, there were only sporadic references to its impact and many of these were simply stories and images that had been filtered through national media.[40] These included references to part of the Shercock-Castleblayney road being built in 1846 by poorer farmers who had to provide their own wheelbarrows. There were references to 'porridge houses' for the distribution of oat-meal porridge in Aghnamullen parish, as well as other houses for the distribution of 'government broth'.[41] On 'Porridge Hill' in Tedavnet parish, Williamson's house provided gruel every second day for the starving poor;[42] 'Stirabout house' was referred to in Magheross. There were many more such sites and places associated with famine landscapes – relief works, relief houses, outbuildings and sheds of the workhouses, graves perhaps – which were part of the traumatic upheaval that marked those years in Monaghan and which have long been forgotten in an exercise of almost universal amnesia. However, an examination of the nature of the population and social catastrophe that was the Famine shows that the very class which was most affected were the people who had least in terms either of material goods or social value – or 'respectability' in Victorian terms. These were the cottiers and landless people, the 'broken down' and 'useless' tenantry on the Shirley estate, the paupers who were 'shovelled out' under emigration schemes. They were certainly rejected by the establishment which saw their disappearance as a benefit; their travails went largely unnoticed by the rest of the community. They lived in cabins of no value, which were destroyed when their owners left – the fourth-class houses of the census, which have left no traces but melted quickly back into the landscape. Like the travellers on the roadside today perhaps, who are unknown to most of the settled community, the impoverished victims of the Famine who died on the roadsides and tramped to the emigration ships disappeared quickly like ghosts from the landscape of memory.

DISTRESS IN THE COUNTRY—BARONIAL SESSIONS.

COUNTY OF TYRONE.

LOWER STRABANE.—On Saturday, sessions were held in the court-house of Strabane. Major Humphrey was called to the chair.

A resolution to the effect that twenty thousand pounds be levied off the barony, to be expended in public works, was passed. A presentment for thirty thousand pounds for a ship canal from Strabane to the Foyle was also passed, with this condition, that the responsibiliy of repayment of the sum be undertaken by the Marquis of Abercorn, and made a rentcharge on his estate, and that no part of it be levied off the cesspayers.

The Chairman, on the part of the noble marquis, having declared himself satisfied with the presentment, it passed unanimously, amidst great cheering.

The Rev. Wm. Knox then submitted a presentment for a sum not exceeding forty thousand pounds for the earthwork, masonry, &c., of that portion of the Londonderry and Enniskillen Railway, which passed through Lower Strabane, which was carried, after which the court adjourned till Tuesday, when it reassembled, and, after much conversation and discussion, rescinded its vote of the previous Friday with regard to presentments for drainage—at least, suspended it in the meantime—and proceeded to present for roads in various divisions of the half barony, but postponed presenting any for the Strabane division until Friday, to which day the court adjourned.

ENNISHOWEN WEST.—The sessions for this barony were held on Friday, D. Todd, Esq., J.P., presiding, when the sum of £15,000 was passed for public works. Rev. Mr. Devlin suggested that a subscription should be commenced for the relief of cases of extreme distress, and said he was authorised to state that his bishop, Dr. Maginn, was prepared to subscribe £5. The proposition was agreed to.

UPPER HALF BARONY OF STRABANE.—An extraordinary presentment sessions for this upper half barony, was held at Gortin, on Friday. The chair was filled by A. W. Cole Hamilton, Esq. As there were no accurate accounts of the amount of destitution to be provided for, it was resolved to vote the sum of six thousand pounds, to meet the present exigency, on the understanding that when this was expended more would be applied for.

WEST OMAGH.—At those sessions on Monday, on the motion of Sir R. A. Ferguson, Bart., M.P., the sum of seven thousand pounds was presented for, to give employment to the poor.

THE FAMINE
IN
COUNTY TYRONE

JIM GRANT

I

Statistical records indicate that Tyrone was among those Irish counties least affected by the Great Famine. The partial failure of the potato in 1845 seems to have had no serious effect in the county; for example, no local efforts were made, in the form of Famine relief committees, to avail of special government assistance. However, the total failure of the 1846 potato crop produced quite different reactions. From early October, local relief committees began to form in response to local needs, though the bulk of the 28 committees in correspondence with Dublin Castle did not begin to operate until November or December.[1] From October, too, calls were made in various localities for the adoption of the government's principal relief measure, the public works scheme. The use of the scheme, however, was comparatively slight, with only four counties in Ireland recording fewer numbers employed than Tyrone. Yet, an estimated 11,500 people in the county were sustained by public works from mid-November 1846 until the end of March 1847.[2]

The abundant statistics for the use of the Temporary Relief Act, which replaced public works in April 1847 with (mostly) free issues of food, show Tyrone as a whole avoiding extreme destitution. The worst-affected areas, on the basis of those statistics, were Omagh and Clogher Poor Law Unions, each of which had nearly 21 per cent of its population in receipt of food. Yet, in a 'distress' table of all 130 Poor Law unions in Ireland, Omagh and Clogher were well down the list, in 75th and 76th places respectively. Strabane Poor Law Union had over 18 per cent of its population receiving food during the same period, placing it, with Omagh and Clogher, above the Ulster average which was 17.5 per cent; Castlederg had just over 16 per cent, Dungannon and Cookstown around 11 per cent and, lastly, Gortin, with just over nine per cent.[3]

Like workhouses all over the country, those serving the Co. Tyrone unions were inundated by applicants from mid-October 1846 onwards, a clear sign of the social collapse of the labourers and small farmers. Many contemporaries, like Rev. James Disney of Charlemont in Co. Armagh, remarked on the extraordinary resistance to the workhouse among the poor. Rev. Disney saw recourse to the workhouse as 'no small evidence ... of the destitution which exists, as the most unreasonable reluctance prevails ... to taking shelter in the poor-houses'.[4] None of the Tyrone unions was exempt from the stresses of overcrowding, disease and the extraordinary expenses of the Famine period.

Finally, population decrease between 1841 and 1851 can be used as a rough guide to the disruptive effect of the Famine. The average for the nine counties of Ulster was 17.33 per cent. The heaviest losses, between 25 and 30 per cent, were in counties Monaghan, Cavan, and Fermanagh. Tyrone showed a loss of 18.26 per cent, the only other Ulster county above the provincial average.[5]

While most of the 'broad indicators' show Co. Tyrone as coping with the Famine better than most counties in Ireland, this is not to say that many local communities were not affected at one time or another by serious dislocation and suffering. A look behind the generalisations will show this.

II

An analysis of the financial outlay on public works in Co. Tyrone shows that the most substantial sums were expended in Upper Strabane barony (centred on Gortin); £7,771 was laid out on 76 roadworks, of which 19 were new and the remainder improvements. In East Omagh (a long narrow barony running north-east to south-west from Carrickmore, through Omagh to Dromore and Trillick), £4,323 was spent on 93 roadworks, all but 28 of them improvements. Lower Strabane (stretching from Dunnamanagh

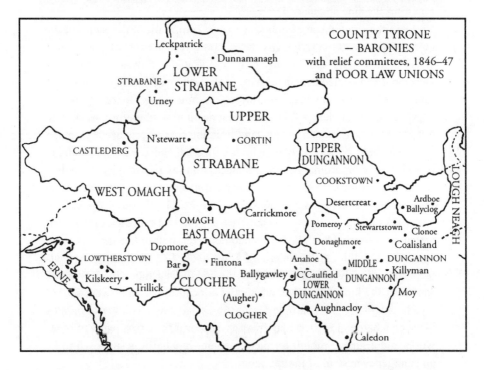

through Strabane to Newtownstewart) was allocated just under £2,500 for 30 road improvements, six new road sections and one stone-breaking scheme. The three recognised sub-divisions of the large barony which occupied the east of the county, namely, Upper, Middle and Lower Dungannon, were each allocated about £2,000. The smallest expenditures were in West Omagh (the area south and west of Castlederg) and Clogher (centred on the cathedral town), where roadworks numbered 45 and 20 respectively.[6]

A few examples from the barony of East Omagh show how far presentment monies would go. Of £218 levied in Beragh division, £142 was earmarked 'to form, level, drain and make 700 perches of a new line of road from Beragh to Balligawley, in the townlands of Clogherney and Redargan ...; £16 to repair 59 perches of road in the townlands of Coolesker and Beragh'. In Dromore division, £35 was set aside 'to cut down two hills and fill two hollows on the road from Dromore to Ederney' and £50 'for repairing the side streets of Dromore'.[7]

Even the limited use of public works in Tyrone illustrates some of the common problems in this heavily bureaucratic system of relief. While most works in the county seem to have progressed satisfactorily, a report in mid-December 1846 noted that, in the barony of East Omagh, while an additional number of gangs had been employed, in some parts Board of Works' approval had been delayed. Despite great destitution, therefore, works had not yet started.[8] A meeting of the landlords and cess-payers of East Omagh had been held on 13 October which called on the Lord Lieutenant to proclaim an extraordinary presentment session (as required by the public works legislation). This session was held at Omagh courthouse on 26 October and voted nearly £5,000 for road works. The Board of Works took five weeks to make its report to the Treasury on the first batch of works of which there were 44 in all. It was another week before the first Treasury sanction came through, accounting for just under £2,000. Smaller amounts were subsequently sanctioned around the end of December, but it was late January 1847 before the next substantial allocation was approved, £1,700 on 38 roadworks. This example demonstrates that it took nearly two months between a baronial request and Treasury approval for a first batch of relief works and a further month for the remainder in what was supposed to be an emergency system of famine relief.[9]

A more common complaint was that works provided were insufficient. In Upper Strabane barony, for example, it was reported that while almost all the destitute poor who applied for work had got it – about 1,200 were employed – 'Some of the amounts presented for these works (especially in the parish of Cappagh) ... are nearly all expended, making new presentments a necessity'.[10] Clogher Relief Committee, which took seriously its duty under the scheme of providing lists of destitute for employment, had enrolled

500 labourers by early January 1847, 'Notwithstanding that they (had) rejected a vast number of applicants'. The committee further believed that numbers would certainly rise each subsequent week, more rapidly than they could be employed.[11] Nearby Fintona had similar problems, exacerbated by the late start of the works. Charles Eccles, the chairman, wrote in late February, 'Our list of destitute labourers contains upwards of 700 names, but only about 160 are employed'. This occurred in a large area with a population of 12,000, 'of whom at least one third have not a single day's provision in reserve' and this at a time when 'fever, dysentery and diarrhoea are prevailing to an alarming extent among the poor'.[12] At about the same time, employment on public works around Omagh was gradually falling off, which 'heightened ... the gloomy prospect' for the poor in a union whose workhouse, designed for 800 paupers, contained 1,200. Most of the excess numbers were 'so hurriedly admitted that they (were) not as yet provided with clothing of any kind except their own rags'.[13]

Yet another problem was insufficiency of wages on the works. This was due to two principal factors; first, government policy which required wages to be 2d. a day less than the local rate (in order not to draw labourers from farm work) and, secondly, the steep increase in the cost of food of all kinds. Clogher Relief Committee had to support labourers on the works who had large families by supplying them with cut-price meals: half of the 500 employed required such help.[14] Similarly, Urney Relief Committee provided food tickets every Saturday to such labourers. It was a practice which officialdom disapproved of strongly enough to threaten to withhold grant-aid from the committee's fund.[15] The Board of Works inspecting officer for Tyrone, Capt. Oldershaw, reported visiting a quarry near Strabane where the labourers complained that the stone that they were required to break was so hard that they could not earn a moderate day's wages at the prices fixed. Oldershaw agreed that the stone was 'uncommonly hard' and he asked the engineer to allow the men something extra.[16] Similar problems were reported to Oldershaw's colleague, Lt. Colomb, by the inspectors of drainage: 'in harsh and stony ground or where large stones frequently occur in the line of a drain, it is impossible for the men to earn enough for the support of their families at the rate of 4d. per perch'.[17]

One of the most serious problems with the public works system – and often a source of great delay – was disagreement among landlords as to what action should be taken to relieve distress. Many landlords were worried about some aspects of the public works scheme, especially government's insistence that the work be unproductive, that is, undertaken purely as relief work or as a test of destitution for those employed. Another landlord anxiety was the compulsory character of the extraordinary presentment session which followed the Lord Lieutenant's proclamation of a distressed area. The danger was that such sessions could be intimidated by large crowds – mobs – which had happened already at a few sessions in counties Cavan and Monaghan.[18]

Extraordinary presentment sessions in Tyrone, while generally restrained, did not escape the excitement which characterised such meetings all over the country. They were invariably well-attended. At Clogher, on 12 October 1846, within a few minutes of the doors opening, 'the galleries were filled to suffocation ... but the people well-behaved'.[19] At Gortin (Upper Strabane barony, 16 October), the attendance was 'most numerous ... the room crowded to excess ... '. Similarly, on the following day at Strabane (Lower Strabane), 'The attendance of the rate-payers, and of the labouring classes was very numerous, the galleries and the body of the court being densely crowded'. These scenes were repeated at Castlederg a few days later, where 'The court was crowded to suffocation'.[20] An exception was the Lower Dungannon sessions at Aughnacloy on 4 November, where 'The attendance of magistrates and gentlemen was very thin'. With only one magistrate present and the proceedings were delayed for an hour but, with the help of the cess-payers, the business of the meeting was done.[21]

The Clogher session illustrates the volatility of an expectant crowd, despite their good behaviour, especially in an atmosphere in which 'Considerable anxiety was manifested (among the rate-payers) ... regarding the nature and results of the approaching proceedings'. At first there was quick agreement that the barony should opt for drainage works, but a roll-call of electoral divisions represented showed that more than half of them wanted some road works as well as drainage. An adjournment was agreed upon, when:

> The Rev. Mr. McDuogh, P.P., wished to know what the starving poor were to do in the interim before the public works were commenced. The people were starving in that town, in Augher, and throughout various parts of the country, and many of them were living solely on cabbages. (Cheers from the galleries.)

The meeting adjourned 'amidst considerable cheering from the galleries, and shouts of "relief for Ireland" – "no adjournment," etc.'.[22]

The session held at Cookstown on 2 November for the barony of Upper Dungannon was quite uncontrolled. Despite unfavourable weather, a 'vast multitude' had assembled outside and made 'an immense rush' into the courtroom when the doors were opened. The crowd cheered the chairman, Col. Stuart of Killymoon, when he announced that one of their objectives – echoed at several Tyrone sessions – would be 'to bring the work as near as possible to every poor man's door ...'. They quickly became impatient with discussions among magistrates, at one point 'shouting that they wanted some person to speak for them as otherwise their wants and wishes would not be fairly represented'. Their wrath was provoked a short time later by a cess-payer from Drumaney who suggested that there was not much destitution in his part of the county: 'The crowd immediately caught hold of this observation ... ' and disrupted the proceedings 'for a considerable period'. A spokesman for the Belfast, Dublin and Coleraine Junction Railway had hardly begun to speak when 'he was assailed by the most unearthly cries from the multitude, who kept up a continual shouting of "no more jobs", etc.'. Finally, when Col. Stuart brought the meeting to a close and asked everyone to disperse quietly, 'the crowd refused to comply ... and several of them said that they would keep the magistrates in for a week (there being no passage to the door except over the heads of the crowd) if they would not do something for them'. Several members of the session forced their way successfully through the crowd, but one gentleman, having been 'rudely pushed on the stairs', called on a policeman to make an arrest. 'This was the signal for an almost universal riot', which the local press condemned as 'a scene of insanity' caused by 'a love of licentious riot' on the part of those – 'principally of the labouring classes and the uninformed and less intelligent portion of the population ... utterly destitute of every feeing of propriety' – for whose benefit the sessions was being held.[23] Fortunately, this sessions appears to have been an exception.

Arrangements for the barony of Middle Dungannon provide a good illustration of landlord disagreement. The proprietors had had a series of discussions about whether to ask the Lord Lieutenant for an extraordinary session. At their final meeting, in late October 1846, Lord Northland, on behalf of himself and his father Lord Ranfurly (they were the proprietors, *inter alia,* of the town of Dungannon) objected to an extraordinary session (that is, to the use of public works) and proposed instead 'to take charge of,

and secure from want and privation, the poor on his estate both tenantry
and cottier so that no man living on the property, in the town or on the
estate, shall know want'. He further proposed, on behalf of his father, a
private subscription of £5 per week as a fund to be distributed among the
poorer classes 'of all sects and parties who may be in destitution in the
town of Dungannon, irrelevant of our own householders or tenantry'. One
condition was that the fund should be administered by his agent with the
leading clergymen of the three main denominations. Northland called on
the other landlords to take similar action but, instead, they prevailed on
him to withdraw his objection to public works.[24] A few days later,
extraordinary sessions were announced for Upper Dungannon at Cookstown
(2 November), Middle Dungannon at Dungannon (same date) and Lower
Dungannon at Aughnacloy (4 November).[25]

Interestingly, all of the works decided upon in Upper and Middle
Dungannon and two thirds of those for Lower Dungannon were reproductive
drainage works.[26] Reproductive public works were a significant concession
forced from government by a sustained campaign supported by influential
Irish landlords of every party. The central argument of this movement was
that, since by compulsory sessions they were obliged to pay out money,
they ought to be allowed to do so to the benefit of the land. The concession,
communicated in a letter of Henry Labouchere, Chief Secretary for Ireland,
on 5 October 1846, was, in the words of a well-informed contemporary, 'so
guarded as to be not clearly intelligible'. As a result, in Ireland as a whole,
only five per cent of the monies expended on the public works scheme
were for 'Labouchere drainage' as it was commonly called. The principal
requirement was that each individual proprietor using the concession had
to give a written undertaking that funds expended should be 'a charge
exclusively on the lands ... to be improved'. This written undertaking
probably deterred many landlords, eager for easy access to public funds.
Another deterrent was the unanimity required in practice to make public
arrangements for drainage worthwhile.[27] In such a context, the landlords
of Dungannon barony displayed considerable persistence and unanimity,
the latter a rare commodity among landlords when money was involved.
However, arrangements 'under Labouchere's letter', while good for the
land, were not good for destitute labourers and small farmers, for
'Labouchere' arrangements were notoriously slower than ordinary public
works. As a member of the Lower Strabane sessions warned, 'the carrying

out of the drainage plan solely would not give immediate employment to the people... Cries of "it will, it will."' [28] Landlords were always cautious about laying out money, particularly when they were unsure of the outcome. The words of Henry Corry, M.P., to his agent Daniel Auchinleck, on his realisation of the extent of the 1846 potato failure, are very typical:

> There is no share of reasonable responsibility which I ... am not prepared to undertake. Come what will, the people must not be allowed to starve if we can help it, but unhappily the same visitation which inflicts the disease, deprives us in a great measure of the means of meeting it.[29]

There appears to have been an almost universal desire among the members of extraordinary presentment sessions in Co. Tyrone to engage in 'Labouchere drainage'. In two instances they failed to do so, Clogher and West Omagh. There was a serious lack of agreement in Clogher and in West Omagh, the session seems to have taken the advice of the influential Sir R.A. Ferguson, MP, and opted for road works, 'as unfortunately the barony required them'.[30]

The conduct of the public works in Co. Tyrone gave constant satisfaction to the Board of Works officers who supervised them. The principal inspecting officer, Capt. Oldershaw, routinely reported, between mid-November 1846 and the end of February 1847, 'The works in general are going on satisfactorily. The country is quiet, and the people orderly and well-behaved'. He appreciated that such good order was maintained in spite of great difficulties, 'There are a great many destitute poor in the county, yet no instance of misconduct has occurred', a view corroborated by his colleague Lt. Colomb, 'The county, although in a great state of destitution, is perfectly quiet'.[31] Oldershaw was complimentary about the attitude to work of the labourers: ' ... the people work very well and very hard and the gangers chosen from among them are in general very attentive'. He was also effusive about the relief committees (in their statutory role of providing properly scrutinised lists of destitute applicants for employment) 'The committees have been indefatigable in their duties in the rural districts and have given great satisfaction ... (They) are very active and transact their business promptly and efficiently ... (and) impartially ...'. They were 'zealous and, I believe, disinterested in the discharge .of their duties'.[32] Oldershaw was the only county inspecting officer in Ulster who was so complimentary to local committees.

This officer's journal gives several glimpses of the severe weather of that winter of 1846-7, a reminder that, in addition to the trauma of total potato failure, the people had to contend with 'the only natural (winter) we have had in years', as a contemporary expressed it.[33] In late November, Oldershaw reported from the neighbourhood of Omagh: ' ... the snow falling thick and the wind blowing strong at daylight, the gangs ... knocked off work, but upon being encouraged, they set to again with very goodwill'. Two weeks later, he noted 'The snow ... falling and now upwards of six inches deep and in many places much more'. In January, heavy rain 'caused many of the new embankments raised as fences to slip before they could be covered with sods', and in early February, heavy snow and 'continued frost' interrupted both farming and drainage work.[34]

There is a further aspect of public works activity in Co. Tyrone which is worth noting, if for no other reason than its curiosity value. In general, the works undertaken in Tyrone were entirely typical of the scheme in the country at large; that is, they were predominantly road improvement works – 183 of them – with 94 new sections. Tyrone was atypical in the extent of 'Labouchere drainage' works, 43 in all, which accounted for the exceptionally high proportion of 27.8 per cent of public works funding in the county.[35] In addition to roadworks and drainage, there were two serious attempts, both by the extraordinary session for Lower Strabane barony, to secure canal and railway undertakings as public works. The session proposed a £30,000 outlay on a ship canal from Strabane to the Foyle on condition that the landlord, the Marquess of Abercorn, should take responsibility for the sum, making it a rent charge on the estate and no part of it to be levied off the county cess. These stipulations appeared to fit the 'Labouchere' conditions perfectly. A maximum of £40,000 was presented for the 'earthwork, masonry, etc. of that portion of the Londonderry and Enniskillen Railway' which passed through the barony.[36]

Of the two projects, only the railway one was seriously pursued. It was supported by a joint petition to the Prime Minister, Lord John Russell, from the Londonderry and Enniskillen, and Londonderry and Coleraine, railway companies. The petition argued that railway construction would prevent many labourers from being thrown on the public works. It also highlighted the benefits of each line, the case for the Enniskillen line being by far the more convincing. The petition further suggested that railway construction would provide 'an immense extent of country' (the greater parts of Tyrone, Fermanagh and Donegal) with easy access to Derry, ' their

accustomed port for communication with England and Scotland'. Such a
link would stimulate labour in the whole area. A similar attempt was made
at the sessions for Upper Dungannon on behalf of the Dublin, Belfast and
Coleraine Junction Railway.[37] Following 'careful consideration',
government decided that loans to railway companies were not the way to
relieve 'distress arising from the scarcity of food', which was a way of
signalling that it was not sympathetic to private companies joining forces
with baronial sessions to make use of public funds.[38]

III

Following the total failure of the 1846 potato crop, numerous relief
committees began to form, a sure sign that the leadership of local
communities perceived a need for extraordinary help to those most reliant
on the potato as their staple food. As the chairman of Clogher Relief
Committee wrote, in October 1846, ' ... the farms in this neighbourhood
are generally very small, and the persons holding them have with their
families depended almost entirely on potatoes for their food'.[39]

However, the formation of relief committees did not depend exclusively
on local leadership. Because of previous famines, the mechanism of
government-supported local effort was well established and had already
been activated in 1845. Early in October 1846 all county lieutenants were
requested by the government's relief commission in Dublin (administered,
in practice,by the Commissary General for Ireland, Sir Randolph Routh)
to divide their counties into relief districts and nominate local committees.
The county lieutenant for Tyrone, the Earl of Charlemont, nominated 24
committees in a series of appointments at the end of October. With the
exception of five, for which the records do not survive, the committees, in
order of Charlemont's appointment were: Cookstown, Gortin, Omagh,
Castlederg; Trillick, Stewartstown, Fivemiletown, Fintona, Newtownstewart
(at this point, 28 October, Charlemont noted he had then appointed 14
committees), Caledon, Moy, Aughnacloy, Dungannon, Pomeroy, Augher,
Camus, Urney, Dunnamanagh and Leckpatrick.[40]

However, using the correspondence of local committees as a guide, it is
possible to establish the following approximate chronology of their
operation. Aughnacloy and Clogher committees appear to have been the

first into action, around mid-October, certainly a fortnight before
Aughnacloy was formally appointed. In early November, Fintona,
Ballygawley, Dungannon, Moy, Carrickmore, Dromore, Leckpatrick and
Urney were functioning, followed by Omagh, Dunnamanagh and
Newtownstewart. During December, Trillick, Stewartstown, Desertcreat,
Anahoe, Ardboe and Coalisland began operating. Caledon and Pomeroy
followed early in the new year. Apart from the fact of their appointment,
there was no further correspondence between Augher, Fivemiletown and
Cookstown committees and the Relief Commission, though it seems that
Augher and Clogher were one and the same.[41]

If the foregoing suggests a degree of confusion in the appointment and
operation of local relief committees, it is only reflecting reality. While there
was a considerable degree of uniformity of response – due largely to the
government's *Instructions* for the formation and guidance of local
committees published on 8 October 1846 – in practice there was considerable
confusion and duplication of activity.[42] A letter from the rector of Desertcreat
parish, in which he appealed unsuccessfully for government grant-aid, gave
a good picture of such confusion which derived, in his view, from the fact
that landlords' properties were spread over various parishes. The result
was that

> ...in the beginning of the distress there was no one concerted plan of relief,
> nor any regularly constituted relief committee. That which meets in
> Cookstown is for the whole petty sessions district including the greater
> part of this and three or four other parishes. It confines its labours to
> selecting names for the Public Works. Various local subscriptions have
> been raised and partly expended in different parts of this parish. Some of
> these are on particular estates, only parts of which, in some instances, are
> in the parish or district. These several funds are generally managed by
> local committees. In one case, a soup kitchen has been in operation for the
> benefit of the neighbourhood; another is just about to be opened. In two or
> three instances meal has been given weekly to the poorest gratuitously and
> at half price to those who have any means of paying. So much has been
> hitherto done in these ways and in employing the people in private and
> public works that no application has yet been made to government for
> assistance. ... I am aware that the rules laid down for such applications
> have not been hitherto complied with, but perhaps, where so much has
> been done independently, some latitude may be allowed in seeking for
> public aid now that it is becoming necessary.[43]

It is evident from this letter that several independent committees were operating in the district ('Various local subscriptions have been raised'), none of them 'regularly constituted' by the lieutenant of the county and so ineligible for grant-aid. The exception was Cookstown whose committee, appointed by Lord Charlemont on 26 October 1846, covered the petty sessions district, but whose activities were limited 'to selecting names for the Public Works'. This would suggest that the Cookstown committee did not raise a relief fund, an omission which was not only not in keeping with government's *Instructions* but also very unusual. That they did not establish a fund is supported by the absence from the records of any application from the committee for government grant-aid. The implication is that the Cookstown committee was not prepared to extend relief beyond those destitute labourers whom it nominated for employment on public works, unless the others could have recourse to the 'several funds' in the district. The fact that 'there was no one concerted plan of relief' and that some subscriptions were raised and expended 'on particular estates' suggests that the outlook of the landed interest, the leaders of society, did not extend beyond their own estates, an attitude that was not confined to the Famine period. In a mixture of altruism and desire for control, they regarded the destitute on their estates as their own problem. To bring government into the situation was, for many, an invitation to subsequent taxation to which there might be no limits. So, like Rev. J. R. Moore, Earl Annesley's trustee at Castlewellan, they were anxious to 'prevent the poor falling into the hands of government.[44]

Another illustration of local confusion is provided by the case of the parish committee of the perpetual curacy of Moy, caught between the Moy and Dungannon relief districts. On one hand, the curate, Rev. John Leach, was treasurer of Moy committee. Moy did not establish a soup kitchen, but the curate established one with a small parochial fund which was 'of much advantage to the neighbourhood'. It distributed 'about 90 quarts gratuitously each day of the week, Sunday excepted'. Yet his request for grant-aid to his fund was rejected. On the other hand, part of the curacy lay within the Dungannon relief district; sub-committees of Dungannon included the parish of Killyman whose fund was grant-aided. Rev. Leach pleaded – in vain – for similar treatment.[45]

There are two aspects of organisation and outlook which distinguish relief committees in Co. Tyrone from those in other parts of Ulster. The organisational difference was the widespread use in the county of relief

districts based on petty sessions districts. The difference in outlook relates
to the very strenuous objections raised by a number of committees to one
aspect of government relief policy, namely, the insistence that where the
committees sold food they should charge at least 'first cost'.

In the appointment of local committees and the delineation of the relief
districts they were to supervise, county lieutenants were given a free hand.
The *Instructions* of October 1846 preferred smaller districts (including,
however, at least two parishes), though larger central committees, much
used in relief operations in the previous season (and preferred, as
administratively convenient, by Sir Randolph Routh), could be retained if
county lieutenants found them 'more desirable'. In practice, the lieutenants
followed their own preferences. For example, central committees were
widely used by the Earl of Erne in Fermanagh and by John Young MP,
acting lieutenant for Cavan. In Donegal, vice-lieutenant Sir James Stewart
adhered to two-parish districts; in Co. Londonderry, Sir Robert Ferguson
preferred electoral divisions of Poor Law Unions, while the strong preference
of Lord Charlemont in Tyrone was for petty sessions districts. All three
relief districts in Clogher barony, namely, Clogher, Ballygawley and Fintona
were certainly petty sessions districts. So too were Omagh and Carrickmore
in East Omagh barony. Trillick was probably one, which later broke down
into the sub-districts of Trillick, The Bar and Kilskeery. Cookstown in
Upper Dungannon and Aughnacloy in Lower Dungannon were also petty
sessions districts. In Middle Dungannon, there was a serious attempt to
use central committees. Dungannon Relief Committee embraced the
parishes of Drumglas, Donaghmore, and Killyman, with the district of
Castlecaulfield/Edencrannon. Stewartstown had sub-committees at Ardboe,
Clonoe and Ballyclog. However, in the barony of Lower Strabane, all the
districts were parochial, namely, Camus (embracing the town of Strabane),
Dunnamanagh, Leckpatrick, East Urney and Newtownstewart (Ardstraw
parish).[46]

The result of such local relief arrangements over the country as a whole
was the emergence of a higgledy-piggledy patchwork of districts. This was
no great harm in itself, but such irregularity became a serious administrative
liability when, at the turn of 1846-7, government lost faith in its scheme of
public works and took the first step, through the Temporary Relief Act,
towards expanding the Poor Law system to handle famine as well as ordinary
poor relief. There was a period of chaos and confusion while Poor Law

electoral division uniformity was forced upon the irregular patchwork of districts. For the Temporary Relief Act, popularly known as the Soup Kitchens or Rations Act, was to be financed out of the poor rates and administered by the local relief committees, reorganised on a uniform system of single or multiple electoral divisions of Poor Law Unions.

Apart from their role – where relevant – in providing properly scrutinised lists of applicants for employment on the public works, local relief committees were expected to provide food – 'supplies of Indian corn, or Indian-corn meal, or other food <u>for sale</u>'. This they were to finance from their locally-raised relief fund supported, if they adhered to the official *Instructions*, by a government grant. Up to mid-January 1847, this grant was usually 50 per cent; thereafter it was usually 100 per cent. The *Instructions* were quite specific that committees should <u>sell</u> food, but only in 'small quantities' and only 'to persons who are known to have no other means of procuring food'. Further, the price they charged 'should be the same as the market prices which prevail in the neighbourhood'; committees had the discretion to give 'gratuitous assistance to persons not capable of making a return in labour of any kind', but only when the local workhouse was full.[47]

There is abundant evidence that there was widespread disagreement with this aspect of government relief policy. In Ulster, the most forthright critics were several Tyrone committees, particularly Moy and Dunnamanagh, who made no secret of their disagreement with policy and of their breach of the *Instructions*, while boldly requesting government grants in aid of their funds.

Moy Relief Committee anticipated at the beginning of November 1846 that they would have to give money and food to 'a large class of poor ... who from infancy, infirmity or old age cannot work', despite the fact that Dungannon Union workhouse, to which Moy belonged, was not full.[48] In early January 1847, the chairman, James Eyre Jackson, admitted that the practice was continuing (though by then it was legal, since the workhouse was full); but the committee was also supplying meal to, 'poor families' at a 'reduced price' – in fact, at a penny a pound at a time when the local price was at least twopence a pound. Jackson acknowledged that the practice was not in accord with the *Instructions*, but argued that his committee were unable to devise any other plan that was not 'equally or more objectionable'. Many schemes for giving employment had been considered, but set aside as being more expensive than their plan of selling meal at a penny a pound. The only people refused relief by the committee were those 'holding so much as four acres'. By the time these admissions were made, things had worsened considerably in the area, for now there was 'great and general distress'. On these grounds, Jackson was pressing for a government donation towards their fund of £319, of which £120 had been spent since the end of November on their meal scheme. In reply, he was furnished with a new circular of 20 January in which the existing policy on gratuitous issues and the sale of food was re-stated. Where food was sold, 'the price to be charged should be the first cost'. If the committee conformed, Sir Randolph Routh would recommend a donation.[49]

Undaunted, Jackson replied that his committee was unanimous in its opinion that their system had worked well. And he went further, '... the poor are more careful of the article that they buy (though at a price under its value) than they are of what they do not pay for ...', which principle, he claimed, was recognised by Routh himself, 'for you apportion the government grants not to the extent of distress only, but also with reference to the sum raised by private subscriptions'. In other words, just as government helped in proportion to local efforts at self-help, so the committee wanted to help the destitute by affording them the (moral) 'stimulus to exertion' which buying at a penny a pound would give. The committee were fully aware that the main object of the 'sale at first cost' policy was, at worst, not to frighten off the private supplier of food or, at best, to encourage him. In the Moy area, this point did not apply: 'it is not retail traders that are wanting, but money wherewith to buy food'.[50]

Henry Colthurst, secretary to the Dunnamanagh committee, was even more deliberate and assured in his challenge to Routh on the grounds that, ' ... A literal adherence to the *Instructions* (on the sale of food) would be impracticable in this district, consistently with due regard to the assistance which it is the very object of the relief fund to afford to the labouring classes'. If the committee gave gratuitous relief to the destitute, as the *Instructions* allowed, they would be bringing 'in collision two charitable institutions (i.e. the Relief Commission and the Poor Law) which were designed for different classes of recipients'. They could well understand the necessity of committees 'affording relief in aid of the Poor Law' in the south and west of Ireland, 'where the destitution was so overwhelming as to be beyond the reach of the ordinary legal provision'; but circumstances were different 'in this part of the country'. Again, if the committee were to sell meal only at first cost, as the *Instructions* required, 'the whole amount of the relief fund would remain undiminished ... at the termination of their labours, which neither they nor their subscribers desire'. Therefore, with 'absolute paupers' being taken care of in the workhouse, the committee – with a fund to spend on relief – directed their 'bounty towards persons with large families wholly dependent upon them, where the parents are but partially employed, and owing to the combined operation of low wages and high prices, are unable to earn sufficient to support their families'.

Such cases, argued Colthurst, were so numerous as to be 'the common rule', for the usual custom in the area was for the farmer 'to employ his cottiers or labourers two or three days in the week and leave them to seek work during the remainder of the time wherever they can find it'. Another numerous class in the area were the weavers who were 'but partially employed owing to the depression of the linen business'. Neither labourers nor weavers could earn more than tenpence a day 'even if fully employed' and 'with meal at 2° d. a pound, it would be utterly impossible for them to afford an ordinary sized family more than a single meal a day without such assistance as the committee extend to them'.

Finally, the committee were anxious to impress upon Routh that their bounty was not open-ended. When they sold Indian corn at the reduced price of 1s. per peck (of 10lbs), they never supplied an unlimited quantity nor allowed an applicant to obtain a whole week's supply at the reduced price. Their practice was to limit the allowance to 2° lbs per week for each member of a family, and only for families which were 'in absolute distress' and proven to the committee 'to have neither cows, corn nor any other means of support'. The committee reckoned that their policy enabled them 'to add materially to the resources of the poorer classes without interfering with the legitimate profits of the retail trader'. They freely admitted that their system was 'tantamount to an augmentation of wages', but 'without producing the evils to be apprehended from a direct resort to that expedient'. What they did was 'barely sufficient to place the recipients beyond absolute starvation', to which many would otherwise be exposed. The secretary concluded 'his full and candid exposition' of the committee's practice by assuring Routh that they would continue 'to scrutinize minutely' the merits of every case that came before them.[51]

In addition to Moy and Dunnamanagh, several committees in Tyrone admitted openly or tacitly that they sold meal at reduced prices. From the beginning of its operations in early November, Dungannon wanted 'a discretional power' in regard to food sales, otherwise they could 'procure no subscriptions'.[52] Newtownstewart admitted: 'we have three depots for selling meal at reduced price'.[53] Camus 'sold meal at 1s. a peck in quantities varying from half a peck to two pecks according to the number of the respective families and the extent of their destitution'.[54] Clogher had a similar sliding scale for selling meal 'at a reduced price', while Pomeroy sold 'at 1d. and 1° d. (per lb)'.[55]

Some committees were anxious to demonstrate their efforts to follow government guidelines, like Clonoe, which claimed to give relief in such a way as 'not to interfere with the current market price of provisions, namely, by the issue of tickets to three retailers of meal in different parts of our district, the committee paying one moiety and the purchaser the other'.[56] This was similar to an earlier scheme of East Urney's to help 'those destitute labourers on the public works whose families are so large that their weekly earnings will not meet the expense of providing them with food sufficient to sustain nature'. On Saturday nights, the committee would issue tickets 'for so many pecks (of) meal' which would 'pass current at the shops of the provision merchants in every part of our district and come into use early in the week when we shall give payment to those merchants'. The scheme, in the opinion of the committee, would not only not injure the 'fair trader' but be of 'decided advantage' to him. Routh rejected this scheme. As he told the committee, it involved 'the adoption of the aid-of-wages system which produced so much evil in England under the late poor laws'. This was a reference to the evils of the 'old' Poor Law which, it was erroneously believed, had been rooted out by the reform of 1834 (on which the Irish Poor Law of 1838 was modelled). For this reason, Routh was not 'authorised to recommend a government donation' to the Urney relief fund.[57] Yet he had no hesitation in recommending grant-aid to Clonoe. The difference in treatment – both committees were breaking the rules – is explained by the timing of the two applications. East Urney applied at the beginning of December, Clonoe at the beginning of January. Between the two dates the situation in the country at large had seriously worsened, with the result that the application of government policy was considerably relaxed. This is shown clearly in the government decision in January to increase grant-aid – or donations in aid – to committees from 50 per cent to 100 per cent.

East Urney subsequently received grant-aid, like all the other rule-breaking committees named above.

The correspondence of local committees with Dublin Castle reflects clearly the worsening situation in the Irish countryside around the turn of the year 1846-7. The following extracts from Co. Tyrone give some first-hand impressions of the deepening crisis as perceived in many local communities, particularly in January and February 1847. One of the earliest warnings was from Urney parish in early November 1846: 'The people are almost in despair at no work having commenced ... hunger, like necessity, has no law and we know not the moment we shall hear of a break out'.[58] Five weeks later, from nearby Strabane, the cry was, ' ... destitution in this town and neighbourhood is very great ... we have 340 families on our list to be relieved' (or about 1800 individuals). By early February, the same correspondent described the privations of a peaceful people as 'heartrending'.[59]

Early in the new year several committees echoed the observation of the Hon. and Rev. Robert Maude, Dean of Clogher that, ' ... the circle of destitution is rapidly increasing and extending itself to a higher class of the agricultural population according as their little store is reduced and expended'.[60] Aughnacloy committee pleaded that their fund was altogether inadequate to:

> preserve from perishing from want of food many, not only of the labouring class, but of the smaller farmers in the district ... several cases ... have come to the knowledge of the committee where persons possessed of from 3 to 4 acres of land have been compelled to sell the corn which ought to have been reserved for seed and to part with almost every article of furniture to furnish means of subsistence and whose wasted forms and emaciated countenances give too sure evidence confirming the truth of their statement.[61]

Similar sentiments were expressed from Coalisland ' ... with our present funds <u>we cannot hold out</u> as the distress is daily <u>increasing</u> and new application from families now in <u>starvation</u> continually coming in who at first never were contemplated as likely to be reduced to such extreme destitution'.[62] From Ardboe, a communication contained...

> brief statement of facts, show(s) the extent to which the distress prevails here ... On our last day of meeting we selected from the list of applicants <u>193 families</u>, cottier tenants, without land or any means of support, and

gave them some gratuitous relief. But there is another class comprising
not less than <u>300 families</u> in nearly a similar state, holding from 1 to 6
acres of land. These we have refused assistance from want of funds. Against
this fearful amount of destitution we are utterly unable to contend with our
present limited funds.[63]

In nearby Clonoe, 'the distress ... is beyond all description, ... the
majority are now in a state of the greatest destitution and many of absolute
starvation'.[64] The Moy chairman reported, 'There is great and general
distress in our district; ... the linen manufacture is depressed and the farmers
have very generally discharged their servants'.[65] Around Pomeroy: ' ...
much distress is now prevailing ... Every day presents fresh scenes of distress
and misery and the misfortune is the poor have not the money to give, be
the price of provisions ever so small'.[66] As far as the Leckpatrick secretary
could see, ' ... The fact is starvation is at the doors, ay in the houses of
some of our labouring population. The universal cry is, "We, our wives
and children must die of hunger"'.[67] In Dunnamanagh, ' ... destitution and
sickness pervade the whole district to a terrible degree'.[68] Finally, one of
the most poignant accounts of distress, from Rev. Henry Lucas St George,
Rector of Dromore, who wrote in the middle of March 1847:

> ... Many have died of actual want. Coroners have not been applied to, for
> the neighbours said there was no use to do so. ... Multitudes of children
> have dropped off from their parents being unable to give them more than a
> drink of gruel once a day, and mothers with infants at their breasts,
> themselves starving.[69]

One or two of these extracts may be dismissed as theatrical exaggeration;
indeed, many of them are part of the texts of begging letters, seeking
government help for diminishing or inadequate funds; but the overall tone
of correspondence from relief committees is too consistently serious for
their evidence to be ignored as a record , however subjective, of how the
crisis was perceived in their communities.

IV

The use of the Temporary Relief Act provides a useful method of showing
how varied the stress of the Famine was in different parts of the county. As
indicated earlier, a full range of statistics for the operation of the act between

April and August 1847 was compiled. Because the Act was administered through the Poor Law system, statistics were presented by Poor Law unions and by electoral divisions within these unions.[70]

The most immediately useful statistic as a comparator is the 'Maximum or highest Number of Persons supplied with Food in any one day' expressed as a percentage of the population of the union or electoral division as given in the 1841 census, hence the figures quoted in the introduction, which suggested that Omagh and Clogher Unions were worse off than Strabane, Castlederg, Dungannon, Cookstown and Gortin.[71] A closer look behind union figures reveals, for example, that numerous electoral divisions in Strabane Union were as badly off as some divisions in Omagh or Clogher and that the figures for occasional divisions within other unions were much greater than the union average. As examples in the latter category, Moyle division of Gortin Union had 35.5 per cent of its population receiving food (as a maximum) as against a union average of 9.24 per cent and, in Castlederg Union where the average figure was 16.22 per cent, Drumquin West division had 25.64 per cent on rations.

The following arrangement should give the reader a bird's eye view of 'stress points' within the Poor Law unions of Co. Tyrone, arranged in descending order of percentages of population receiving food. Within unions, figures for electoral divisions are similarly arranged in descending order, with an arbitrary cut-off point of 20 per cent which is close to the highest figure of 20.77 per cent for any union in the county and, at the same time, represents a degree of distress worth noting.

OMAGH UNION (average 20.77 per cent in 29 electoral divisions):
    Killyclogher 30.93; Mountjoy Forest West 30.3; Mullaghslin 29.26;
    Drumquin 27.87; Athenry 27.37; Derrycard 26.67;
    Mountjoy Forest East 25.48; Fintona 24.47; Camowen 23.72;
    Seskinore 23.14; Dromore 22.77; Omagh 22.55;
    Gortnacreagh 23.72; Camderry 20.65.[72]

CLOGHER UNION (average 20.77 per cent in 17 electoral divisions):
    Augher 38.82; Aughnacloy 32.86; Aughintain 24.39;
    Ballygawley 24.14; Tullyvar 23.25.[73]

STRABANE UNION (average 18.44 per cent in 24 electoral divisions):
    Newtownstewart 35.98; Camus 31.66; Douglas Burn 25.61;
    Strabane 25.44; East Urney 23.57; Mountcastle 20.11.[74]

CASTLEDERG UNION (average 16.22 per cent in 14 electoral divisions):
    Drumquin West 25.64; Killeter 22.99; Clare 22.46; Killen 21.89.[75]

DUNGANNON UNION (average 11.27 per cent in 19 electoral divisions):
Brantry 21.48. [76]

COOKSTOWN UNION (average 10.74 per cent in 16 electoral divisions):
No electoral division over 20 per cent.[77]

GORTIN UNION (average 9.24 per cent in 13 electoral divisions):
Moyle 35.5.[78]

A further broad comparator provided by the statistics for the Temporary Relief act is the way in which the Act was funded. There were actually seven different funding methods. The two major ones were, first, loans ('advances' in the official jargon) made to individual electoral divisions by government on credit of subsequent rates and, secondly, the raising of further local subscriptions to which government continued to give 100 per cent donations. As a rule of thumb, poorer areas where there were weak local economies – often indicated by a multiplicity of landowners or a considerable degree of absenteeism or, at least, a lack of local unanimity about relief measures – tended to rely on loans from government. Conversely, more prosperous areas, where local economies were strong and where there was positive local leadership, tended to provide for themselves by further local subscriptions. The irony here is that prosperous areas had the benefit of 100 per cent government support of their funds while less prosperous divisions were burdened with the debt of the full amount of government loans.

The statistics show that of the unions more seriously afflicted by famine stress (on the basis indicated above), Omagh, Strabane and Castlederg relied exclusively on government loans. Clogher needed loans to defray two-thirds of the expense, but managed the remainder locally. Lesser-burdened Dungannon and Cookstown raised all of their funds by local subscription. Gortin was exceptional in that only five of its 13 electoral divisions used the act, a clear sign that, with the exception of Moyle division, it was not seriously affected by the Famine.[79]

V

Serious pressures on the workhouses in the autumn of 1846 were presaged by the discovery of extensive blight in the growing potatoes 'during the last two or three days of July and the first six or seven days of August'.[80] In those unions where potatoes were grown on the workhouse grounds, boards of guardians rushed to use the crop before it became diseased. In Clogher, for example, where the potatoes had only been planted in May, the Guardians ordered five lbs to be given daily to each inmate instead of meal, so long as they lasted.[81] Similarly, 'the whole produce of the workhouse ground' at Omagh, totalling 760 stones, was consumed during three weeks in August.[82]

The influx into workhouses all over Ireland began in October 1846, with the greatest number of admissions in December 1846 or January 1847. By the turn of the year, 21 of the 43 Ulster unions were filled to more than their capacity, seven others were close to it, while 15 reported no pressure, the latter including Castlederg and Strabane.[83] Omagh was the first of the Tyrone unions to report its workhouse full, on 28 November 1846; on 12 December it was Clogher's turn and, on 26 December, Cookstown, Dungannon and Gortin were full. Castlederg did not fill until 6 February 1847 and, finally, Strabane on 20 February.[84]

As workhouses filled up, all kinds of temporary devices were used to extend accommodation. The most common were the erection of 'sleeping galleries' around the larger common rooms such as dining halls or dormitories. Alternatives were the use of wooden sheds in workhouse grounds or the hiring of houses in the town, as in Dungannon, or the conversion of outbuildings, as in Clogher, where the guardians 'fitted up the straw store (and) put a fire-place in it'. Castlederg 'entered into contracts for enlarging the workhouse'. Some boards of Guardians resisted the advice of the Poor Law Commissioners on expanding accommodation. The commissioners had 'strongly and repeatedly' prompted the Omagh board to provide more places or limit their admissions, 'especially of children without their parents', but to no avail.[85]

By the beginning of February, Omagh workhouse was very overcrowded. It contained nearly 400 over its capacity of 800, despite the repeated and emphatic warnings of its medical officer, Dr White, about the dangers of overcrowding to the health of the inmates. In the third week of December there had been 16 deaths and during Christmas week a further 23 died, of whom 16 were children. The Commissioners attributed this mortality to the Guardians' illegal admission of children without their parents. The Guardians stoutly defended their practice as an extraordinary remedy in 'these extraordinary times'.[86] The medical officer's fear was that the already debilitated state of newly admitted paupers, especially children, among whom diarrhoea, dysentery and measles were rife, ('some have died on the

same day and the day following their admission', he had noted) would be
the source of a serious fever outbreak. The bathrooms had been appropriated
as probationary wards, that is, for new admissions. They contained 'an
immense number of individuals with scarce a rag to cover them and lying
on a little straw at night as thick as they can'.[87] In early February 1847, the
Commissioners intervened and ordered the workhouse to be closed to further
admissions from 25 February. It was to remain closed until 22 July despite
the provision, in late March, of 200 sleeping places 'over the dining hall'.[88]

In the meantime, the steadily increasing numbers of inmates stricken
with fever were treated in the original probationary wards. They were lying
so close together on the floor that the doctor had to 'walk over one to see
another'. He commented: 'No medical man's life is worth anything while
attending fever patients under those circumstances'.[89] Fortunately, while
fever in the union was serious, the epidemic which Dr White feared did
not materialise, due largely to his own careful arrangements. The availability
of the nearby Omagh fever hospital was also a help, since serious cases
could be referred there until it became full in March. By early June fever
sheds had been placed in the workhouse grounds, followed in the middle
of the month by a temporary fever hospital in Drumquin electoral division.[90]
Similar temporary hospitals were arranged for Omagh, Fintona and
Dromore divisions in the first half of July. The Fintona hospital, with
provision for 60 patients, also catered for the divisions of Tattymoyle,
Derrybard, Seskinore and Fallaghearn, while Dromore also served Greenan
and Tullyclunagh divisions. In all, the temporary hospitals in Omagh Union
provided 190 extra beds for fever patients, the sixth highest of any union
in Ulster after Lurgan, Cavan, Armagh, Enniskillen and Banbridge. In
Dungannon Union, where 140 extra beds were provided at temporary
hospitals for the divisions of Dungannon, Donaghmore, Moy with Benburb
and Tullyniskan with Drumnaspil, the fever had peaked in early June. Two
temporary hospitals were provided in Clogher Union at Aughnacloy, serving
Aughnacloy and Tullyvar electoral divisions and at Fivemiletown, serving
the divisions of Fivemiletown, Cole and Aughintain. There was one small
hospital, with provision for 20 patients, established at Pomeroy in Cookstown
Union and, finally, Trillick division, which belonged to Lowtherstown Union,
shared a large hospital with Lowtherstown and Moorfield.[91]

While unions like Omagh had chronic problems induced by famine
conditions, even favoured ones like Cookstown did not escape the intense

pressure of the winter of 1846-7. Cookstown workhouse, built to hold 500 paupers and declared full on 26 December, was considered by its medical officer to be dangerously overcrowded a month later. His opinion was that 650 was 'as many as the house can contain'. Presumably responding to this warning, the board on that date – 23 January – admitted only seven paupers and turned away 89. Rejection by guardians of sometimes large numbers of applicants, due to lack of room, was not uncommon at this time. The question arises as to what became of such unfortunate beings. Given the widespread abhorrence of the workhouse among the poor, it must be assumed that they presented themselves for admission as a last resort. That the Cookstown Guardians were aware of this is borne out by the fact that they wrote – in vain – to ask the Poor Law Commissioners if they might give 'a little food' to such applicants turned away.[92]

The cumulative effect of full and overfull workhouses, the need to provide extra accommodation, the replacement of the potato in the diet by expensive meal and bread and the care of large numbers of sick inmates meant that all unions were under severe financial pressure. In February 1847, the Assistant Poor Law commissioners were asked to report on the financial state of the unions under their care. Edward Senior, responsible for most of the northern unions, reported pessimistically on the Tyrone unions. Only in Castlederg did he expect the whole rate to be collected, 'but the cost of ... maintenance will probably exceed the estimate'. Of the others, Strabane and Gortin 'must be assisted by the government'; Clogher, Cookstown, Dungannon and Omagh would collect only two thirds of their rate and Omagh would 'depend on Government aid' in the ensuing months.[93]

In due course, those unions which funded the Temporary Relief Act by loans from government (like Omagh, Strabane, Castlederg and Clogher) were required to strike rates in order to repay. Hence, yet another financial burden was added. Moreover while the Temporary Relief Act was running its successful course, the Whig government introduced a new Irish Poor Law which was to be implemented on 15 August 1847. This new law allowed outdoor relief – hitherto anathema in Ireland – and proposed, for each union, several salaried relieving officers to supervise it. These officers replaced the voluntary wardens of the previous Poor Law. While the new relief was to be strictly limited, there was a widespread reaction against it, particularly among boards of guardians in east Ulster, some of whom set themselves against implementing the new law. Others showed their displeasure by making the appointment of relieving officers as difficult as possible for the commissioners. Such was the attitude of the Omagh Guardians, the most strenuous opponents in Tyrone of the new arrangements. Divided within itself between *ex-officio* landlord guardians and elected members, the latter drawn from the tenant farmers and shopkeepers, it had always been at odds with the Poor Law Commissioners. The elected guardians, over a period of weeks between mid-July and the end of August, produced a series of deliberately confusing proposals and counter proposals, aimed at delaying the appointments. Eventually, only the intervention of Assistant Commissioner Senior brought an agreed conclusion.[94]

VI

A vast amount of local research needs to be done before we can arrive at a comprehensive account of the Great Famine in Co. Tyrone. I have attempted, using the abundant official statistics, to provide a comparative framework within which Tyrone could be measured against other counties and localities in the county identified where the stress of the early Famine period was felt more keenly than others. The various government relief mechanisms were explored – particularly the public works scheme and the activity of local relief committees – for the light their records throw on local perceptions of the effects of the potato failure of 1846. These serve as a reminder that, despite the relatively light impact of the Famine on the county as a whole, there were localities where considerable, even extreme, distress and suffering were experienced, especially in the winter of 1846-7.

SOURCES AND BIBLIOGRAPHY

INTRODUCTION

1 Examples of recent local studies of the Famine include, Michael O'Gorman, *A Pride Of Tigers. A History of the Great Hunger in the Scariff Workhouse Union from 1839-1853*, (Clare, 1994); Swinford Historical Society, *An Gorta Mor. Famine in the Swinford Union,* (Swinford, 1995); Kildare County Council *Lest We Forget. Kildare and the Great Famine,* (Kildare, 1995); Cork Archives Institute, *Great Famine Facsimile Pack* (Cork, 1996); Stewartstown and District Local History Society, *The Famine in East Tyrone,* (Stewartstown, 1996); Gerard MacAtasney, *This Dreadful Visitation. The Famine in Lurgan and Portadown,* (Beyond the Pale, 1997).

2 Exceptions are an unpublished thesis by James Grant, 'The Great Famine in the Province of Ulster: the mechanisms of relief' (Queen's University, Belfast, 1986) and Jonathan Bardon's seminal work *A History of Ulster* (Belfast, 1992). Also, Patrick Campbell, *Death in Templecrone. An Account of the Famine Years in Northwest Donegal* (New Jersey, 1995) and John Killen's *The Famine Decade. Contemporary Accounts 1841-1851.* (Belfast, 1995) which includes many contemporary reports from Ulster newspapers.

3 Jim Smyth 'The Men of No Popery. The Origins of the Orange Order' in *History Ireland* (vol. 3, Autumn 1995), pp. 48-53.

4 L. A. Clarkson, 'Famine and Irish History' in E. M. Crawford (ed.) *Famine: The Irish Experience 900-1900,* (Edinburgh, 1989) p. 225.

5 It is possible that blight was first observed in the Botanic Gardens in Dublin on 20 August 1845, E. Charles Nelson, *The Cause of the Calamity. Potato blight in Ireland, 1845-47 and the role of the National Botanic Gardens, Glasnevin* (Dublin, 1995); P. M. Austin Bourke, *The Visitation of God ? The potato and the Great Irish Famine,* (Dublin, 1993) p.157.

6 *The Nation,* 19 September 1846.

7 Christine Kinealy *A Death-Dealing Famine. The Great Hunger in Ireland,* (Pluto Press, 1997).

8 Christine Kinealy, *This Great Calamity. The Irish Famine 1845-52,* (Gill and Macmillan, 1994) pp 366-371.

9 *ibid.,* pp. 210-216.

10 Michael Gould, *The Workhouses of Ulster,* (Belfast, 1983) p.6

11 Christine Kinealy, 'The Role of the Poor Law during the Famine' in Cathal Porteir (ed.) *The Great Irish Famine,* (Mercier Press, 1995) pp. 119-121.

12 James S.Donnelly 'Mass Eviction and the Great Famine' in Cathal Porteir (ed.) *The Great Irish Famine* pp.155-173.

13 *Transactions of the Central Relief Committtee of the Society of Friends during the Famine in Ireland in 1846 and 1847,* (Dublin, 1852, reprinted 1996).

CO. ANTRIM

1 PRONI, D.2977/6, *Second Report on the Antrim Estates 1845...*John Lanktree, Agent, p.12.

2 M. J. Murphy, *Rathlin: Island of Blood and Enchantment* (Dundalk, 1987) p.30.

3 PRONI, D.2977/6, Lanktree's Report, 1845 *op.cit.*

4 *Coleraine Chronicle,* 5 Aug. 1845.

5 PRONI, BG 1/A/1, Antrim Guardians' meeting, 17 July 1845.

6 PRONI, BG 1/A/1, Antrim Guardians' meeting, 14 Oct. 1845.

7 PRONI, BG 5/A/3, Ballymoney Guardians' meeting, 17 Aug. 1845.

8 PRONI, BG 5/A/3, Ballymoney Guardians meeting, 7 Sept. 1845.

9 *ibid.*

10 PRONI, BG 5/A/3, Ballymoney Guardians' meeting, 1 October 1845.

11 PRONI, BG 5/A/3, Ballymoney Guardians' meeting, 8 October 1845.

12 PRONI, BG 5/A/3, Ballymoney Guardians' meeting, 12 October 1845.

13 PRONI, BG 5/A/3, Ballymoney Guardians' meeting, 7 Dec. 1845.

14 *Coleraine Chronicle,* 28 December 1845

15 PRONI, BG 1/A/1, Antrim Guardians' meeting, 6 Nov. 1845.

16 PRONI, BG 1/A/1, Antrim Guardians' meeting, 13 Nov. 1845.

17 *ibid.,* BG 1/A/1, Antrim Guardians' meeting, 13 Nov. 1845.
18 PRONI, BG1/A/1, Antrim Guardians' meeting, 20 Nov. 1845.
19 PRONI, BG19/A/5, Lisburn Guardians' meeting, 21 Oct. 1845.
20 PRONI, BG 19/A/5, Lisburn Guardians' meeting, 4 Nov. 1845.
21 PRONI, BG 19/A/5, Lisburn Guardians' meeting, 20 Jan. 1846.
22 PRONI, BG 19/A/5, Lisburn Guardians' meeting, 24 Feb. 1846.
23 PRONI, BG 1/A/1, Antrim Guardians' meeting, 19 Mar. 1846.
24 PRONI, BG 17/A/2, Larne Guardians' meeting, 23 April 1846.
25 Minutes of Ballycastle Dispensary Committee 1823-47, in private hands and made available to the author.
26 *ibid.*
27 J. Irvine, 'Glenarm Soup Kitchens', *The Glynns,* vol 2 1974, p. 38-40.
28 *ibid.*
29 PRONI, BG 10/A/5, Coleraine Guardians' meeting, 12 Dec. 1846.
30 PRONI, BG 10/A/5, Coleraine Guardians' meeting, 19 Dec. 1846.
31 *Coleraine Chronicle,* 12 Jan. 1847.
32 PRONI, BG 5/A/4, Ballymoney Guardians' meeting, 21 December 1846.
33 *Coleraine Chronicle,* 5 June 1847.
34 *Fourteenth Report from the Select Committee on Poor Laws, Ireland.* H. C. 1847 Vol xv Pt 1, pp. 222-3.
35 *Papers relating to the Relief of Distress and State of the Unions in Ireland,* Seventh Series, 1848, pp.196-7. H. C. 1847-8, Vol liv.
36 Evidence of Edward Senior, to *Select Committee on Poor Laws (Ireland),* 15 Mar. 1849, Q. 2361. H.C. 1849 [237] Vol xv Pt 1.
37 PRONI, D.2977/6, Lanktree to Lady Londonderry, April 1846.
38 PRONI, D.2977/6, 'Antrim Estate, Statistical Report for the year 1847'.
39 PRONI, *ibid.*
40 *ibid.*
41 *ibid.*
42 *ibid.*
43 PRONI, D. 2977/6, 'Statistical Report for the year 1848' (Antrim Estate).
44 *ibid.*
45 *ibid.*
46 J. Irvine, 'The Famine Stone or Lettered Rock', *The Glynns,* Vol. 3, 1975 p. 37.
47 P. Magill, *Garron Tower,* (Belfast 1990), p. 7.
48 J. Irvine, 'John Langtree'. *The Glynns* Vol. 8, 1980 p.53.

49 *ibid.*
50 *Coleraine Chronicle,* 25 October 1845.
51 *ibid.*
52 Catherine Gage, *A History of the Island of Rathlin (*1851) (Impact Printing, Ballycastle, 1995), p. 87.
53 PRONI, T.1883/63, J & J Cooke to Rev. Robert Gage, 19 April 1847.
54 *ibid.*
55 Mrs Gage, op.cit. p.87.
56 PRONI, D.2892/1/1.
57 *British Parliamentary Papers: Population 13, 1851 Census Ireland,* Part 1, p.15. Irish University Press Series.
58 M. J. Murphy, *Rathlin: Island of Blood and Enchantment* (Dundalgan Press, Dundalk, 1987) p.31.
59 Rev. H. I. Law, *Rathlin: Island and Parish* (1961) p. 21.
60 *ibid.,* p. 22.
61 *ibid.,* p. 23.
62 *ibid.,* p. 30.
63 *ibid.*
64 Cathal Porteir, *Famine Echoes* (Dublin, 1995), p. 245.
65 *ibid.,* p.184-5.
66 *ibid.,* p.167.
67 PRONI, BG 4/A/2, Ballymena Guardians' meeting, 18 Sept. 1851.
68 PRONI, BG 1/A/2, Antrim Guardians' meeting, 11 Sept. 1851.
69 PRONI, BG 1/A/2, Antrim Guardians' meeting, 18 Sept. 1852.

CO. ARMAGH

1 *The Newry Telegraph,* 6 March 1849
2 *Northern Whig,* 22 May 1847.
3 *ibid.,* 20 March 1847.
4 *ibid.,* 2 January and 30 March 1847.
5 *Evidence taken before the Commissioners appointed to enquire into the occupation of land in Ireland,* 1844, The Devon Commission. Digest of Evidence, Part 1, H.C. 1845 (605), vol xix. Evidence of John Hancock, Q. 55
6 *First Report of Commissioners for inquiring into the condition of the Poorer Classes in Ireland.* Supplement of Appendix D., p.285 H.C. 1836, vol xxxi, Evidence of Rev. C. T. Irwin, Drumcree.
7 *ibid.,* Rev. W.H. Wynne, Tullylish and Fr. James O'Neill, Drumcree.
8 *ibid.,* Rev. Ivers, Tartaraghan.
9 PRONI, BG22/A/4, pp.50, 60, 68-9, Lurgan Guardians.
10 PRONI, BG22/A/4, p.249.
11 National Archives, Relief Commission Papers, Woodhouse to Capt. Kennedy, 4 April 1846.
12 PRONI, BG22/A/3, 1845, p.255.

13   *ibid.*, 1846, p.79.
14   National Archives, Constabulary Reports 1846, Cos Armagh, Down, and Antrim.
15   *ibid.*, Maralin/Moira, 30 May 1846.
16   National Archives, Relief Commission Papers, Lord Gosford to the Lord Lieutenant, 24 April 1846.
17   *Northern Whig*, 8 September 1846.
18   *ibid.*, 3 September 1846.
19   13th Annual Report of the Poor Law Commissioners, 1847, Appendix A., No 9, pp. 182, 188, 196, (L.H.B.)
20   PRONI, BG22/A/4, p. 391.
21   *ibid.*, pp 361, 371, 381.
22   *ibid.*, pp 321-391.
23   *Newry Telegraph*, 21 September 1847.
24   PRONI, BG22/A/4, weekly attendance of Guardians for the year ending 25 March 1847.
25   PRONI, BG22/FO/2, 14 March 1847.
26   *Belfast Vindicator*, 6 January 1847 (L.H.B.).
27   National Archives, Relief Commission Papers, Reports from throughout the Union, 1846-7.
28   *ibid.*, D. Babington to R. J. Rarth, 3 February 1847.
29   *ibid.*, Woodhouse to Dublin Castle, 12 December 1846.
30   National Archives, Distress Papers, Gosford to T.N. Redington, 26 January 1847.
31   National Archives, Relief Commission Papers, James Brown to Dublin Castle, 27 February 1847.
32   *ibid.*, Robert Hill to R.J. Routh, 5 January 1847.
33   *ibid.*, Reports from Relief Committees in Cos Armagh, Antrim and Down, 1847.
34   *ibid.*, Rev. Clements to R.J. Routh, 1 January 1847.
35   *ibid.*, Wm Morris to W. Stanley, 14 April 1847.
36   *ibid.*, Alexander Miller to R.J. Routh, 27 February 1847.
37   *ibid.*, Rev. Outton to W. Stanley, 4 February 1847.
38   *ibid.*, D. Babington to R.J. Routh, 3 February 1847.
39   *ibid.*, D. Babington to R.J. Routh, 3 February 1847.
40   *ibid.*, Henry Wynne to R.J. Routh, 5 February 1847.
41   *ibid.*, Rev. Francis Clements to R.J. Routh, 1 January 1847.
42   *ibid.*, Clements to R.J. Routh, January 1847.
43   *ibid.*, Clements to R. J. Routh, January 1847.
44   National Archives, Portadown Constabulary Report, 13 January 1847. Outrage Papers.
45   *ibid.*, Portadown 23 January 1847.
46   *ibid.*, Tandragee 23 February 1847.
47   *ibid.*, Tandragee, 23 February 1847.
48   PRONI, BG22/A/4, pp 401, 411, 421.
49   PRONI, BG 22/FO/1. Lurgan Workhouse,

Chaplain's notebook, January/February 1847.
50   PRONI, BG22/A/4, p.426.
51   *ibid.*, p.426.
52   *ibid.*, p.426.
53   *ibid.*, p.426.
54   *ibid.*, p.426.
55   *ibid.*, pp 431, 441, 457, 461.
56   *Correspondence relating to the state of the Union Workhouses in Ireland*, Third Series, H.C., 1847 (863), vol. iv, p. 5.
57   *ibid.*, pp 9, 15.
58   *ibid.*, pp 19, 23.
59   *Newry Telegraph*, 30 January 1847.
60   PRONI, BG22/A/4, p.435.
61   *ibid.*, p.455 and p.456.
62   *ibid.*, p.450.
63   *ibid.*, p.449.
64   *ibid.*, p.459.
65   *ibid.*, p.450.
66   *ibid.*, p.459.
67   *ibid.*, p.449.
68   *ibid.*, p.460.
69   PRONI, D1817/2. Hancock to Mr Hanley, 15 February 1847. Letter Book of John Hancock, p.309.
70   *ibid.*, p. 309.
71   *Newry Telegraph*, 9 February 1847.
72   *Belfast Vindicator*, 10 March 1847.
73   PRONI, BG22/A/4, p.456.
74   *Report of Dr Smith to the Board of Health, Dublin, on the state of the Lurgan Union Workhouse*, H.C., 1847 (247) lv. ii, p.13.
75   *ibid.*, pp 13-14.
76   *ibid.*, p.14.
77   *ibid.*, p.14.
78   *ibid.*, p.16.
79   *ibid.*, p. 14.
80   *ibid.*, p. 14.
81   *ibid.*, p. 14.
82   *ibid.*, p. 15.
83   *ibid.*, p. 14.
84   *ibid.*, p. 15.
85   *ibid.*, p. 15.
86   *ibid.*, p. 15.
87   *ibid.*, p. 15.
88   PRONI, BG22/A/4, p. 469.
89   *ibid.*, p. 469.
90   *ibid.*, p. 469.
91   *ibid.*, p. 469.
92   *ibid.*, p. 469.
93   *ibid.*, p. 470.
94   *ibid.*, p. 470.
95   *ibid.*, p. 470.
96   *ibid.*, p. 470.
97   *ibid.*, p. 470.
98   *ibid.*, p. 470.
99   *ibid.*, p. 471.

100 *ibid.*, p. 475.
101 *ibid.*, p. 476.
102 *ibid.* p. 477.
103 *ibid.*, pp. 478-479.
104 *ibid.*, pp. 478-479.
105 *ibid.* pp. 478-479.
106 National Archives, Relief Commission Papers. Henry Wynne to R.J. Routh, 5 February 1847.
107 PRONI, BG22/A/4, p. 480.
108 *Belfast Vindicator*, 10 February 1847.
109 *Newry Telegraph*, 1 May 1847.
110 *Armagh Guardian*, 11 May 1847.
111 *Belfast Vindicator*, 28 April 1847.
112 *Armagh Guardian*, 11 May 1847.
113 PRONI, BG22/A/4, p. 419.
114 *Belfast Vindicator*, 28 April 1847.
115 Transactions of the Central Relief Committee to the Society of Friends during the Famine in Ireland in 1846 and 1847; Appendix III; p.192 (A.L.H.).
116 *Belfast Newsletter*, 2 April 1847.
117 *ibid.*, 2 April 1847.
118 Society of Friends, Appendix III, p. 192.
119 *ibid.*, p. 192.
120 PRONI, BG22/A/4, p.509.
121 *ibid.*, p. 520.
122 *ibid.*, p. 520.
123 *ibid.*, pp. 528-529.
124 *ibid.*, pp. 530.
125 *ibid.*, pp. 538.
126 *ibid.*, pp. 550.
127 *ibid.*, pp. 550.
128 *ibid.*, pp. 550.
129 PRONI, BG22/A/6, p. 9.
130 *ibid.*, p. 10.
131 *ibid.*, p. 267.
132 PRONI, BG22/A/5, p. 535.
133 *ibid.*, p. 535
134 PRONI, BG22/A/6, p. 1.
135 *ibid.*, p. 1.
136 *ibid.*, p. 16.
137 Appendix A to Third Report from the Relief Commissioners, p. 13, H.C., 1847 (836) vol. xvii.
138 PRONI, BG22/A/6, p. 65.
139 Appendix iii to Fourth Report from the Relief Commissioners p. 26, H.C., 1847 (859) vol xvii, Appendix to Fifth Report from the Relief Commissioners, p. 22., H.C., 1847-8, (876), vol xxix.
140 PRONI, BG22/A/5. p.310.
141 PRONI, BG22/A/7, 1848, p.169.
142 PRONI, BG22/A/8, p. 249.
143 Reports from Assistant Handloom Weavers' Commissioners, Part III, p. 714, H.C., 1840 (220) xxiii, 49. See also W.H. Crawford, *The Handloom Weavers and the Ulster Linen Industry* (Ulster Historical Foundation, 1994), p. 63.
144 *Northern Whig*, 22 May 1847.
145 *Report of Dr Smith for the Board of Health...on the state of the Lurgan Union Workhouse.* H.C. 1847 (247) lv ii p.13.

CO. CAVAN
1 *Report of the commissioners appointed to take the census of Ireland for the year 1841* (hereafter *Census Ire*) H.C. 1844 (504) xxiv.
2 *ibid.*
3 *Report of commissioners for enquiring into the condition of the poorer classes in Ireland* (hereafter *Poor Enquiry Ire*), H.C. 1836, xxx-xxxii, Appendix E, p.294
4 *ibid.*
5 *ibid.*, p.293
6 Gerard Alwill, '1841 Census of Killeshandra Parish', *Breifne (Journal of the Breifine Historical Society)*, v. no. 17, (1976), pp 7-19. Margaret Crawford, 'Poverty and Famine in County Cavan,' *Cavan: Essays on the history of an Irish county*, (ed.) Raymond Gillespie, (Irish Academic Press, 1995), pp 143-149.
7 *Freeman's Journal* (hereafter *FJ*), 28 October 1845. Abraham Brush, Dunbar, Cavan was secretary to the Cavan Royal Agricultural Improvement Society. *FJ*, 30 October, 14, 15, 20 Nov., 6 Dec. 1845. Some of the reports in papers tried to play down the extent of the potato failure throughout the winter of 1845-6. Even as late as May-June 1847 the *Dublin Evening Mail* maintained that the 'potato panic' was an illusion and disputed the figures given by the *Anglo-Celt. Anglo-Celt* 15 May, 5 and 12 June 1847.
8 *Anglo-Celt*, 20 February and 3 April 1846.
9 In recognition of his efforts Morton was presented with an address and testimonial from numerous people on 10 April 1848. *Anglo-Celt*, 10 Dec. 1847, 14 April 1848.
10 Margaret Crawford, 'Poverty in Co. Cavan' *op.cit.*, p.150.
11 Terence P. Cunningham DCL, 'The Great famine in County Cavan', *'Breifne*, v.11, no. 8, (1966), p. 516. National Archives, Relief Commission Papers, Cavan, 1845-7, no 2142, McKiernan to Sir Robert Peel, 31 Jan. 1846.
12 *Anglo-Celt.*, 18 Sept., 4, 11, 18 Dec. 1846.
13 *ibid.*, 14 Aug, 23 Oct. 1846.
14 *ibid.*, 28 Aug. 1846.
15 *ibid.*, 21 and 31 Aug. 1846
16 *ibid.*, 25 Sept. 1846
17 National Archives, Relief Commission Papers 1845-7, Cavan, letter from Archdeacon J.C. Martin, Rectory House, Killeshrandra, 4 Sept. 1846.
18 *Anglo-Celt*, 25 Sept. 1846.

19   *ibid.*, 2 October 1846.

20   *ibid.*, 18 Dec. 1846.

21   *F.J.*, 25 March 1847.

22   *ibid.*, 23 March, 30 April, 5 May, 27 April, 10 June, 2 July 1847.

23   *Anglo-Celt*, 9 April 25 June, 16 July 1847, *F.J.*, 23 June 1847.

24   *Minute Book of P L Guardians,*Cavan, 30 March; *ibid.*, Cootehill, 2 April., (Cavan Co. Library).

25   *Meath Herald*, 13 November 1847, *Anglo -Celt*, 20 August 1847, F.J., 12 October 1847.

26   *Dublin Quarterly Journal of Medical Science*, v.vii, (Febr.-May 1949), p.107 ff.

27   *Anglo-Celt*, 23 April 1847.

28   See Report on Drs Halpin and Mease in *Anglo-Celt*, 23 April 1847.

29   *Anglo-Celt*, 23 April, 4 June 1847.

30   *Anglo-Celt,* 23 April, 28 May, 2 July 1847, *F.J.*, 31 May 1847.

31. *Anglo-Celt*, 2 July 1847.

32   *ibid.*, 23 April, 25 June 1847.

33   Terence P. Cunningham DCL, *op.cit.*, *Breifne* v.ii, no8, (1966), p.427.

34   *Minute-Book P.L.G.*, *Cavan* 28 Sept., 12 Oct., 23 Nov., 30 Nov. 1847.

35   *Anglo-Celt*, 18 Febr. 1848.

36   *Minute-Book, P.L.G.*, *Cavan*, 5 April, 1 May, 8 May, 15 May 1849. *A.C.*, 26 May, 23 June, 4 Aug., 11 Aug. 1848 *Thom's Directory* 1851.

37   *Anglo-Celt*, 4 Aug. 1848.

38   *ibid.*, 17 March 1848.

39   *F.J.*, 25 July 1848.

40   *Anglo-Celt,* 4 Aug. 1848.

41   *F.J.*, 3 March 1848.

42   *ibid.*, 4 Jan. 1848.

43   *ibid.*, 27 Jan., 1849.

44   *Anglo-Celt*, 1 June 1849.

45   *ibid.,* 7 April, 9, 23 June 1848.

46   *Census of Ireland for the year 1841*, H.C. 1844 (504), xxiv and the *Census of Ireland for the year 1851*, pt vi, H.C. 1856 (2134), xxxi.

47   *Anglo-Celt*, 9 April 1847, 13 Aug. 1848, 10 Dec. 1848, *Minute Book P.L.G.*, Cavan, Nov.-Dec. 1848, F.J., 25 Oct. 1848.

CO. DONEGAL

1   C.W.P. MacArthur, 'Visit to Some of the Distressed Districts in Ireland', *Donegal Annual 1994*, p.64.

2   Anthony Begley, 'Poverty, Famine and the workhouse at Ballyshannon', *Donegal Annual 1989,* p.59.

3   Mary McDaid, 'History of Land Ownership and Agrarian Structure of the Estate of William Connolly', *Donegal Annual 1994*.

4   John Ewing, *Statistical returns, Ordnance Survey Memoirs, Co. Donegal*, Royal Irish Academy,

Ref. Box 21 XIII.

5   *Report of the Devon Commission of Inquiry into the Occupation of Land in Ireland, Part II*. Evidence of witnesses pp. 155-156.

6   John O'Connor, *The Workhouses of Ireland*, (Anvil Books, Dublin 1995).

7   John Mitchell, *The Last Conquest of Ireland*, p.116.

8   PRONI, BG 97/A/1, Inishowen Guardians' meeting, 26 Jan. 1846.

9   PRONI, BG 109/A/1, Letterkenny Guardians' meeting, 17 July 1846.

10   PRONI, BG 9/A/1, Glenties Guardians' meeting, 1 May 1846.

11   PRONI, *ibid.*, 17 Nov. 1845.

12   PRONI, *ibid.*, 17 July 1846.

13   PRONI, *ibid.*, 7 Aug. 1846.

14   MacArthur, *op.cit.*, *Donegal Annual* 1994, p.64.

15   Christine Kinealy, *This Great Calamity. The Irish Famine 1845-52* (Gill & Macmillan 1994) pp.87-8.

16   James Hack Tuke, *Narrative of the Second, Third and Fourth Weeks of William Forster's visit to some of the Distressed Districts of Ireland, Pamphlet* (London 1847).

17   Caitlin Mhic Amhlaigh, b. Carrick.

18   Conall MacCuinneagain, 'The Great Famine in Glencolmcille', *Donegal Annual* 1995.

19   *Famine Echoes*, (ed.) Cathal Porteir, (Mercier Press, 1995). William Torrens, b. 1872, Lisminton, Ballintra, Co. Donegal. He heard it from his father William Torrens, 1828-1912 in the townland of Rath.

20   *Statement Showing...Workhouse Accommodation...9 Jan. 1847*. HC 1847 Vol. lv p.147.

21   PRONI, BG 92/A/1, Glenties Guardians' meeting, 26 March 1847.

22   PRONI, *ibid.*, 6 July 1847. Rates were struck of up to 15s, in the case of Malinbeg and 12s 6d in the case of Derryloughan; elsewhere the rates were 8s 6d (Meenevally), 7s 4d (Ardara) and 6s (Glenties).

23   J.V. Stewart, *Evidence to Select Committee on the Poor Laws*, 20 April 1849 q.5337. HC Vol. xv Pt 1.

24   Ulster Museum, *First Report of the Committee of the Belfast Ladies' Association for the Relief of Irish Destitution, 6 March 1847*. (Belfast, 1847) p.20.

25   *ibid.*, p.13.

26   *Papers relating to the proceedings for the relief of distress, and state of the unions and workhouses in Ireland*, Glenties Union p. 56.

27   Padraig Ua Cnaimhsi, 'The Great Famine in the Rosses', *Donegal Annual* 1995.

28 *ibid.*, p.16.
29 Asenath Nicholson, *Letter to Londonderry Journal* 1847.
30 National Archives, Dublin, Relief Commission Correspondence, RLFC 1A/50/50.
31 *The Ballyshannon Herald,* May 1846.
32 *Minutes of the Ballyshannon Union Board Guardians 1846-51.*
33 Edwards and Williams (eds), *The Great Famine* (New York, 1956) p.266.
34 *ibid.*, p.1.
35 John B. Cunningham, 'The Ballyshannon Herald 1845-1850', *Donegal Annual* 1993.
36 Porteir, *op.cit.*, p.24.
37 Cunningham *op.cit.*, pp. 99-113.
38 Sean Beattie, 'Workhouse and Famine in Inishowen (1845-49)', *Donegal Annual* 1980.
39 Porteir, *op cit.*, p.22.
40 *ibid.*, p.13, Sean O Domhnall, b.1873, Cahir, Co Tipperary.
41 *Barney's Report on the Execution of contracts for Certain Union Workhouses in Ireland.*
42 Porteir, *op cit.*, p.26
43 *ibid.*, p.13, Michael Gildea, b. 1872, Dromore, Ballintra, Co. Donegal.
44 *ibid.*, p.26.
45 *ibid.*, p.6.
46 *ibid.*, p.28.
47 *ibid.*, p.13, (William Torrens)
48 *ibid.*, p.21; for more on the orphan emigration scheme see Kinealy, *op.cit*, pp. 315-27, and Trevor McClaughlin, *Barefoot and Pregnant? Irish Famine Orphans to Australia* (Melbourne, 1991)
49 William Allingham, *Diary*, (Centaur Classics 1967).
50 *Letters to William Allingham* (Ed.) H. Allingham and E. Baumer (Williams London 1911).
51 *ibid.*, p.37.
52 Introduction to *The Hungry Voice* (ed.) Chris Morash, (Irish Academic Press 1989).
53 Anthony Begley, 'The Diary of a Ballyshannon Lady 1844-1848', *Donegal Annual 1993.*
54 James Hack Tuke, *op.cit.*, p.1.
55 Begley, *op. cit.* Donegal Annual 1993.
56 *ibid.*, p.26.
57 National Archives, TR 8, p 201.

CO. DOWN
1 *Banner of Ulster*, editorial, 5 Feb. 1847.
2 *The Vindicator*, 22 April 1846; *Belfast Penny Journal*, 19 July 1846 printed in J. Killen (ed), *The Famine Decade, Contemporary Accounts 1841-1851* (Belfast, 1995), pp. 60, 31 (hereafter, Killen, *Famine Decade*).
3 *Abstract of the Census for Ireland taken in 1841 and 1851, arranged according to the Counties*, H.C., 1851 (673) 1.

4 John Andrews (1792-1864) was educated at Crumlin Academy and Glasgow University. In 1812 he was taken into partnership in the family firm John & James Andrews of Comber, linen bleachers. He owned the townland of Carnesure, and he and his three brothers owned a 400-acre farm. In 1828 he became a JP, in 1830 he became agent to Lord Londonderry's County Down estates, in 1833 he was appointed to the Committee of Appeals on the Valuation of the Barony of Ards, and in 1846 to the Committee of the Chemico-Agricultural Society of Ulster. In 1857 he was made High Sheriff of County Down and in 1863 he founded the firm of John Andrews & Co. Flax Spinners. He was the grandfather of J. M. Andrews, Prime Minister of Northern Ireland, 1941-3. See Burke's *Irish Family Records* (London, 1976).
5 A. Day and P. McWilliams (eds) *Ordnance Survey Memoirs of Ireland* Vol 7. *Parishes of County Down II 1832-34, 1837 North Down and the Ards* (Belfast, 1991) notes on the parish of Newtownards (hereafter, *O.S. Memoirs*).
6 A. Bourke, *'The visitation of God?' The potato and the Great Irish Famine* (Dublin, 1993) pp. 114-25 (hereafter, Bourke, *Visitation of God.*
7 *Report from H. M. Commissioners of Inquiry into the State of the Law and Practice in respect to the Occupation of the Land in Ireland (*B.P.P. 1845), Evidence of John Andrews, 27 March 1844.
8 PRONI, D.714/7/2, 'The Marquess of Londonderry's observations on inspecting the towns of Newtownards and Comber. Addressed to the Improvement and Management Committees of the Towns', 31 Oct. 1841.
9 PRONI, BG25/A/1, Newtownards Guardians' meeting, 19 Aug. 1846.
10 *The Northern Whig*, 18 April 1846.
11 'The State of the Poor of the North', *Banner of Ulster*, 5, 23, 26 Feb. 1847.
12 William Sharman Crawford (1781-1861) was the eldest son of William Sharman of Moira Castle, the MP for Lisburn in the Irish Parliament. In 1805 he married the daughter and heiress of John Crawford of Crawfordsburn, who owned an estate of 5,700 acres, and added the surname Crawford. As MP for Dundalk between 1835-7, he was a firm advocate of radical measures, eg, seeking legislation to make the 'Ulster Custom' a statutory requirement and extending it to all Ireland, and a federal parliamentary system for the United Kingdom. He accepted all the principles of the Chartist petition and was invited by Rochdale to be its MP, a constituency which he represented from 1841-1852. He continued to press for the legalisation of the Ulster custom,

and on this platform he attempted to win one of the seats for County Down in 1852 but in this, as in all his political goals, he failed. See L. Stephen, S. Lee (eds) *The Dictionary of National Biography V* (London, 1922), pp.58-9.

13 *Northern Whig*, 12 Jan. 1847.

14 *Downpatrick Recorder*, 28 Nov. 1846.

15 *ibid.*, 9 Nov. 1850.

16 'Chatterdom: Recollections of the Famine in Newtownards', in *The Newtownards Independent*, 15 June 1872.

17 *The Newtownards Independent*, 29 June 1872.

18 C Kinealy, T*his Great Calamity. The Irish Famine 1845-52* (Dublin, 1994), p.95 (hereafter, Kinealy, Great Calamity).

19 *Minute Book.*

20 *ibid.*, 18 Nov., 9, 16 Dec. 1846.

21 PRONI, Londonderry Papers, D 654/N2/24. Copy of letter from John Andrews to the editor of the *Londonderry Standard*, 16 January 1847.

22 *ibid.*

23 Robert was the son of David Gordon, who had moved from Summerfield in Dundonald to Florida Manor in 1809. The Gordons were on of Belfast's leading commercial families, founding the Belfast Banking Company, later the Northern Bank, in 1808. The family owned a couple of townlands in each of the parishes of Kilmood and Comber. Robert ran his estates feudally, still insisting on duty hens in 1852! He was very unpopular with the local Tenant Right organisations. See P. Carr, '*The Most Unpretending of Places. A history of Dundonald, County Down* (Dundonald 1987) pp. 113, 123, 125; *Ordnance Survey Memoirs*: entries on parishes of Kilmood and Comber.

24 PRONI, D.654/N2/24, Andrews to Lord Londonderry 10, 18 Jan. 1847.

25 *Northern Whig*, 6 Feb. 1847.

26 *Banner of Ulster*, 5 Feb. 1847.

27 *Newtownards Independent*, 22 June 1872.

28 PRONI, D/654/N2/24, Andrews to Lord Londonderry, 2 5 Feb. 1847.

29 *ibid.*, 10, 18 January, 2, 5 Feb. 1847; *Banner of Ulster*, 'State of the Poor of the North', 26 Feb. 1847.

30 *Banner of Ulster*, 23 Feb. 1847.

31 *ibid.*, 26 Feb. 1847.

32 *ibid.*, 5 Feb. 1847.

33 *Northern Whig*, 25 Feb. 1847.

34 *ibid.*, 'Notes on the state of the country and progress of the spring agricultural labour', 10 April 1847.

35 *Banner of Ulster*, 5 Feb. 1847.

36 PRONI, D/654/N2/24, Andrews to Lord Londonderry, 18 Jan. 1847.

37 *ibid.*, Andrews to Lord Londonderry, 14 March 1847; Andrews to [Lord Castlereagh?] 21 Feb. 1847.

38 *ibid.*, Andrews to Lord Londonderry, 14 May 1847.

39 Article entitled 'The Three Marquises' from 'a correspondent', printed in the *Londonderry Standard*, 8 Jan. 1847.

40 *ibid.*, 19 Jan. 1847.

41 *ibid.*, Andrews to [Lord Castlereagh ?], 21 Feb. 1847.

42 Letter of John Andrews, Comber, to the editor, 12 Feb. 1847 printed in the *Londonderry Sentinel.*

43 *ibid.*, 12 Feb. 1847, letter of Lord Londonderry, Seaham, to John Andrews, Agent's Office, Newtownards, 6 Feb. 1847.

44 *Londonderry Standard,* 19 Feb. 1847, 'John Andrews Esq., the Marquis of Londonderry and the Derry Standard'.

45 PRONI, D.654/N2/24, Andrews to [?] Lord Castlereagh, 11 Dec. 1847.

46 *ibid.*, Andrews to Lord Londonderry, 25 Jan. 1847; Andrews to [Lord Castlereagh?], 21 Feb. 1847.

47 *ibid.*, Andrews to Lord Londonderry, 21 Feb. 1847; J. Bardon, *A History of Ulster*, (Belfast, 1992), p.314 (hereafter Bardon, *Ulster*).

48 PRONI, D.654/N2/24. Statement of Income and Expenditure, August 1847.

49 Letter from the Marquess of Londonderry, Mount Stewart, to John Andrews, Agent's Office, Newtownards, 17 Nov. 1846, printed in *The Downpatrick Recorder*, 28 Nov. 1846.

50 *ibid.*, 2 Dec. 1848.

51 *ibid.*

52 See n.48.

53 PRONI, D.654.N2/24, letter from the Belfast Banking Company, Belfast, to Lord Londonderry, Holdernesse House, London, 8 June 1847.

54 *ibid.*, 6 March 1847.

55 *ibid.* Andrews to Lord Londonderry, 14 March 1847.

56 *Northern Whig*, 6 March 1847.

57 PRONI, BG25/A/1, Newtownards Guardians' meetings, 13 Jan., 10 March, 8 April, 12 May, 7 June 1847.

58 PRONI, D.654/N2/24, Andrews to Lord Londonderry, 21 March 1847.

59 Kinealy, *Great Calamity*, p.140.

60 PRONI, D.654/N2/24, Andrews to Lord Londonderry 14 May 1847.

61 *ibid.*, Andrews to Lord Londonderry, 5 Aug. 1847.

62 PRONI, BG25/A/1, Newtownards' Guardians' meetings, 21, 28 July 1847.

63   Andrews to Lord [? Castlereagh], 11 Dec. 1847.
64   Robert Steele Nicholson was born in 1809, the eldest surviving son of Robert Steele of Ballymacarrett. He assumed the surname Nicholson in compliance with the will of his uncle who had married the last surviving Nicholson. The Nicholson family had come to the Bangor area in the late seventeenth century. They lived at Balloo House, off today's Balloo Road, in a three-storey 18th century house which was demolished in 1976. Robert was called to the bar in 1836 and was appointed a J.P.
65   PRONI, BG25/A/1, letter of resignation from Robert Nicholson to the Poor Law Commissioners, 4 Oct. 1847.
66   PRONI, BG25/N2/24, Andrews to [Lord Castlereagh ?], 11 Dec. 1847.
67   *The Banner of Ulster*, 5 Feb. 1847.
68   PRONI, BG25/A/1, 15 Nov. 1848.
69   J.S. Donnelly in 'The Great Famine: its interpretations old and new', *History Ireland*, 1 No. 3, (1993).
70   PRONI, D.654/N2/24, Andrews to [?] Lord Castlereagh, 11 Dec. 1847.
71   *ibid.*, Andrews to Lord Londonderry, 21 March 1847.
72   *ibid.*, Andrews to Lord Londonderry, 2 Feb. 1847.
73   *ibid.*, Andrews to Lord Londonderry, 5 Aug. 1847.
74   *ibid.*, Andrews to Lord Londonderry, 21 Aug. 1847.
75   *ibid.*, Andrews to Lord Londonderry, 20 Nov. 1847.
76   PRONI, BG25/A/1, Newtownards Guardians' meetings, 1 Dec. 1847, 5 Jan. 1848.
77   Those in favour of outdoor relief were as follows:
Name of Guardian; Electoral division represented
William Sharman Crawford of Rademon, Ex officio
Hugh Montgomery of Rosemount, Greyabbey, Ex officio
Major Francis Montgomery of Newtownards, Ex officio
George Dunbar of Woburn, Millisle, Ex officio
Samuel Delacherois Crommelin of Carrowdore, Ex officio
Colonel John Robert Ward of Kircubbin, Ex officio
Robert Edward Ward of Bangor, Ex officio
Robert Steel Nicholson of Balloo House, Bangor, Ex officio
Guy Stone of Barn Hill, Comber, Ex officio
Dr William Moore of Ballyvernon, Bangor
John Neil of Bangor, Bangor
John Boyd of Ballyree, Bangor
John McKittrick of Newtownards, Newtownards
John Miller of Comber, Comber
Frederick Sharman Crawford, Crawfordsburn
William Orr of Roddens, Ballyhalbert
Those who voted against outdoor relief were:
John Sinclair of Ballymeglaff
Andrews of Comber, Ex officio
John Cooper of Cunningburn, Mount Stewart
John Hutton of Ballygrainey
John Robert Gordon of Florida Manor, Kilmood, Ex officio
Robert Carse of Ballyminstra, Kilmood
Jacob Gibson of Ballykeel, Kilmood
Arthur McGraddy of Carrickmannon, Greyabbey
Samuel McKee of Kilbright, Carrowdore
William Orr of Ballyrickard, Comber
John Cooper of Donaghadee, Donaghadee
James Kelly of Donaghadee, Donaghadee
William Campbell of Ballyalton, Newtownards South
John Moore of Killarn, Newtownards South
James White of Newtownards, Newtownards
William Shaw of Kircubbin, Kircubbin
James Dalzell of Newtownards, Tullynakill
78   PRONI, BG25/A/1, Newtownards Guardians' meeting, 1 Dec. 1847
79   PRONI, BG3/A/1, Banbridge Guardians' meetings, 13 March, 10 April 1847, 8 Jan. 1848; *Banner of Ulster*, 19 March 1847.
80   PRONI, D.2918/3/7/154, 162, 165-6, John Doran P.P., Aghaderg, to J.J. Whyte, 21 Dec. 1848; P. O'Connor to J.P. Kelly, 7 March 1849; J.P. Kelly to J.J. Whyte 14 March 1849. I wish to thank Catherine Loney for pointing me to the sources in this and the preceding note.
81   A.M. Wilson, *Saint Patrick's Town: a history of Downpatrick and the Barony of Lecale* (Belfast 1995), p.170; Bardon, *Ulster*, p. 285.
82   *The Vindicator*, 24 Oct. 1846, printed in Killen, *Famine Decade*, p.74.
83   Bardon, *Ulster*, p.287.
84   *The Parliamentary Gazetteer of Ireland*: entry on Newtownards; see n.3.
85   PRONI, D.654/N2/24, Andrews to Lord Londonderry, 21 Feb. 1847.
86   *The Newtownards Chronicle*, Obituary notice of David McKean, 2 Dec. 1893.
87   T. McCavery, *Newtown, a history of Newtownards* (Belfast, 1994), pp.133-142.
88   PRONI, D.654/N2/24, Andrews to Lord Londonderry, 5 April, 25 April, 10 May 1848; *Downpatrick Recorder*, 13 May 1848.
89   *The Newtownards Independent*, 13 July 1872.
90   Bourke, *Visitation of God*, p.184.

CO. FERMANAGH
1   W. E. Vaughan and A. J. Kirkpatrick (eds) *Irish Historical Statistics: Population 1821-1971* (Dublin, 1978) p. 12.
2   British Parliamentary Papers. 1851 Census,

Ireland: Part 1, Ulster & Connaught, pp. 201-226. (IUP, 1970).

3   Malachy McRoe has drawn to my attention two sources which may throw some light on the arrival of potato blight in the county. A report in the *Impartial Reporter* as early as 12 Dec. 1844 states that ...'in the neighbourhood of Florencecourt...there is extensive rot in the potatoes'. The confirmation of blight having been detected in Co. Fermanagh in the late summer of 1845 is evident in a letter of 6 September 1845 addressed to Lord Erne 'with regard to the potato failure', published in the *Impartial Reporter*, 18 Sept. 1845.

4   *Enniskillen Chronicle and Erne Packet*, 20 Nov. 1845.

5   *Enniskillen Chronicle and Erne Packet*, Letter of A. Graham, 3 Dec. 1845, 4 Dec. 1845.

6   *Enniskillen Chronicle and Erne Packet*, 20 Nov. 1845.

7   PRONI, BG14/A/2, Enniskillen Guardians' meeting, 14 July 1846.

8   PRONI, BG14/A/2, Enniskillen Guardians' meeting, 18 Aug. 1846.

9   PRONI, BG14/A/2, Enniskillen Guardians' meeting, 15 Sept. 1846.

10 PRONI, BG21/A/1, Lowtherstown Guardians' meeting, 7 Jan. 1846. See also C. Kinealy, *This Great Calamity. The Irish Famine 1845-52* (Dublin, 1994), p. 67.

11 *Enniskillen Chronicle and Erne Packet*, 14 Nov. 1846.

12 *Enniskillen Chronicle and Erne Packet*, 13 Nov. 1845.

13 Peadar Livingstone, *The Fermanagh Story* (Enniskillen, 1977) p.197. Local folklore: source, George McFarland.

14 *Enniskillen Chronicle & Erne Packet*, 18 Dec. 1846

15 P. Livingstone, *op.cit.* p.198.

16 *ibid.*, p. 198.

17 *ibid.*, p. 198.

18 *ibid.*, p. 199.

19 Livingstone, *op.cit.*, p.200.

20 PRONI, BG 14/A/2, Enniskillen Guardians' meetings of 16 Dec. 1847, 27 May 1848. See also Neil McAtamney 'The Great Famine in Co Fermanagh', *Clogher Record* 1994, pp. 3-16.

21 PRONI, BG 14/A/2, Enniskillen Guardians' meeting, 5 Jan. 1847.

22 *Correspondence relating to the State of Union Workhouses in Ireland*, Third Series, H.C. 1847, Vol. lv.

23 Appendix to *Fourteenth Report from the Select Committee on Poor Laws, Ireland*. Return of Paupers in the workhouses...week ended 30 December 1846-8. H.C. 1849, Vol. xv, Pt 2.

24 ibid.

25 PRONI, BG 14/A/2, Enniskillen Guardians' meeting, 3 April 1847.

26 PRONI, BG 14/A/2, Enniskillen Guardians' meeting, 6 and 11 May 1847, 1 June 1847

27 PRONI, BG 14/A/2, Enniskillen Guardians' meeting, 17 Aug. 1847.

28 C. Kinealy, *op.cit.* p.138.

29 C. Kinealy, *op.cit.* pp 211-214.

30 C. Kinealy, *op.cit.* p.268

31 PRONI, BG15/A/2, Lowtherstown (Irvinestown) Guardians' meeting, 18 Mar. 1849.

32 *Enniskillen Chronicle and Erne Packet*, 20 Feb. 1845, printing a letter from John Irvine, Clerk, Lowtherstown Board of Guardians, 29 Nov. 1843.

33 Report of Mr Phelan, Medical Inspector, to Poor Law Commissioners, 24 July 1847.

34 PRONI, BG20/A/3, Lisnaskea Guardians' meeting, 3 March 1849.

35 BG15/G/1, Admission Register of Lowtherstown Union workhouse. These statistics were compiled by 7 Fermanagh schools in an Education for Mutual Understanding project. See also *Computer Education*, February 1992, pp5-7, for description of project.

36 *ibid.*

36 *ibid.*

37 *ibid.*

38 *ibid.*

39 PRONI, BG 14/A/2, Enniskillen Guardians' meeting, 27 April 1847.

40 *Impartial Reporter*, 1 May 1847.

41 PRONI, BG 14/A/2, Enniskillen Guardians' meeting 5 Jan. 1847.

42 Joan Vincent, 'A Political Orchestration of the Irish Famine: County Fermanagh, May 1847', in *Approaching the Past: Historical Anthology Through Irish Case Studies*, (eds) Marilyn Silverman and P. H. Gulliver (New York, 1992), pp.75-98.

43 *Impartial Reporter*, 8 May 1847.

44 PRONI, BG 14/G/1.

45 Joan Vincent, *op.cit.* p.93.

46 PRONI, BG14/G/1, p.1.

47 PRONI, BG14/A/1, correspondence of Enniskillen PLU.

48 BG14/A/1, correspondence of Enniskillen PLU.

49 *Enniskillen Chronicle and Erne Packet*, 20 Nov. 1845.

50 *Fourteenth Report from the Select Committee on Poor Laws, Ireland*. Return of Paupers in the workhouses. H.C. 1849, Vol xv, pt 2, p.447.

51 *ibid.*

52 *ibid.*

53 *ibid.*

54 See, for example, Edward Senior's circular on

the risk of female orphans becoming 'permanent deadweight', as discussed by Ballymoney Guardians, 23 April 1849, PRONI, BG 5/A/5.

55 Trevor McClaughlin, *Barefoot and Pregnant? Irish Famine Orphans in Australia.* Melbourne, 1991).

56 H. C. 1847-8, Vol. xxxiii, p.16.

57 *Enniskillen Chronicle and Erne Packet*, 11 Jan. 1849.

CO. LONDONDERRY

1 National Archives, Dublin, Relief Commission Papers, RLFC 3/2/442

2 PRONI, T.2890/1, D. McGregor, Inspector General, Dublin, 16 Sept. 1845.

3 PRONI, T.2890/3, George Fitzmaurice, County Inspector, 25 Sept. 1845.

4 PRONI, T.2890/4, John H. Babington MB, Medical Officer, Coleraine Union workhouse, to Chief Secretary, 13 Oct. 1845

5 PRONI, T. 2890/5, Sub-Inspector T. Thornley, Coleraine, to Inspector General, 14 Oct. 1845.

6 PRONI, T. 2890/8, Thornley to Inspector General, 28 Oct. 1845

7 PRONI, T. 2890/9, Thornley to Inspector - General, 4 Nov. 1845

8 PRONI, T.679/201/30, entry by Rev. Samuel Montgomery in baptismal, marriage and burial register of Ballynascreen Church of Ireland church. I am grateful to Robert McClure for his help in identifying this source.

9 PRONI, BG10/A/4, Coleraine Guardians' meeting, 13 Sept. 1845.

10 PRONI, BG21/A/2, Londonderry Guardians' meeting, 18 Oct. 1845.

11 PRONI, BG10/A/4, Coleraine Guardians' meeting, 18 Oct. 1845.

12 PRONI, T.2890/15, A. Moore to Capt. Kennedy, Newtownlimavady, 13 March 1846

13 PRONI, T.2890/14, Sir Robert Ferguson to Sir William Fremantle, 5 Jan. 1846.

14 C. Kinealy, *This Great Calamity* (Dublin, 1994), p. 84

15 PRONI, T. 2890/21, Abstract of Co. Londonderry Relief Committees, 24 Oct. 1846.

16 *Coleraine Chronicle*, 18 April 1846.

17 *ibid.*

18 National Archives, RLFC 3/2/442, C. Maxwell to Capt. Nott R.N., 18 Feb. 1847

19 National Archives RLFC series. I am grateful to Jim Grant for allowing me access to his research on the amounts raised by the respective relief committees in Co. Londonderry. See also J. Grant, 'The Great Famine in the Province of Ulster 1845-49 - The Mechanisms of Relief', unpub. Ph.D. thesis (Q.U.B. 1986).

20 *Coleraine Chronicle*, 18 April 1846.

21 PRONI, T. 2890/28, Charles Knox to William Stanley, 20 Feb. 1847.

22 T. H. Mullin, *Aghadowey. A Parish and its Linen Industry* (1972) p.112-113.

23 PRONI, T. 2890/29, Alex. Barklie, Aghadowey & Agivey Relief Committee, 25 Feb. 1847.

24 *First Report of the Commissioners for Inquiry into the Condition of the Poorer Classes in Ireland*, Appendix C, p.76. H.C. 1836 Vol. xxx.

25 PRONI, D. 3632/J includes a series of c. 38 petitions relating to requests for abatement or reductions of rent 1832-9.

26 'The London Companies as Progressive Landlords', by O. Robinson. *Economic History Review*, Second Series, Vol. XV (1962-3) pp 103-118.
There is evidence that other London companies were aware of the problem of poverty among their tenantry. Edward Oseland's third report to the Clothworkers' company, refers to 'the present distressed state of the country'. He suggested that the company should consider 'grants in aid of emigration of the small occupiers' and that 'an arrangement...should be made either with the Canada or British Land Company to receive emigrants from the estate...'. See PRONI T. 656/449

27 PRONI, D. 3632/J/10/10, petition of Jean Convey, August 1832.

28 PRONI, D. 3632/E/20/7, 21 Nov. 1845.

29 *ibid.*, 26 Feb. 1846.

30 PRONI, D.3632/J/19/1, May 1847.

31 PRONI, D.3632/J/20/1, May 1848.

32 PRONI, D.3632/G/5/2/2, 2 March 1847.

33 James S. Donnelly Jnr, 'The Great Famine: its interpretations, old and new'. *History Ireland* Vol. 1 No. 3, pp 127-133.

34 PRONI, D. 654/N2/24, Andrews to Lord Londonderry, 5 Feb. 1847.

35 PRONI, D. 654/N2/30, Spottiswood to Lord Londonderry, 19 April 1847.

36 *Londonderry Standard* 8 Jan 1847, 'The Three Marquesses'; *Londonderry Sentinel* 12 Feb. 1847

37 PRONI, D. 654/N2/24, Andrews to Lord Londonderry, 20 Jan. 1848.

38 PRONI, T.2603/1, Rt Hon. George Dawson, Castledawson, to Sir William Fremantle, Dublin, 17 Jan. 1847..

39 PRONI, T. 2603/7, Dawson to Fremantle 27 Dec. 1847.

40 PRONI, T.2890/28, Charles Knox to W. Stanley, 20 Feb. 1847.

41 PRONI, T.2890/30 Alex Barklie, Sec. Aghadowey & Agivey Relief Committee, 6 March 1847

42 *Coleraine Chronicle* 13 January 1847

43 PRONI, D. 1118/12, quoted in *The Great Famine*, PRONI Facsimile series 1 - 20 (1969).

44 *ibid.*

45 National Archives, RLFC 3/2/442/2, John Jackson, Ballinderry Glebe, to Sir Randolph Routh, 2 March 1847.

46 National Archives, RLFC 3/2, Barony of Coleraine. Rev. Mitchell Smyth, Garvagh Relief Committee to Routh, 24 Oct. 1846.

47 *ibid.*, Barony of Coleraine, 27 February 1847.

48 National Archives, RLFC 3/2, Barony of Loughinsholin, John Jackson, 9 March 1847.

49 *ibid.*, 24 March 1847.

50 National Archives, RLFC 3/1/783, Barony of Keenaght, 16 Nov. 1846 (not 16 March, as given in Search Room catalogue).

51 National Archives, RLFC 3/2/442/2, John P. Hewitt, Rectory, Moneymore, to W. Stanley, 3 Feb. 1847.

52 National Archives, RLFC 3/1/353, Adam Boyle, Bovedy Presbyterian Church, 13 Jan. 1846.

53 PRONI, MIC 1P/90/1, entry of 15 September 1848 in Castledawson Presbyterian Church Session Book.

54 *Correspondence Relating to the State of the Union Workhouses in Ireland, Second Series.* 9 Jan 1847. H.C. 1847 Vol lv.

55 *Correspondence Relating to the State of Union Workhouses in Ireland, Third Series.* H.C. 1847 Vol lv.

56 *ibid.*

57 *Report from the Select Committee on Poor Laws, Ireland.* Appendix No. 2, Return of Paupers in the Workhouses...week ended 30 December 1846-8. H.C 1849 Vol. xv, Pt. 2.

58 *ibid.*

59 PRONI, BG23/A/1-2. See particularly the extracts from minute books, compiled by Brian Trainor, available on Search Room shelves.

60 PRONI, MIC 1P/90/1.

61 *Papers Relating to the Relief of Distress, Seventh Series: Paupers in Workhouses.* H.C. 1847-8 Vol. liv, pp.220-1.

62 *ibid.*

63 *Coleraine Chronicle,* 14 Sept. 1844.

64 Edward Senior to the Select Committee on the Poor Laws, 15 March 1849. H.C. 1849 Vol xv Pt 1 Q. 2449.

65 PRONI, BG5/A/6, Ballymoney Guardians' meeting, 23 April 1849.

66 PRONI, BG21/A/5, Londonderry Guardians' meeting, 30 June 1849.

67 PRONI, BG10/A/7, 12 May 1849, meeting of Coleraine Guardians. Two cases of workhouse-assisted group emigrations from Coleraine and Letterkenny workhouses are described by Brian Trainor, 'Emigration from Irish Workhouses during the Great Famine' in *Directory of Irish Family History Research,* No. 17, 1994, pp 75-88.

68 Christine Kinealy, op cit, p.310.

69 *ibid.*

70 Trevor McClaughlin, *Barefoot and Pregnant? Irish Famine Orphans in Australia.* (Melbourne, 1991.)

71 *ibid.* For an account of the Ulster workhouses' contribution, see Trevor Parkhill, 'Permanent Deadweight: Ulster Female Pauper Emigration to Australia, 1848-50' in *Ulster Local Studies* Vol. 10 No. 1 Summer 1988, pp.

72 PRONI, BG21/A/4, Londonderry Guardians' meeting, 17 June 1848.

73 *ibid.*, Londonderry Guardians' meeting, 8 July 1848.

74 *Papers Relating to the Relief of Distress and State of the Unions in Ireland, Eighth Series,* Appendix A, p.xc. H.C. 1849 Vol xlviii.

75 *Fourteenth Report from the Select Committee on Poor Laws, Ireland.* H.C. 1849 Vol xv Pt 2 p. 447.

76 PRONI, D. 2892/1/1-4, passenger books.

77 *Irish Historical Statistics: Population 1821-1971.* (eds) W. E. Vaughan and A. J. Fitzpatrick. Dublin 1979, p. 325.

78 Sholto Cooke, *The Maiden City and the Western Ocean* (Dublin, 1952) pp.103-4.

79 PRONI, T.3789 contains a list of passengers known to have been on board the *Exmouth* when it sank. See also *The Times,* 4 June 1847

80 *Correspondence on the Treatment of Passengers on board the Emigrant Ship Washington. Minutes of Evidence given before the Select Committee on the Passengers' Act, 1851,* q. 424 - 438. H.C. 1851 Vol. xix.

81 *Belfast Newsletter* 5 December 1848. See also W. H. Crawford, 'An Emigrant Ship Disaster', in *Ulster Local Studies* Vol. 18 No. 1 Summer 1996. I am grateful to Bill Crawford for a full transcription of this newspaper account.

82 *ibid.*

83 PRONI, T. 2890/14, Sir Robert Ferguson to Sir William Fremantle, Chief Secretary, 5 Jan. 1846.

84 National Archives, RLFC 3/1/446. F. H. Hemming, Secretary in London of the Dublin and Enniskillen Railway, to Capt. J. P. Kennedy, Relief Commission, Dublin, 2 Feb. 1846.

85 *ibid.*

86 PRONI, T. 679/201/30

87 PRONI, T.2603/3, George Dawson, Castledawson, to Sir William Fremantle, 14 Nov. 1847.

88 *Papers relating to the Relief of Distress and State of the Unions in Ireland,* Seventh Series, 1848, pp 196-7. H.C. 1847-8, Vol. liv.

89 PRONI, D. 654/N2/30, A. Spottiswood, Magherafelt, to Lord Londonderry, 23 October 1847.

90 PRONI, T. 2603/14, Dawson to Fremantle, 11 December 1850.
91 PRONI, D. 3632/1/1, letter from agents, Moneymore, 17 May 1849.
92 'The London Companies as Progressive Landlords', by O. Robinson. *Economic History Review*, Second Series, Vol xv (1962-3) pp 103-118.
93 *Statistical Statement for Each Poor Law Union in Ireland*. H.C. 1849 Vol. xlvii. For Sept. 1848 statistics, see *Appendix to Minutes of Evidence before the Select Committee on the Operation of the Irish Poor Law*, H.C. 1849 Vol. xv.
94 PRONI, T. 2603/9, Dawson to Fremantle, 26 July 1849.
95 PRONI, T.2297/1. Henry Keenan, parish of Ballyscullion, to Daniel Keenan, Baltimore, 15 July 1849.
96 *Irish Historical Statistics: Population 1821-1971.* (eds) W.E. Vaughan and A .J. Fitzpatrick (Dublin 1978) p. 325.
97 *ibid.*, p. 13.
98 IUP Series, *Population 13* (1970). Census of Ireland for the Year 1851...County Londonderry, pp 239-265.
99 C. Ó Gráda, *Ireland Before and After the Famine: Explorations in Economic History* (Manchester, 1988) p. 83.
100 IUP Series, *Population 14* (1970). Census of Ireland for the Year 1851. General Report, Table XXXIII, p. li, Showing by Provinces, Counties...the number of deaths...1841 to 1851.

CO. MONAGHAN
1 Ordnance Survey Memoirs, Parish of Currin, unpublished mss., Institute of Irish Studies, Queen's University, Belfast.
2 John O'Donovan, *Ordnance Survey Letters*, Co Donegal, p.197.
3 T.W. Freeman, *Pre-famine Ireland*, (Manchester, 1957), p.18.
4 Clogher Diocesan Census, 1985.
5 P. J. Duffy, 'The evolution of estate properties in south Ulster 1600-1900' in W J Smyth and K Whelan, *Common Ground*, (Cork, 1988).
6 W. H. Crawford, 'The significance of landed estates in Ulster 1600-1820' *Irish Economic and Social History*, xvii (1990) p.61.
7 Devon Commission (*Commission of Inquiry into the state of the law and practice in respect of the occupation of land in Ireland*, Parliamentary Papers, 1845, 885.
8 Devon Commission, Appendix (Part IV), p.491-3.
9 *ibid.*, p.873, 884.
10 PRONI, D.3531/A/4, Shirley Estate Papers.
11 From document in Warwick County Record Office, Box 3/1(19).

12 PRONI, D.3531/P.
13 R. J. Scally, *The end of hidden Ireland: rebellion, famine and emigration*, (Oxford, 1995), chapter 2.
14 *Report of the commissioners for inquiring into the condition of the poorer classes in Ireland*, quoted in A. Gailey, 'Vernacular dwellings of Clogher diocese', *Clogher Record*, 1977, p.212.
15 Although is it worth noting that the OS Memoirs (1835) for Magheracloone parish in the south of the Shirley estate described the cottages of the poor as being 'of a better description and more efforts have been made to plant the country and assist nature in giving it a more civilised appearance'.
16 W. J. Smyth, *Social and economic geography of nineteenth century Co. Armagh*, unpublished Ph.d. thesis (National University of Ireland, 1974) p.191.
17 PRONI, D.3531/P/box 1.
18 W. S. Trench, *Realities of Irish Life* (London, 1868).
19 PRONI, D.3531/S/55.
20 The petitions are contained in unsorted boxes in the Shirley papers, PRONI, D.3531/P/boxes 1-3. See P. J. Duffy, 'Assisted emigration from the Shirley estate 1843-54', *Clogher Record*, xiv (2) (1992), 7-63.
21 Devon Commission, p.923.
22 *ibid.*, p.889.
23 PRONI, D.3531/M/5/1-22.
24 Chris Morash, *Writing the Irish Famine* (Oxford, 1995) p.3 on the 'textual creation' of the Famine.
25 B. O Mórdha, 'The great famine in Monaghan: a coroner's account.' *Clogher Record*, 1962, p.176, although this could be expected in inquests.
26 Variation in potential crop failure is suggested in the shooting of a man 'watching potatoes' near Smithboro in September 1847, O Mórdha, *op cit.* p.176.
27 P. Livingstone, 'Castleblayney Poor Law Union', *Clogher Record*, 1964, p.238.
28 C. O Gráda, 'Across the briny ocean' in T. Devine and D. Dickson (eds) *Ireland and Scotland* (Edinburgh, 1983), p.127.
29 *First report of the commission for inquiry into the poorer classes*, H.C., vol xxxii, 1835, 386.
30 Unpublished mss, Institute of Irish Studies, QUB.
31 *ibid.*
32 B. O Mórdha, 'The great famine in Monaghan: a coroner's account' *Clogher Record*, 1960-61, p.40.
33 *ibid.*, p.33.
34 *ibid.*, p.32.

35 L. O Mearáin, 'The Bath Estate 1777-1800', *Clogher Record*, 1968.
36 *The Nation*, 8 Sept. 1849.
37 Correspondence from Lord Lismore to his agent, May 1838. Personal communication.
38 See P. J. Duffy, 'Assisted emigration from the Shirley estate 1843-54' *Clogher Record*, 1992, p.7-62.
39 *ibid*.
40 See C. Morash and R. Hayes (eds) *Fearful Realities, new perspectives on the Famine* (Dublin, 1996), p.113 for discussion of the 'encoding' of famine icons in literature.
41 IFC S940, p.13.
42 IFC S954, p.75.

CO. TYRONE
*   The chronological scope of this article is limited to the point where, in August 1847, extraordinary Famine relief measures were terminated and responsibility for all relief was transferred to the 'extended' Irish Poor Law system.
1   National Archives, Relief Commission Papers - hereafter Rlf Com Papers - (Co. Tyrone) *passim*.
2   *Report of the Commissioners of Public Works in Ireland, on the Subject of the Returns ordered by the House of Commons 11 February 1852, relating to the Employment of the Poor in Ireland, etc.,* p 595, H.C. 1852(169)xviii.
3   *Supplementary Appendix Part II to the Seventh Report of the Relief Commissioners*, pp 18-21, H.C. 1847-48(956)xxix.
4   National Archives, Rlf Com Papers (Co. Armagh) II/2b/8541, Rev James Disney, Sec., Charlemont Relief Committee to The Commissary General, 26 Dec 1846.
5   *Abstract of the Census, etc.*, Pt I, H.C. 1851(673)l.
6   *Return of Number and Description of Works applied for, recommended and sanctioned in each District of Ireland in the Year 1846*, pp 523-559, H.C. 1847 (764)l; *Report of the Commissioners of Public Works in Ireland, 11 February 1852, etc.,* p 595, H.C. 1852(169) xviii (Hereafter *Return of Works*).
7   *Tyrone Constitution*, 6 Nov 1846.
8   *Belfast Newsletter*, 15 Dec 1846.
9   *Return of Works*, pp 523-559, H.C. 1847(764)l. A check, in this return, of some 21 early presentments in Ulster shows an average delay of nearly eight weeks between proclamation and Treasury approval.
10 *Belfast Newsletter*, 15 Dec 1846.
11 National Archives, Rlf Com Papers (Co. Tyrone) 2b/8882, (Hon and Rev) Robert Maude, Dean of Clogher, Chr, to Routh, 8 Jan 1847.
12 *ibid.,*/12241, Charles Eccles, Chr and David

Lindsay, Sec, to Routh, 27 Feb 1847.
13 *ibid.,*/10829, (Rev) W T Cuthbert, Sec to Routh, 10 Feb 1847.
14 *ibid.,*/8882, Maude to Routh, 8 Jan 1847.
15 Wm. Stanley to Rev. Robert Hume, 3 Dec 1846, p. 281, H.C. 1847 (796)lii.
16 Extracts from Journal of Capt Oldershaw for week ending 30 Jan 1847, p. 94, H.C. 1847(797)lii.
17 Extr jnl Lt Colomb, Insp Officer Co. Tyrone, week ending 6 Feb 1847, p. 239, ibid. (For the benefit of younger readers, a perch measured five and a half yards, or about five metres.)
18 J. Grant, 'The Great Famine in the Province of Ulster 1845-49 - The Mechanisms of Relief', unpublished Ph.D. thesis, (Q.U.B. 1986), p. 156.
19 *Tyrone Constitution*, 16 Oct 1846.
20 *ibid.*, 23 Oct 1846. Clogher and Fintona Relief Committees offered employment at stone breaking until the public works should start. See Rlf Com Papers (Co. Tyrone) 2b/D7191, Maude to Labouchere, 26 Oct 1846 and D/12241, Charles Eccles, chr to Routh, 17 Feb 1847.
21 *Tyrone Constitution*, 6 Nov 1846.
22 *ibid.*, 16 Oct 1846
23 *ibid.,* 6 Nov 1846.
24 *Northern Whig*, 24 Oct 1846.
25 *ibid.*, 27 Oct 1846.
26 *Return of Works*, pp 523-559, H.C. 1847 (764)l.
27 The text of Labouchere's letter (addressed to Col. Jones, Chr of the Board of Works) is given in O'Rourke, Rev. J., *The History of the Great Irish Famine of 1847 with notices of earlier Irish famines*, 3rd edition (Dublin 1902), pp 549-551. The well-informed contemporary was George Poulett Scrope, the economist and MP for Stroud in Gloucestershire.
28 *Tyrone Constitution*, 23 Oct 1846.
29 PRONI, D.674/218G, Henry Corry, MP, to (Daniel) Auchinleck, 12 Sept (1846), (PRONI). I am grateful to Mr Trevor Parkhill for bringing this document to my attention.
30 *Tyrone Constitution*, 23 Oct 1846.
31 Extrs jnls inspecting officers Co. Tyrone, Capt. Oldershaw for weeks ending 5 Dec 1846, 9 and 16 Jan 1847; Lt. Colomb for week ending 20 Feb 1847, p. 325, H.C. 1847(764)l; pp 74, 239, H.C. 1847(797)lii.
32 Extrs jnl Capt.Oldershaw for weeks ending 28 Nov, 5, 12 and 19 Dec 1846, pp 286, 325, 382 and 415, H.C. 1847(764)l.
33 Mr (James) Stronge to Mr Trevelyan, Tynan, Co. Armagh, 27 Dec 1846, p. 451, *ibid*.
34 Extrs jnl Capt. Oldershaw for weeks ending 28 Nov, 12, 19 Dec 1846, 23 Jan, 13 Feb 1847, pp 286, 382 and 415, H.C. 1847(764)l, p. 239, H.C. 1847 (797)lii.

35 *Return of Works*, pp 523-559, H.C. 1847(764)l.
36 *Northern Whig*, 24 Oct 1846.
37 *Correspondence relating to Applications for Loans for the Construction of Railroads*, pp 31-4, H.C. 1847(764)l; *Tyrone Constitution*, 6 Nov 1846.
38 *ibid.*, p. 34.
39 National Archives, Rlf Com Papers (Co. Tyrone) 2b/D7179, (Hon and Rev) Robert Maude to Chief Secretary Labouchere, 26 Oct 1846.
40 *ibid.*, 2a/6678, 6734, 6807, Charlemont to Routh, 26, 28 and 30 Oct 1846.
41 National Archives, Rlf Com Papers (Co. Tyrone) *passim*.
42 *Instructions for the Formation and Guidance of Committees for Relief of Distress in Ireland consequent on the Failure of the Potato Crop in 1846*, pp 104-7, H.C. 1847(764)l. (Hereafter *Instructions.*)
43 National Archives, Rlf Com Papers (Co. Tyrone) 2a/12365, Thomas H. Porter, D.D., Rector of Desertcreat, to Routh, 26 Feb 1847. It is clear that some local relief committees were already operating before Charlemont made formal appointments.
44 PRONI, D.1854/6/3, p. 130, Rev J.R. Moore (no addressee) 26 Apr 1847.
45 National Archives, Rlf Com Papers (Co. Tyrone) 2a/15192, 19119, (Rev) John Leach to Routh, 20 Mar, 17 Apr 1847.
46 *ibid., passim* for the counties named.
47 *Instructions*, 8 Oct 1846, pp 104-7, H.C. 1847(764)l; *Treasury Minute*, 31 Aug 1846, pp 67-71, ibid.
48 National Archives, Rlf Com Papers (Co. Tyrone) 2a/6952, James Eyre Jackson, Chr, to The Commissary General, 2 Nov 1846.
49 *ibid.,* 2a/9377, Same to Same, 21 Jan 1847, with draft reply, 22 Jan 1847.
50 *ibid.*, 2b/9983, Same to Same, 1 Feb 1847.
51 *ibid.,* 2b/9758, Henry Cotthurst, Sec. to Wm. Stanley (Secretary to the Relief Commission), 28 Jan 1847.
52 *ibid.*, 2a/704? (number incomplete), Robert Wray, Chr to Wm. Stanley, 4 Nov 1846.
53 *ibid.,* 2b/9795, John Rogers, Chr to Routh, 27 Jan 1847.
54 *ibid.*, 2a/10567, printed handbill dated 25 Jan 1847. A peck was commonly computed at 10 lbs. weight in contemporary Ireland. This implies half-price meal.
55 *ibid.,* 2b/8882, Maude to Routh, 8 Jan 1847; 2b/9862/James Robinson, Sec (Pomeroy) to Routh, 29 Jan 1847.
56 *ibid.*, 2b/8803, Rev Wm. Atwell to Routh, 5 Jan 1847.
57 *ibid.*, 2a/7874, Rev Robert Hume, Chr to Routh,

1 Dec 1846, with draft reply, 3 Dec 1846.
58 *ibid.,* 2a/7344, Same to Same, 12 Nov 1846.
59 *ibid.*, 2a/8428, 2b/10628, (Rev) James Smith, Chr to The Commissary General, 21 Dec 1846, 3 Feb 1847.
60 *ibid.,* 2b/8882, Maude to Routh, 8 Jan 1847.
61 *ibid.*, 2b/D297, Memorial to His Excellency the Earl of Bessborough "Lord Lieutenant General and General Governor of Ireland', 8 Jan 1847.
62 *ibid.*, 2a/11371, (Rev) Isaac Ashe, Sec to Routh, 28 Jan 1847.
63 *ibid.*, 2b/9117, Thomas Sandels, Curate, Sec to Routh, undated, but received at Routh's office 16 Jan 1847.
64 *ibid.*, 2b/8803, 9112, (Rev) Wm. Atwell, Chr to Routh, 5, 14 Jan 1847.
65 *ibid.*, 2a/8989, James Eyre Jackson, Chr to Routh, 11 Jan 1847.
66 *ibid.*, 2a/9181, (Rev) Alex. George Stuart, Curate, to Routh, 5 Jan 1847.
67 *ibid.,* 2a/9175, W. Chambers, Sec to Routh, 18 Jan 1847.
68 *ibid.*, 2a/12009, (Hon. and Rev.) Charles Douglas, Chr to Routh, 24 Feb 1847.
69 *ibid.*, 2a/14624, Rev Henry Lucas St George, Rector, Chr to Routh, 16 Mar 1847.
70 Poor-law unions, established by the Irish Poor Law of 1838, did not recognise county boundaries. It is, therefore, incorrect to speak of 'Tyrone poor-law unions'. But, while part of Strabane union was in Co. Donegal, part of Clogher in Co. Monaghan - and small parts of Co. Tyrone in Armagh, Enniskillen and Lowtherstown (now called Irvinestown) unions, still the unions of Dungannon, Omagh, Cookstown, Castlederg and Gortin were entirely within the county.
71 The census figures for 1841 cannot, of course, be accurate for 1847, but it can be argued that comparisons based on them are broadly useful.
72 *Supplementary Appendix Part III to the Seventh Report of the Relief Commissioners*, p.75, H.C. 1847-48(956)xxix. (Hereafter *Suppl App Pt III.*)
73 *ibid.*, p. 39.
74 *ibid.*, pp 80-81.
75 *ibid.*, p. 36.
76 *ibid.*, p. 46
77 *ibid.*, p. 41.
78 *ibid.*, p. 52.
79 *ibid.*, See pages as above for respective unions.
80 *Thirteenth Annual Report of the Poor Law Commissioners, 1 May 1847*, p. 27, H.C. 1847(816)xxviii.
81 PRONI, BG9/A/2, Clogher Guardians' meetings, 9 May, 22 Aug 1847.
82 PRONI, BG26/A/3, Omagh Guardians' meeting,

1 Oct 1847.

83 *Thirteenth Annual Report of the Poor Law Commissioners, 1 May 1847*, p. 27-28, H.C. 1847(816)xxviii.

84 *Statement showing the Amount of Workhouse Accommodation in Ireland, the Number of Inmates on the 9th. of January 1847, etc.*, pp 7-13, H.C. 1847(790)lv. (Hereafter, *Statement 9 Jan 1847*.)

85 *ibid*; for Castlederg, see Edward Senior, Assistant Poor Law Comissioner, to the Commissioners, 24 Mar 1847, p. 1, H.C. 1847(863)lv. Admission of children without their parents was illegal. The Irish poor law required whole families to enter the workhouse as a proper test of destitution and to prevent fraud.

86 PRONI, BG26/A/3, Omagh Guardians' meetings, 10, 17, 24 Dec 1846; 14 Jan 1847 and see 29 Oct 1846.

87 *ibid.*, 24 Dec 1846; 4 Feb 1847.

88 *ibid.*, 25 Feb to 22 July 1847; see 25 Mar 1847.

89 *ibid.*, 29 Apr 1847.

90 *ibid., passim*, May to July 1847 and see 18 Mar 1847; *Suppl App Pt III*, p. 75.

91 *List of Orders on Certificates from the Central Board of Health in Ireland for providing Hospital Accommodation or Dispensaries, pursuant to Act 10 Vic. cap. 22*, in *Third Report of the Relief Commissioners, 17 June 1847*, Appendix A, pp 7-15, H.C. 1847(836)xvii; *Fourth Report ditto, App Pt III*, p. 24-28, H.C. 1847(859)xvii; *Sixth Report ditto, App Pt III*, p. 20, H.C.1847-8(876)xxix.

92 PRONI, BG11/A/2, Cookstown Guardians' meeting, 23 Jan 1847. The commissioners' reply was that the law allowed for only to those actually admitted to the workhouse.

93 Edward Senior, Assistant Poor Law Comissioner, to the Commissioners, 24 Mar 1847, p. 2, H.C. 1847(863) lv.

94 PRONI, BG 26/A/3, Omagh Guardians' meeting, 29 July; 5, 12, 19 and 26 Aug 1847.

INDEX

Abercorn, James Hamilton, *2nd Marquess of*, 206
Act of Union, 3
Aghabog, 189
Aghadowey, 150, 151, 154, 166
Aghadrumkeen, 190
Aghanloo, 156
Aghinillard, 131
Aghnamullen, 186, 188, 189, 195
Agivey, 150, 154
Ahoghill, 22
Allingham, Mary, 94
Allingham, William, 94-7
Alts, 171
America, 5, 27, 29, 30, 32, 94, 152, 160, 183, 188, 193
Anahoe, 208
Andrews, John, 12, 100, 103, 105, 106, 108, 110-13, 115, 116, 118-22, 125-7, 153
Anglo-Celt, 63, 66, 68, 71, 73
Anketell estate, 183
Annageliff, 75
Annagh, 60, 75
Annaghybane, 190
Annesley, William Richard Annesley, *4th Earl*, 209
Annie (ship), 31
Antrim, Co., 4, 5, 10, 15-34, 36, 162, 164, 185
Antrim (*town*), 5, 16, 18-20, 24, 25, 34, 100, 115
Antrim, Hugh Seymour McDonnell, *4th Earl of*, 25
Antrim, Laura Cecilia, *Countess of*, 21
Arboe (Co. Londonderry), 166
Ardboe (Co. Tyrone) 208, 210, 215, 216
Ardmillan, 102
Ardragh, 171
Ards Farming Society, 110
Ardstraw, 210
Armagh, Co., 2-5, 12, 34-57, 171, 179, 185
Armagh (*town*), 7, 8, 220
Armagh Guardian, 52
Army, British, 186
Arranmore, 84, 85
Arva, 73
Ashfield, 67, 70
Athenry (Co. Tyrone), 217
Auchinleck, Daniel, 205
Augher, 202, 207, 208, 217
Aughintain, 217, 220
Aughnacloy, 202, 204, 207, 208, 210, 215, 217, 220
Aughnamullen, 178
Australia, 29, 94, 97, 145, 159, 160, 194

Babington, *Mr (of Drumcree)*, 42
Babington, Dr John H. 147, 148
Bailieborough, 60, 61, 66-71, 73, 75
Balligawley, 200
Ballinagh, 65, 68
Ballinamallard, 135
Ballinamore and Ballyconnel, 63
Ballinascreen, 148, 163
Ballinderry (Co Antrim), 40, 42
Ballinderry (Co Londonderry), 13, 154, 156
Ballintemple, 75
Ballintoy, 22, 32
Ballinure, 192
Ballyblack, 109
Ballycastle, 5, 16, 20-5, 32
Ballyclog, 210
Ballycloghan, 109
Ballygawley, 200, 208, 210, 217
Ballygilbert, 109
Ballygowan, 100, 109
Ballygrooby, 152
Ballygrot, 109
Ballyhaise, 61, 65, 66, 68
Ballyhalbert, 100
Ballyhinney, 109
Ballyjamesduff, 61, 63, 66, 68, 69
Ballykelly, 165
Ballymacaldrick, 26-8
Ballymachugh, 65, 75
Ballymaglaff, 100
Ballymena, 22, 24, 25
Ballymoney, 5, 11, 16-20, 24, 25, 148, 157-9, 165
Ballymullan, 109
Ballyrashane, 147
Ballyscullion, 166
Ballyshannon, 9, 77, 78, 82, 83, 85-98
Ballyshannon Herald, 85, 88, 96
Ballyvaddy, 28
Ballyvennaght, 22
Ballywalter, 100, 102
Baltimore (USA), 166
Banbridge, 123, 220
Banbridge Choral Society, 123
Bangor, 100, 102, 108, 109, 121
Banner of Ulster, The, 99, 107-10, 112, 119
Bantry, 46
Bar, The, 210
Barklie, Alexander, 150
Barndonagh, 171

Bath estate, 174, 183, 193, 194
Bathlodge, Ballycastle, 20, 21
Bawnboy, 11
Begging, 73, 114, 183, 188
Belfast, 1-3, 5, 7, 10, 24, 25, 99, 100, 125, 166
Belfast and County Down Railway Co., 110
Belfast Banking Co., 113
Belfast, Dublin, Coleraine and Junction Railway, 203, 207
Belfast Ladies Association for the Relief of Destitution, 83, 84
Belfast Newsletter, 53, 112, 162
Belfast Protestant Journal, 29
Belfast Relief Fund, 41
Belfast Vindicator, 40, 46, 52
Belgium, 4
Bell, *Dr*, (*of Lurgan workhouse*), 7, 37, 43-7, 50, 51
Belleek, 129, 130
Belmore, Armar Lowry-Corry, *3rd Earl*, 130
Belturbet, 9, 60, 61, 64, 67-70, 73
Benburb, 220
Beragh, 200
Beresford, *Rev*. Charles, 69
Beresford, John Barre, 154
Beresford, *Ven*. M.G., 66
Berry, Joseph, 38
Betty, Stewart, 142
Black, Andy, 30
Blacklion, 60
Blackwood, *Rev*. Townley, 105
Blankets, 3, 181, 182
Blayney estate, 183
Board of Works, 63, 64, 124, 200, 201, 205
Boards of Guardians, 5-11, 16-18, 20, 61, 69, 86, 90, 92, 116, 137, 145, 159, 221
- Antrim, 16, 18-20, 34, 100, 115
- Armagh, 8
- Ballycastle, 5, 16, 20, 21, 25, 32
- Ballyshannon, 86-92
- Carrickmacross, 194
- Castleblayney, 186
- Cavan, 11, 69, 70
- Clogher, 219
- Coleraine, 9, 22, 23, 149, 159, 160
- Cookstown, 221
- Cootehill, 11
- Derry, 148, 149, 159, 166
- Enniskillen, 132, 136-8, 142, 144, 145
- Larne, 20
- Lisburn, 19, 20, 34
- Lisniskea, 11, 140, 141, 145
- Lowtherstown, 8, 11, 137, 138
- Lurgan, 8, 37, 39, 44, 45, 47-51, 54, 55, 57
- Newtownards, 102, 104-6, 113-22
- Omagh, 222
Bocks, 193
Bogle, Robert, 17, 18
Boston, 32

Bourke, Austin, 127
Bovedy, 156
Boyd, *Mrs*, (*Matron of Cavan Workhouse*), 169
Boyle, *Rev*. Adam, 156
Brachan Bray, 98
Brackagh Rully, 152
Bradley, (*Widow, of Ballygrooby*), 152
Brady, *Dr* George Frazer, 85
Brady, *Rev. Fr*. Tom, 72
Bragan, 185
Brantry, 218
Brereton, *Capt*., 124
British Relief Association, 44, 66, 84
Brooke, *Sir* Arthur, 131, 145
Brookeborough, 131, 133
Broughshane, 22
Brown, *Mr* (*of Donaghcloney*), 39
Brown, *Rev. Dr.*, John, 154
Brown, *Messrs*, S.R. & T., 107, 126
Browne, *Dr* James, *Bp of Kilmore (RC)*, 11, 73
Brownlow, Charles, *see* Lurgan, Charles Brownlow, *1st Baron*
Brownlowsderry, 55
Bruce estate, 166
Brush, Abraham, 60
Bullock, *Mr (of Lurgan)*, 49
Burials, of paupers, 52, 119
Burtonport, 85

Calcutta Fund, 41
Caledon, 207, 208
Camderry, 217
Camowen, 217
Camus, 207, 210, 214, 217
Canada, 94, 159
Canals, Work on, 63, 206
Cappagh, 200
Carbery, Jane, 94
Carleton, Jane, 94
Carndonagh, 85, 88
Carnlough, 15, 28
Carre, *Rev*. Henry, 84
Carrickadooey, 171
Carrickaslane, 184
Carrickmaclim, 181
Carrickmacross, 174, 181, 184, 186, 188, 193, 194
Carrickmannon, 109
Carrickmore, 199, 208, 210
Carrigart, 84
Carrowdore, 100
Castleblayney, 184, 186, 188, 195
Castlecaulfield, 210
Castledawson, 153, 156, 165
Castlederg, 7, 198, 199, 202, 217-9, 221
Castlerahan, 64, 75
Castlesaunderson, 64
Castleshane, 179
Castetara, 75

Castleward, 74
Castlewellan, 124, 209
Cavan Co., 2, 5, 13, 14, 59-75, 130, 170, 185, 198, 202, 210
Cavan (*town*), 7, 8, 11, 60, 61, 63-71, 73, 74, 210
Cave Hill, 5
Central Board of Health, 45, 46, 55
Charlemont, Francis William Caulfield, *2nd Earl of*, 207, 208, 210
Charlemont, 55, 198
Children, in Workhouse, 8, 144, 145, 158, 159
Chism, *Mr (of Ballyshannon)*, 96
Cholera, 124, 162
Clanawley, 129
Clandeboye, 108
Clankelly, 129
Claraghy, 190
Clare, Co., 185
Clare (Co. Tyrone), 217
Clarendon, George William Villiers, *4th Earl of see* Lord Lieutenant of Ireland
Clark, *Mr (supplier of potatoes to Lisburn Workhouse)*, 19, 20
Claudy, 150
Clements, *Rev. Mr.*, 13, 41, 42
Clergy, 13, 155-7
Clogher, 198-202, 205, 207, 208, 210, 214, 217-21
Clogherney, 200
Clones, 130, 140, 179, 180, 186, 188, 192
Clonmacate, 40
Clonmany, 94
Clonoe, 210, 214, 216
Clonsedy, 171
Clontibret, 179, 187, 188, 192
Clor na Scriobach, 30
Clothworkers' Company, 149, 154
Clough, 22
Cloughcorr, 32
Coalisland, 208, 215
Cole, 220
Colebrooke estate, 130, 131, 145
Coleraine, 9, 11, 22, 23, 147-50, 157-60, 163, 165, 166, 206
Coleraine Chronicle, 18, 24, 149, 159
Collum, *Dr (of Enniskillen)*, 134
Columb, *Lieut.*, 201, 205
Colonial Office, 160
Colthurst, Henry, 212, 213
Comber, 100, 102, 108, 109, 115, 118, 127
Condon, *Dr (of Enniskillen)*, 136
Connacht, 2, 35, 53, 159, 176, 195
Connanger, 97
Connolly, Edward, 78, 79, 82, 87
Connolly estate, 78
Convey, Jean, 152
Conynghan, (*landlord of Burtonport*), 85
Cooke, J and J., 30, 162
Cookstown, 198, 203, 204, 207-10, 217-21

Coole, (Co. Fermanagh), 129
Coole Brae, 22
Coolesker, 200
Cootehill, 11, 60, 61, 64, 67-73
Coragh, 72
Corragarry, 190
Corranewy, 190
Corbane, 182
Corcuilloge, 171
Cordressigo, 189
Cork, Co. 7, 54
Cork, (*City*), 44, 46
Cork Abbey, 176
Corlea, 172
Corlough, 75
Corn Laws, Repeal of 119, 120, 125
Cornawall, 189
Corry, Henry, 205
Cottiers, 2, 64, 174, 178-88, 191, 192, 195
Craig, Frank, 15, 30, 31
Craigmacagan, 32
Crawford, William Sharman, 10, 12, 103, 116, 117, 120, 122, 126, 127
Crawfordsburn, 103, 109
Cremourne, 180
Crime, 42, 43, 96, 97, 132, 186
Crossbane, 72
Crossdoney, 63
Crosserlough, 60, 75
Crosslea, 190
Cullies, 73
Cumming, *Dr.*, 45
Cummins, *Rev. J.*, 78
Currin, 135

D'Arcy, *Mr (Inspector of workhouses)*, 89, 91
D'Arcy, *Mr (owner of site for Lowsterstown workhouse)*, 140
Dartrey, 171, 184
Dawson estate, (Co. Monaghan), 174, 183
Dawson, George, 153, 154, 163-5
Deaths, numbers of 44, 68, 88, 89, 143, 166
Denn, 65, 75
Dernamoyle, 196
Derry (*city*), 2, 94, 148-50, 157-63, 165, 206
Derry, Co., *see* Londonderry, Co.
Derry Standard see Londonderry Standard
Derrybard, 220
Derrycard, 217
Derrygonnelly, 129, 133
Derryheen, 60
Derrykinard, 190
Derrylossett, 190
Desertcreat, 208
Desertlyn, 166
Devon Commission, 36, 79, 154, 176, 179, 180, 182, 183
Diarrhoea, 6, 43, 50, 106, 201, 219

Dickson's distillery, 61
Disney, *Rev.* James, 198
Diver, *Mr, (of Ballyshannon)*, 91
Dolling, Robert, 35, 36
Donacloney, 39-42
Donagh, 85, 187, 189
Donaghadee, 100, 102
Donaghmore, 210, 220
Donegal, Co., 9, 26, 44, 77-98, 113, 162, 164, 170, 185, 206, 210
Donegal *(town)*, 79, 83, 87, 94
Donegal Historical Society, 98
Donegan family, 32
Donnelly, J.S., 12, 119, 153
Douglas, Burn, 217
Down, Co., 5, 6, 20, 36, 99-128, 185
- South 124
Downings, 85
Downpatrick, 7, 100, 123, 124
Downpatrick Recorder, 103, 113, 125
Downshire, Arthur Hill, *4th Marquess of*, 111, 124, 174
Drainage Schemes, 6, 63, 204-6
Drapers' Company, 151-4, 164, 165
Draperstown, 151
Dromore (Co. Tyrone), 199, 200, 208, 216, 217, 220
Drumalee, 70
Drumaney, 203
Drumbo, 172
Drumbracken, 172
Drumcall, 189
Drumcree, 40, 42
Drumcrow, 26, 27
Drumglas, 210
Drumgole, 189
Drumgoon, 75
Drumgoosat, 172
Drumhirk, 109
Drumintin, 190
Drumlane, 74, 75
Drumlomman, 75
Drumlona, 190
Drumnaspil, 220
Drumquin, 217, 220
Drumskool, 133
Drumsnat, 189
Drumulla, 190, 191
Drumully, 189
Drung, 72, 74, 75
Dublin, 41, 176
Dublin, Co., 174, 192
Dublin and Enniskillen Railway Co., 163
Dublin Quarterly Journal of Medical Science, 67
Dublin Relief Association, 41
Dufferin and Ava, Frederick Temple, *1st Marquess of*, 108
Dunboe, 150, 154

Dundalk, 188
Dundermot, 22
Dundrennan, 189
Dunfanaghy, 80, 82, 83, 98
Dungannon, 198, 203, 204, 207-11, 214, 217-21
- Lower 199, 202, 204, 210
- Middle 199, 203, 204, 210
- Upper 199, 203, 204, 210
Dunloy, 26
Dunnamanagh, 6, 199, 207, 208, 210-3, 216
Dunourgan, 22
Durham, 113
Dysentery, 6, 44, 46, 47, 50, 55, 67, 87, 88, 109, 115, 125, 156, 201, 219

Earl Grey (ship), 160
East Omagh *see* Omagh
East Urney, *see* Urney (Co. Tyrone)
Easton, *Mr (of Lurgan)*, 55
Eccles, Charles, 201
Edencrannon, 210
Ederney, 129, 135, 200
Ematris, 189-191
Emigration, 2, 3, 12, 14, 27, 28, 74, 84, 94, 114, 120, 125, 130, 145, 152, 159-66, 183, 186, 188, 193, 194
England, 5, 27, 31, 124, 159, 189
Enniskillen, 11, 44, 125, 130, 132, 135-8, 140, 142-5, 163, 206, 220
Enniskillen, William Willoughby-Cole, *3rd Earl of*, 143, 144
Enniskillen Chronicle and Erne Packet, 131-4, 144, 145
Erne, John Crichton, *3rd Earl of*, 132, 133, 210
Evictions, 2, 3, 12, 71-3, 82, 83, 91, 120, 123, 126, 130, 164, 176, 183, 186, 194
Ewing, *Rev.* John, 78
Ewing, Paul and Co., 107
Exmouth (ship), 27, 162
Extraordinary Presentment Sessions, 63, 65, 93, 124, 200, 202-5

Fahan, Upper, 85
Fairly, William, 50
Fallaghearn, 220
Fallyack, 31
Famine Stone, 28
Famines, pre-1845, 2, 4, 20, 21, 59, 207
Farney, 171, 176, 180, 184, 185, 187, 188, 193
Farnham, Henry Maxwell, *6th Baron*, 65, 72
Farranmacbride, 79
Farrelly, P.O., 72
Fay, James, 68
Feely, Ellen, 94
Ferguson, *Sir* R.A., 205
Ferguson, *Sir* Robert, 149, 163, 210
Fermanagh, Co., 5, 10, 11, 14, 97, 129-146, 185, 198, 206, 210

Fever, 6, 8, 11, 20, 21, 43-56, 67-9, 86, 88, 101, 125, 133, 135, 136, 141, 143, 158, 164, 192, 201
Fever Commissioners, 37
Fever hospitals, 9, 21, 37, 46, 55, 56, 68, 69, 85, 88, 104, 115, 136, 143, 192, 220
Finnebrogue, 108
Fintona, 201, 207, 208, 210, 217, 220
Fishmongers' Company, 165
Fitzmaurice, George (*County Inspector, RIC*), 147
Fitzpatrick, Owen, 179
Fivemiletown, 207, 208, 220
Flanagan, *Mr (of Ballyshannon)*, 89
Flax, 36, 56, 191
Flemming, D., *(of Bailieborough)*, 68
Florence Court, 5
Foster, *Mr (of Society of Friends)*, 66
Foster, Vere, 162
Foy, *Rev Fr.*, 72
France, 5
Fremantle, *Sir* Thomas, 163
Freeman's Journal, 60, 61, 71, 72, 74
Frith, *Dr (of Enniskillen)*, 136

Gage, Catherine, 29, 30
Gage, *Rev.* Robert, 29-31
Galway, Co., 179, 185
Garrison, 129
Garron Tower, 13, 15, 28, 164
Garvagh, 155
Garvery Wood, 135
Germany, 5
Gillespie, David, 55
Glangevlin, 74, 75
Glasgow, 30, 101, 107, 126
Glaslough, 174, 179
Glenarm, 5, 21
Glencolmcille, 78, 79, 82, 84
Glens of Antrim, 26
Glenties, 10, 11, 44, 79, 80, 82, 83
Gordon, Robert, 105, 121
Gormley, *Mr (Master of Cootehill workhouse)*, 69
Gort, 9
Gortin, 7, 198, 199, 202, 207, 217-21
Gortnacrea, 217
Gosford, Archibald Acheson, *2nd Earl of*, 40, 41
Gowna, 61, 68
Graham, A., 130
Grand Juries, 20, 39, 100
Grange, Co. Antrim, 22
Greenan, 210
Greenan, Barney, 192
Greer, George, 39
Greer's Distillery, Lurgan, 55
Grey, Henry George Grey, *3rd Earl*, 94, 145, 160
Grey, Roderick, 135
Greyabbey, 100, 110
Griffith's Valuation, 182, 189-91
Grocers' Company, 165

Groomsport, 100, 108
Grosse Isle, 162
Gullian, Hugh, 28
Gweedore, 83

Halpin, *Dr (of Cavan)*, 67, 133
Hamill, Jane, 21
Hamilton, Alexander, 82, 98
Hamilton, John, 87
Hancock, *Capt. (of Enniskillen)*, 135
Hancock, John, 36, 45, 50
Hannay, *Dr (of Lurgan Dispensary)*, 55
Harper, Letty, 160
Headfort, Thomas Taylor, *2nd Marquess of*, 64
Healy, *Sgt.*, 94
Henry, *Lieut.*, 94
Hertford, Richard Conway, *4th Marquess of*, 19, 25, 111
Hewetson, Barry D., 83, 84
Hewitt, *Rev.*, John P., 156, 157
Hill, *Lord* George, 80, 84
Hillsborough, 174
Hinde, Charles, 55
Hughes, *Rev.* William, 156
Hume, William, 79, 82
Humphrey, *Mr (of Ballyhaise)*, 65
Hunt, Leigh, 95
Hurst, *Dr (of Clones area)*, 192

Impartial Reporter, 142
Inchinan (*ship*), 94
Indian corn-meal, 16, 17, 20, 26, 30, 31, 42, 45, 63, 64, 70, 72, 73, 80, 85-7, 135, 156, 210, 213
Inishowen, 79, 83, 85, 88, 92
Iniskeen, (Co. Monaghan), 189
Inniskeen (Co. Cavan), 14, 74, 75
Inny, River, 63
Inspector-General, RIC, 147
Irish Folklore Commission, 195
Irish Poor Law Act 1838 *see* Poor Law Act (Ireland) 1838
Irish Relief Association, 41, 66
Ironmongers' Company, 150
Irvine, Jimmy, 21
Irvinestown *see* Lowtherstown
Ivers, *Rev.*, 4, 37

Jackson, Rev. J., 155, 156
Jackson, James Eyre, 211, 212
John Clarke, (ship), 30

Keadew, 68
Keenan, *Mrs (Matron of Ballyshannon Workhouse)*, 92
Keenan, Henry, 166
Kells, (Co. Antrim), 22
Kells, (Co. Meath), 63, 74
Kelly, *Dr (Medical officer of Ballyshannon Workhouse)*, 87

Kelly, Charles, 28
Kelly, J.P., 123
Kelly, John, 71
Kennedy, *Mr (Baker, of Lurgan)*, 50
Kernan, 40, 52, 55
Kesh, 129
Kilbride, 75
Kilcronaghan, 166
Kildallan, 70, 74, 75
Kilkenny, Co., 185
Kill, 70
Killann, 75
Killanny, 189
Killeevin, 191
Killen, 217
Killeshandra, 64, 68-70, 73, 75
Killeter, 217
Killin Crosserlough, 63
Killinagh, 74, 75
Killinkere, 61, 75
Killough, 124
Killsherdany, 14, 64, 72, 74, 75
Killybegs, 11, 79, 82, 84, 85
Killyclogher, 217
Killyleagh, 123, 124
Killyman, 209, 210
Kilmactrasna, 172
Kilmood, 100
Kilmore, (Co. Cavan), 75
Kilmore, (Co Monaghan), 189
Kilnaleck, 65
Kilrea, 11, 149, 156
Kilrush, Co. Clare, 14
Kilskeery, 210
Kinawley, 74, 75, 135
Kinduff, 190
Kinealy, Christine, 138, 149
Kingscourt, 68
Kircubbin, 100, 102
Kitson, *Mr (of Ballyshannon)*, 90
Knockbride, 74, 75
Knockinny, 129
Knox, C.J., 150

Labouchere drainage schemes, 204-6
Lack, 129
Ladies Dublin Association, 41
Land ownership, 172-8
Landlords, 3, 12, 13, 28, 29, 41, 71, 83, 103, 119, 122, 153-5, 159, 193, 201, 202, 204, 205, 209
Lanktree, John, 15, 25-9, 164
Laois, Co., 185
Lara, 70, 75
Larne, 5, 20, 24, 25
Lavey, 65, 75
Law, *Rev.*, H.I., 31
Leach, *Rev.*, John, 209
Lecale, 123, 125

Leckpatrick, 207, 208, 210, 216
Leinster, 159, 160
Leitrim, Co., 185
Lennon, Sally, 94
Leslie estate, 174, 183
Letterkenny, 79, 82
Levins, Laurence, 193
Lewis' *Topographical Dictionary*, 123
Limavady, 149, 150, 156-8, 163, 165
Lindsey, Alexander, 162
Linen Industry, 2, 3, 6, 10, 14, 36, 56, 60, 74, 151, 152, 171, 177, 179, 180, 191, 213, 216
Lisbellaw, 133, 135
Lisburn, 5, 19, 20, 24, 25, 34
Lislynchahan, 190
Lisniskea, 11, 130, 136, 137, 140-2, 144, 145
Lismore, *Lord*, 193
Liverpool, 162, 188
London, 27
London Companies, 12, 151, 154, 165
Londonderry, Charles William Vane, *3rd Marquess of*, 12, 13, 26-8, 99-101, 103, 105-8, 110-113, 115, 116, 119, 122, 125-7, 153, 154, 164
Londonderry, Frances Anne Vane, *Marchioness of*, 13, 15, 25-9, 101, 105, 111, 113
Londonderry *(City) see* Derry
Londonderry, Co., 2, 4, 5, 12, 26, 113, 147-168, 174, 185, 210
Londonderry (ship), 162
Londonderry and Coleraine Railway, 206
Londonderry and Enniskillen Railway, 206
Londonderry Sentinel, 111
Londonderry Standard, 110-12, 153
Longford, Co., 185
Lord Lieutenant of Ireland, 90, 120, 124, 202, 203
Lough Erne, 63
Lough Foyle, 149, 206
Loughan, 75
Loughbrickland, 123
Louginsholin, 166
Loughrea, 44
Loughriscourse, 100, 109
Lowtherstown (Irvinestown), 8, 11, 129, 130, 132, 133, 137, 138, 142-4, 220
Lucas estate, 177, 179
Lurg, 129
Lurgan, Charles Brownlow, *1st Baron*, 36, 49, 51, 52, 55
Lurgan (**Co Armagh**), 7, 8, 12, 35-56, 210
Lurgan, Co. Cavan, 75
Lurgan Union Farming Society, 49
Lutton, Thomas, 49

McAuley, *Very Rev.*, Bernard, 123
McBride, Ann, 94
McBride, Margaret, 94
McCabe, Francis, 182
Macartney, George, 16

McCausland, Marcus, 149
McClean family, 53, 54
McConaghy, Joe, 32
McCrea, Letty, 94
McCrea, Mary, 94
McCunningham, James, 79
McDermott, Mary Anne (*Emigrant from Ballyshannon*), 94
McDermott, Mary Anne (*of Killeevan*), 191, 192
McDermott, Sally, 94
McDonnell, *Rev. Fr.*, Francis, 77
McDowel, John, 66
McDuogh, *Rev. Fr.*, 202
McElheran, *Mr, of Ballycastle*, 16
McEneaney, Anne, 181
McGimney, Hector, 21
McKean, David, 126
McKiernan, *Rev. Fr.*, Francis, 69
McKiernan, James, 61
McKinley, Maggie, 32
McKittrick, John, 122, 127
McKnight, *Dr* James, 112
McLaughlin, *Dr (of Downpatrick)*, 54
McManus, Bernard, 140
McMenamin, *Rev. I.*, 88
McQuaid, *Rev. Fr.*, Eugene, 69
McQuaid, *Rev Fr.*, Matthew, 64, 71, 72
McVeagh, *Dr (of Lurgan)*, 45, 50

Mackey, *Rev.* John, 85
Macosquin, 150, 154, 166
Magee, Anna, 68
Maghera, 149
Magheraboy, 129
Magheracloone, 171, 182, 185, 187, 192
Magherafelt, 8, 11, 148, 149, 153, 156-8, 164, 165
Magherascouse, 109
Magherasteffany, 129
Magheross, 171, 179, 185, 195
Magill, Henry, 181
Maguire, Mary, 94
Maguire, *Rev. Fr.*, Tom, 74
Maguiresbridge, 135
Maine (USA), 32
Maise, *Dr, (of Cavan)*, 67
Maralin, 40
Marron, Thomas and Mary, 187
Martin, Catherine, 182
Martin, *Rev.*, J.J., 64
Massereene, John Skeffington, *10th Viscount*, 29
Maude, *Hon. and Rev.* Robert, 215
Maxwell, J.W., 103
Mayo, Co., 179, 185
Measles, 219
Meason, John, 47, 51
Meath, Co., 176
Milecross, 119
Milford, 80, 82

Millar, *Mr (of Antrim)*, 16
Millar, *Mr (of Ballinderry)*, 42
Miller, John, 152
Miller, Rowley, 152
Milltown, 68, 71
Mitchel, John, 79
Mitchell, *Mr (agent of Shirley estate)*, 177, 193
Mitchell, *Mrs, (matron of fever workhouse)*, 69
Mohan, Peter, 182, 187
Moira, 38-42, 50, 55
Monaghan, Co., 2-5, 14, 169-96, 198, 202
Monaghan (*town*) 179, 180, 184, 186, 187
Moneymore, 156
Moneyreagh, 100
Monsell amendment, 159
Montgomery, *Rev.* Alexander, 21
Montgomery, *Major*, F.D., 105
Montgomery, *Rev.* Samuel, 148, 163
Monuments, Famine, 28, 30, 97, 98
Moore, *Mr (of Ballycastle Board of Guardians)*, 22
Moore, *Rev.* Hugh, 105
Moore, *Rev.* J.R., 209
Moorfield, 220
Morash, Chris, 95
Morris, William, 41
Morton, Pierce, 60, 61, 63, 140
Mountcastle, 217
Mountjoy Forest, 217
Mountnugent, 69
Mount Stewart, 13, 100, 105, 113
Mourne Mountains, 124
Moville, 88, 93
Moy, 6, 207-13, 216, 220
Moybolgue, 67, 75
Moyle, (Co Tyrone), 217, 218
Muckno, 189
Mullagh, 72, 74, 75
Mullaghnashee, 89
Mullaghslin, 217
Mullanary, 186
Mullarts, 32
Munster, 2, 35, 53, 159, 160, 195
Munterconnaught, 75
Murphy, Patrick, 176
Muslin weaving, 101, 106, 107, 126

Nation, The, 194
National Club, London, 41
Navan, 72
Nesbitt, *Mr (of Crossdoney)*, 63
Nesbitt, *Sub-Inspector, RIC*, 147
Netherlands, 5
New York, 160, 162
Newry, 188
Newry Canal, 42, 43
Newry Telegraph, 45, 46, 51
Newtownards, 6, 7, 10, 100-2, 104-23, 125
- South 100, 105

Newtownards Chronicle, 126
Newtownards Independent, 104, 107, 127
Newtownlimavady *see* Limavady
Newtownsstewart, 199, 207, 208, 210, 214, 217
Nice, 176
Nicholson, Asenath, 85
Nicholson, Robert, 117, 120, 122
Niece, Sally, 85
Nixon, *Dr (of Enniskillen)*, 137
Northern Standard, 183, 193
Northern Whig, 36, 39, 56, 102, 107
Northland, Thomas Knox, *Viscount*, 203, 204

Oatmeal, 5, 17, 32, 45, 64, 87, 132, 195
O'Brien, *Rev. Fr., (of Lurgan)*, 40
O'Connell, Daniel, 118
O'Donovan, John, 170
Ó Gráda, Cormac, 166, 188
O'Hagan, *Rev.* Michael, 21
Oldershaw, *Capt.*, 201, 205, 206
Omagh, 6, 140, 198-201, 205-8, 210, 217-22
O Mórdha, B., 184
O'Neill, Captain, 84
O'Neill, John Bruce Richard, *3rd Viscount*, 29, 115
Ordnance Survey Memoirs, 101, 151, 180, 189, 190
O'Reilly, *Rev. Fr.* Charles, 65
O'Reilly, *Rev. Fr.* Patrick, 63, 69
Otway, G.C., 80
Oulton, *Rev.*, 42, 49
Outdoor relief, 24, 70, 71, 86, 100, 105, 114-6, 118, 119, 121, 122, 186, 221

Park, Lewis and Charles, 107
Parliamentary Gazetteer of Ireland, 100
Peaste, 182
Peel, *Sir* Robert, 5, 26, 61, 133, 134
Pennethorne, *Mr Justice*, 138, 140
Perceval-Maxwell, Robert, 108
Phelan, Denis, 140
Philadelphia, 160, 162
Philips family (of Enniskillen), 135
Phillips, *Dr (of Lurgan)* 54
Plymouth, 94
Poetry, and famine, 95
Pomeroy, 207, 208, 214, 216, 220
Poor Law Commission of Inquiry, 151, 188
Poor Law Commissioners, 8, 9, 18, 19, 23, 24, 43, 46, 50, 54, 69, 80, 82, 85, 86, 88-90, 92, 94, 105, 119-21, 132, 137, 141, 144, 160, 219-22
Poor Law (Ireland) Act 1838, 3, 7, 9, 36, 79, 105, 177, 183, 193, 214
Poor Law (Ireland) Extension Act 1847, 10, 69-71, 94, 114, 116, 121, 135, 138, 159, 221
Poor Law rate, 8, 10, 71, 83, 90, 91, 97, 118, 124, 138, 140, 141, 144, 145, 186, 193, 221
Portadown, 38, 40, 42, 55
Population, decline in, 3, 14, 30, 74, 75, 123-6, 129, 130, 166, 171, 172, 174, 176-8, 184-9, 193-5, 198

Porter, John, 143
Portnoo, 79
Portstewart, 155
Potato blight
- 1845, 4, 5, 15, 16, 25, 39, 60, 61, 80, 102, 130, 131, 147-9, 183, 184, 197
- 1846, 5-7, 26, 39, 61, 64, 79, 80, 102, 132, 148, 184, 197, 218, 219
- 1847, 10, 158, 163
- 1848, 163, 165
- Traces after 1848, 14, 34
Potatoes, price of, 38, 64, 79, 135
Potatoes, varieties of
- Black seedlings, 4, 16
- Cups, 4, 16
- Doe blacks, 4, 16
- Lumper, 4
- Red Downs, 4, 16
Presbyterian church, 156
Protestants, in workhouses, 9, 91
Public Record Office of Northern Ireland, 143
Public works *see* Relief works
Purdon, *Dr.*, 45

Quebec, 159, 162

Radcliff, *Rev.* J., 156-8
Raddins, Mary, 97
Railway Commissioners, 63
Railways, 110, 163, 203, 206, 207
Randalstown, 29
Ranfurly, Thomas Knox, *2nd Earl of*, 203, 204
Rate-in-aid, 11, 122, 125, 140, 141
Rathborne, *Mr (of Virginia)*, 64
Rathfriland, 124
Rathlin Island, 15, 29-32
Rathmullen, 85
Ravara, 109
Read, Tom, 95
Reburn, John, 181
Redergan, 200
Reid, Rose, 94
Relief Commission, 41, 42, 45, 80, 84, 155-7, 163, 207, 208, 212
Relief committees, 4-7, 11, 40-42, 50, 61, 63, 65, 66, 73, 85, 87, 88, 92-4, 96, 100, 107, 108, 123, 146, 149, 150, 154-7, 197, 200, 201, 205, 207-216
Relief works, 2, 5-7, 63, 65, 66, 69, 83, 93, 94, 104, 133, 140, 195, 197, 199-207
Rent reductions, 3, 29, 103, 111, 112, 131, 181
Repeal movement (of Act of Union), 127
Rice, 5, 18, 31, 135
Rockcorry, 191
Rohall, 133
Rooney, Anne, 94
Roscommon, Co., 118, 178, 185
Rosses, 84
Rossmore estate, 183

Rossnowlagh, 98
Rossory, 135
Rothwell estate, 176, 177, 183
Roulston, James, 133, 134
Routh, *Sir* Randalph, 207, 210, 212-14
Royal Irish Constabulary, 42, 43, 147, 148, 178
Russell, *Lord* John, 5, 125, 134, 206
Rutland, 79, 85

St George, *Rev.* Henry Lucas, 216
St John's, Newfoundland, 30
Saunderson, Col., (of Castlesaunderson), 64
Scally, R.S., 178
Schools, 91, 92
Scotland, 71, 109, 159, 162
Scotstown, 184
Scott, *Mr (of Fort Frederick, Virginia)*, 74
Scrabby, 61, 68
Scrabo Tower, 127
Scurvy, 125
Sea foods, 32, 80, 85
Segrett, Francis, 193
Select Committee on Poor Laws (Ireland), 25, 83, 159
Senior, Edward, 23, 25, 55, 116, 145, 159, 221, 222
Seskinore, 217, 220
Shaw, George, 65
Sheil, *Dr* Barclay, 88
Sheil, Mary Anne, 96
Sheil, *Dr* Simon, 88
Shercock, 61, 68, 72, 195
Shirley estate, 3, 174, 176-81, 183, 185-7, 193-5
Sir Charles Napier (ship), 30
Skibbereen, 6, 99
Sligo, Co., 97, 185
Sligo, (*town*), 85, 94, 162
Smallpox, 124
Smith, *Dr (of Central Board of Health)*, 46, 47, 49, 51, 54, 57
Smith, *Dr (of Lurgan)*, 40
Smith, Biddy, 94
Smith, *Rev. Fr.*, James, 69
Smithfield (Belfast), 3
Smyth, *Rev.* Mitchell, 155
Smyth, W.J., 179
Society of Friends, 7, 9, 41, 52, 54, 66, 67, 77, 87
Soup Kitchen Act *see* Temporary Relief of Destitute Persons (Ireland) Act, 1847
Soup kitchens, 7, 9, 10, 21, 22, 24, 32, 66, 69, 86, 94, 98, 105, 107-9, 111, 114-16, 119, 123-5, 135, 155, 156, 192, 195, 208, 209
Spottiswood, Andrew, 153, 164
Stephens, *Dr (Ballyshannon dispensary doctor)*, 88
Stevens, *Dr*, 37, 43, 50
Stewart, *Sir* James, 210
Stewart, John Vandaleur, 83
Stewartstown, 207, 208, 210
Stone, Guy, 117, 122

Stoney Hill, 28
Strabane, 198, 199, 201, 202, 206, 210, 215, 217, 218, 221
- Lower 199, 202, 204, 206, 210
- Upper 199, 202,
Stradone, 61, 66
Stranorlar, 80, 82
Stuart, *Col., of Killymoon*, 203
Sweeney, Margaret, 94
Superior (ship), 162
Swellan, 70
Swinford, 9
Sydney, 94

Tamlaght, 166
Tamlaght O'Crilly, 166
Tamlaght Finlagan, 149, 150
Tamneybrake, 22
Tartaraghan, 13, 37, 41, 42, 52, 54
Tatlow, *Mr (of Crossdoney)*, 63
Tattymoyle, 220
Tedavnet, 195
Teeling, (Teelan), 78, 79
Tehallen, 188
Templecrone, 84
Templeport, 74, 75
Templetown, John Henry Upton, *1st Viscount*, 174
Tempo, 129, 143
Temporary Relief of Destitute Persons (Ireland) Act 1847, 9, 21, 23, 66, 67, 94, 100, 114, 115, 153, 198, 210, 211, 216-18, 221
Tenant Right, 100, 112, 118, 122, 126
Termoneeny, 166
Thompson, *Dr (advises Lurgan Board of Guardians)*, 45
Thompson, William, 159
Tipperary, Co., 89
Tirkennedy, 129
Todd, *Rev.* J.H., 31
Tomregan, 75
Toome, 22
Treasury, H.M., 42, 200
Trench, William Stewart, 177, 179-83, 187, 193, 194
Trevelyan, *Sir* Charles, 87
Trillick, 199, 207, 208, 210, 220
Trimble, William, 142
Tuke, James, Hack, 77, 80, 82, 87, 93, 96
Tullyclunagh, 220
Tullycorbet, 189
Tullylish, 46
Tullynakill, 100
Tullyniskan, 220
Tullyvar, 217, 220
Tullyvin, 67
Turnips, 5
Turnley, Francis, 21
Typhus, 53, 55, 67, 83, 125, 162
Tyrone, Co., 5, 6, 162, 185, 197-222

Ulster, 159, 160, 195
Ulster Canal, 42
United States, *see* America
Urney (**Co Cavan**), 75
Urney, (**Co Tyrone**), 201, 207, 208, 215
- East 210, 214, 215, 217

Vincent, Joan, 142, 143
Virginia (Co Cavan), 64, 68

Wade, *Dr (of Belturbet)*, 68, 69
Walker, *Mrs (of Ederney)*, 135
Wallace, Hugh, 123
Ward, Robert Edward, 108, 120
Warrenpoint, 39
Washington, (ship), 162
Waterford, Henry De La Poer, *3rd Marquess of*, 154, 155
Westport, 9
White, *Dr (Michael Officer of Omagh workhouse)*, 219, 220
Whyte, John Joseph, 123
Williamson's house, Tedavnet, 195
Wingfield estate, 176
Women, in workhouses, 160
Woodhouse, James, 38
Workhouses, 7-10, 16-19, 23, 25, 37, 40, 43, 44, 46, 61, 71, 73, 79, 80, 82, 83, 86, 92, 116, 130, 131, 133, 134, 136, 137, 157-9, 164, 165, 186, 192, 194, 198, 218-222
By place:
- Armagh, 7
- Ballymoney, 157, 158, 165
- Ballyshannon, 82, 86-92, 94, 95, 98, 130
- Banbridge, 123
- Bantry, 46
- Carndonagh, 85, 88
- Carrickmacross, 194
- Cavan, 7, 8, 61, 67-9, 71, 74
- Clogher, 219
- Clones, 130, 140
- Coleraine 148, 157, 158, 165
- Cookstown, 219, 221
- Cootehill, 61, 70, 71
- Derry, 157-9, 165
- Donegal, 83
- Downpatrick, 7
- Dunfanaghy, 80, 82, 83, 98
- Dunannon, 211, 219
- Enniskillen, 44, 130, 132, 136, 137, 140, 142-4
- Letterkenny, 79, 82
- Lisniskea, 130, 136, 137, 140-2, 144
- Loughrea, 44
- Lowtherstown, 130, 132, 136-8, 142-4
- Lurgan, 7, 37-40, 43-57
- Magherafelt, 156-8, 165
- Milford, 80-82
- Newtownards 104-11, 114-22, 125
- Omagh, 140, 201, 219, 220
- Strabane, 219
- Stranorlar, 80, 82
Wynne, Henry, 50

Young, John, 210
Young Ireland, 118, 127